UITGAVEN VAN HET
NEDERLANDS HISTORISCH-ARCHAEOLOGISCH INSTITUUT TE ISTANBUL

Publications de l'Institut historique et archéologique néerlandais de Stamboul

sous la direction de

E. VAN DONZEL,
Machteld J. MELLINK, C. NIJLAND et J. J. ROODENBERG

XLIV

OLD BABYLONIAN TABLETS
FROM ISHCHALI AND VICINITY

OLD BABYLONIAN TABLETS
FROM ISHCHALI AND VICINITY

by

SAMUEL GREENGUS

NEDERLANDS HISTORISCH-ARCHAEOLOGISCH INSTITUUT
TE ISTANBUL
1979

I.S.B.N. 90 6258 044 0
Printed in Belgium

CONTENTS

PREFACE

This book is the culmination of long effort, extending over a period of years; it reflects not only my own labors but incorporates as well the contributions of many other persons. This entire undertaking would not have been possible without this support and assistance.

I would like especially to thank Thorkild Jacobsen. His connection with the Ishchali tablets goes back to the very moment of their discovery. He was the first person to study the Ishchali tablets which Henri Frankfort purchased for the Oriental Institute in 1930; he was the Director of the excavations at Ishchali in 1934-35. He has generously made available all of his previous work; some 86 of his tablet copies were re-worked and incorporated into this book; and his field notes on the excavated tablets have supplied valuable information on Ishchali tablets now in Iraq, which were unavailable for the present study.

Thanks are also due to I. J. Gelb who, as curator of the Oriental Institute Collection, has done everything possible to help my work. His counsel and guidance have been present at every stage of this project.

This project could not have come to completion without financial assistance. In 1970-71, I was the recipient of a Fellowship award from the American Council of Learned Societies. This award, plus a supplementary grant from the American Philosophical Society, enabled me to spend fifteen consecutive months working on the Ishchali tablets. This support is, in a real sense, the "backbone" of the entire undertaking; without it, this book would never have been written. I wish to express my deep feeling of gratitude to these agencies. My intitial work on the Ishchali tablets, in 1969, was made possible by a research stipend provided by the late Nelson Glueck, then President of the Hebrew Union College — Jewish Institute of Religion. The College-Institute has continuously given me strong support. The research of 1970-71 was carried out during a sabbatical leave; and I have received grants to offset the costs of typing and duplicating. I wish to thank Herbert C. Brichto and Kenneth E. Ehrlich for arranging this assistance.

The present publication represents only a part of the work undertaken in this project. There are also transliterations, translations, and notes which remain to be published. A small selection has been incorporated into the present volume; hopefully, the remaining texts will likewise be made available in the not too distant future. A number of scholars have been kind enough to read various parts of the total manuscript: Thorkild Jacobson, Marten Stol, and Johannes Renger. They have contributed a great number of suggestions and improvements. I also wish to thank Robert Whiting for his assistance and collations. All of these men have given most freely of their time and knowledge.

A preliminary description of the purchased Ishchali tablets was prepared by the late Samuel Feigin; this work was incorporated into the Catalogue of the Oriental Institute Collection. Notes on the excavated tablets were prepared by Rivkah Harris for the Assyrian Dictionary. I was able to consult these notes and wish to acknowledge this contribution.

During 1974 I was also able to study the collection of purchased Ishchali tablets in the Collection of the University of California at Berkeley. I want to thank the staff of the Lowie Museum of Anthropology and most especially Anne D. Kilmer, Curator of Tablets, for allowing me access not only to the tablets published by H. F. Lutz in UCP 10/1, but to unpublished tablets as well. Some of the material collected is included in this book.

I also want to thank Brian Sullivan, who assisted me in typing the first draft of the manuscript. Ruth Deemy also assisted in the typing of the Indexes.

I wish to thank the Oriental Institute for permission to reproduce published drawings (figs. 1-3).

This work has been many years in preparation. The time taken to do this work very often required me to absent myself from home and family. I want to thank my wife, Lesha, who has given me steadfast support and encouragement throughout this project. I wish to dedicate this book to her in thanks for her human contributions to this project.

INTRODUCTION

I. THE PROVENIENCE OF THE TABLETS

This volume contains tablets from two collections: (1) Oriental Institute excavations at Ishchali[1] undertaken during 1934-35 (2) tablets purchased in 1930 by Henri Frankfort for the Oriental Institute, which were reported to have been found at Ishchali and Khafaje[2]. The Oriental Institute excavations of these Diyala sites were in fact motivated by the emergence of these and the many other valuable objects and tablets, which came into the hands of antiquity dealers during those years. It was Frankfort's hope "to place these objects and tablets in their proper (archaeological) context"[3].

---

[1] The identification of Ishchali as Neribtum was first put forward by Jacobsen in OIP 43 123[26], based on the occurrence of Neribtum in the treaty found at Ishchali (no. 326) and upon the brick inscription found at Ishchali which states: *a-na* ^dINNIN *Ki-ti-tum* ^d*I-pí-iq-*^dIM ... (text follows Building inscription 13, OIP 43 138, pl. xvi) *Ne-ri-ib-tum i-qí-si-im* (cf. OIP 43 116 and Harris, *JCS* 9 (1955) 33[15]). One would expect the inscribed bricks recording the gift of Neribtum to be situated in the city of Neribtum itself — or at least close by — rather than elsewhere. Lutz, *UCP* 10/1 (1931) 3f, earlier identified Ishchali with Dur-Rimuš on the basis of the phrase *warki mišar Dūr-Rimuš iššaknu*, which occurs in loans of the Ilšu-naṣir archive (see below note 19a). As Harris (*loc. cit.*) remarks, there is a need to account for the occurrence of this phrase. Dur-Rimuš must have been in the vicinity since a *našpakum* of Dur-Rimuš is mentioned in Lutz 48:3-4 and temple storehouses in Lutz 66:5f (É.DUB É DINGIR URU^{KI} BÀD-*Ri-muš*) and in Lutz 89:41 (É.DUB É ^d*Mi-šar*(!) *ša* BÀD-*Ri-muš* (collation)). Yet there are a number of references in the Ishchali texts which note that commodities were shipped *ana Nēribtim*: 137:2, 229:3, Lutz 3:1; these references are not distinguishable from other *ana* GN references to places which are either known or assumed to have been situated outside of Ishchali, e.g.: *ana Agagā* — 101:4, 256:4, 259:4; *ana Tutub* — 253:3, 262:8; *ana Ilbābānim* — 94:19; *ana Maškan-Abi* — 257:8. Yet the texts also show the proximity of Neribtum in that the *kārum* of that city appears in 29:12-13. The available Ishchali tablets, despite their quantity, do not supply a final answer to the question of determining the ancient name of the site. There are many city mounds in the area of Ishchali (cf. Adams, *Land Behind Baghdad*. University of Chicago Press: 1965, fig. 3 — Ishchali is site no. 442) and the proximate sites of Dur-Rimuš, Neribtum, Agaga, Ḫašḫur, and others must eventually be located within this area.

[2] OIC 13 3-4, 57[4]; see further note 87.

[3] OIC 20 74; the discussion in OIC 20 74-99 is the only published report of the excavations at Ishchali; some additional information comes from Frankfort, *Stratified Cylinder Seals from the Diyala Region*, OIP 72 pl. 96 (reproduced as fig. 2 in the present study).

The excavated tablets in this volume come from the Oriental Institute's share of the findings at Ishchali — 138 tablets[4]; there are 142 additional tablets in Baghdad which were not available for study, except for their year date formulas and some other minor data which have been excerpted from Prof. Thorkild Jacobsen's field notes[5]. There were also some inscribed bricks and a clay nail found at Ishchali; a number of these were unearthed in clear stratigraphic contexts and mention Ibalpiel son of Daduša (Ibalpiel II), Ipiq-Adad II, and Sumu-Amnanim[6].

The purchased collection consists of some 390 tablets; only 191 of these are published in this volume. The omission of the balance is due to a number of reasons: (1) tablets being already published elsewhere[7] (2) tablets not belonging to the OB period[8] (3) tablets being in a damaged or unreadable state. The provenience of the purchased collection is of course not so easily established as is the case with the excavated tablets; the assignment of these texts to the site of of Ishchali rests mainly on the testimony of the dealers who sold them[9]. Otherwise, there are only minor points of relationship between

---

[4] This volume contains only 135 out of 138; A 22004, 22005, 22006, which were described by Prof. Feigin as being mathematical texts, are at present missing from the collection.

[5] Prof. Jacobsen has generously made this material available in order to make the presentation here as complete as possible. All references to unpublished Ishchali tablets come from his notes. The only tablet from the Baghdad group that has been made available in its entirety is Ish. 35-T. 1, "An Old Babylonian Charm Against Merḫu", which was copied by Prof. Jacobsen and published by him and B. Landsberger in *JNES* 14 (1955) 14-21.

[6] OIP 43 116f. Prof. Jacobsen's field notes also record 2 fragments of what appears to be a single brick inscription: (1) *a-na* ᵈINNIN (2) ⸢Su⸣-mu-am$_x$(AW)-na-⸢nim⸣ (3) LUGAL *Ša-ad-la-[áš*^{KI}] (4) É ⸢x x⸣ (5) *ù* .... One of these fragments was found at the surface of the mound; the other in the uppermost stratum (6 R 35). These inscriptions belong to the same ruler, whose inscription was published by F. Reschid in *Sumer* 23 (1967) 178 (Arabic part): (1) ᵈ[INNIN] (2) NIN *Ša-ad-la-á*[*š*^{KI}] (3) *ra-im-ti* (4) *Su-mu-am$_x$*(AW)-*na-ni*[*m*] (5) LUGAL *Ša-ad-la-áš*^{KI} (6) *i-qí-iš*. This inscription was found at Tell Dhiba'i (see note 106). On the suggestion of here reading *am$_x$* for AW/WA see Edzard ZZB 107^{528}. A clay nail, Ish. 34-T. 1, was also found on the surface; the inscription is fragmentary and only the last lines are preserved: ... (1') [ ]*šu* (2') [*a-na ba*]-*la-ṭì-šu* (3') [*ib*]-ni(?).

[7] Sixty tablets were published by Gelb in MAD 1 270-336; these are from the OAKK period and are said to have come from Tell Asmar (see Gelb MAD 1 p. xi). Also previously published are A 7762 and 7677, which are YOS 10 60-61; no. 278 in this volume also belongs to the genre of OB liver omens treated in YOS 10. A 7873 has been incorporated in tablet xvii of *Šumma izbu* by Leichty, TCS 4 pp. 174-176; and the mathematical text A 7897 is published (without copy) in MCT 24-26. A 7754 is a list of year dates of Samsu-ditana and has been published by Feigin-Landsberger in *JNES* 14 (1955) 137-160; the tablet copy is labelled Išš 1, but this tablet probably does not come from Ishchali but, rather, from Khafaje.

[8] There are a number of tablets in the collection which appear to belong to the Kassite and NA periods, in addition to the OAkk tablets discussed in the previous note.

[9] The dealers' information regarding Ishchali and other Diyala sites was found to be extremely reliable and was most helpful to Frankfort in preparing the Oriental Institute's plan of excavation. This

the excavated tablets and the purchased collections; these are mainly established through the use of the seal of Abizum, the SANGA of the Kititum temple[10]. There are, however, numerous points of contact between the purchased collection of Frankfort and the purchased collection published by Lutz in UCP 10/1; this group of tablets was also reported to have been found at Ishchali and was acquired in Baghdad in 1929[11]. The contacts consist of prosopographic overlaps between the collections. Most of these are found in tablets belonging to the archives of Ilšu-naṣir, his father Bur-Sin, and his associate Nanna.arḫuš; and there are, in addition, a number of other persons whose names occur both in and outside of the archive texts[12]. But there are no clear links that can be established between the Lutz tablets and the excavated tablets; these two corpora can be united only via the fact that they mutually share connections with the collection purchased by Frankfort.

was the evaluation and clear recollection of Prof. Pinhas Delougaz (oral communication Summer 1974) who was with Frankfort when he visited the shops in 1930 and bought the collections for the Oriental Institute. Prof. Delougaz said that at that time they were able to assign each collection of tablets in the hands of the Baghdad dealers to a particular site — including the tablets purchased by the Oriental Institute. The tablets published by Lutz in UCP 10/1 also came from Baghdad and were also reported to have come from Ishchali. These tablets were apparently acquired by Alfred Kohlberg, a New York antiquities dealer, in 1929. The University of California Lowie Museum of Anthropology (Berkeley), the present custodians, have no records beyond the fact of their own acquisition of the tablets from Kohlberg. Prof. Delougaz was confident that he could recall and corroborate the origin point of the Lutz tablets if he could be told the name of the dealer who sold them to Kohlberg. But, unfortunately by that time, both Kohlberg and Lutz had already died.

[10] The Abizum archive is discussed below. Other points of contact between the collections are: (1) the PN, Anum-pi-Šamaš s. of Bur(!)-dSin (see index) (2) Šamaš-rabi NA.QÀD, 116:3 and 179:5 (3) the geographic name Agaga (see index) and TIM 2 7:8.

[11] See note 9.

[12] The archives of Ilšu-naṣir, etc., are discussed below. The additional persons, beyond the principals, whose names occur in both collections but within the archives are: (1) Abum-ilum s. of Sin-eriba(m) — see index in this volume and index in Seif, *Ishchali* p. 39; also UCLMA 9/2826:10 and seal, 9/2858 + 2863 and seal, 9/2862: rev. 1-2, 9/2866:2', TIM 3 126:12-13 and seal, TIM 5 21:24 and seal (2) Abum-waqar s. of Eribanum — see index in this volume and index, Seif, *Ishchali* p. 39 (3) Ipiq-Ištar s. of Ili-wedeku — 34:15 and perhaps Lutz 46:15f (Ip-qi-EŠ₄.DAR). (4) Munanum DUB.SAR — see index in this volume, index in Seif, Ishchali p. 43 sub PN and sub PN s. of Gullubija; also UCLMA 9/2826:13 and TIM 5 21:31; he uses the seal of Munawwirum his brother (cf. Lutz 25:13, 42:5, and 52) in Lutz 11, 107, UCLMA 9/2826, and TIM 5 21 (5) Riš-Šamaš s. of Nur-Šamaš — 69:4 and Lutz 17:12 (6) Šamaš-naṣir GÌR.NITÁ s. of Sin-iqišam — see 68:10 and index in Seif, Ishchali p. 45 (especially Lutz 8:6, 13:8), UCLMA 9/2826:12, 9/2858:15f. Outside of the archives there are connections in Ṣilli-Ištar s. of Imgurum — see index and Lutz 51:14; and in Šamaš-muštepiš s. of Ušepi — see index and UCLMA 9/2827:14f; in Anum-piša s. of Imguja — see index and Lutz 46:17; and in Imgur-Enlil s. of Enlil-abum — see index and UCLMA 9/2878:3f and perhaps Lutz 51:5. In addition to the personal names, the granary *našpak Ḫašḫur* is mentioned both in 137:13f, 229:20, and in Lutz 10:18.

II. The Reconstruction of Archives

A. The Archive of the *SANGA* *ᵈKititum*

The core of the archive consists of tablets which bear the seal of Abizum[13], the head priest (SANGA) of Kititum, son of Igmil-Sin. Nos. 114-117 are administrative transactions which did not directly involve the head priest but only needed his authorization. The seal, however, is also found on letters both sent and received by Abizum himself: no. 1 and TIM 2 5, a letter sent by Nanna.mansum disclaiming any use or appropriation by him of wooden wheels (GIŠ *ma-ga-ri*) belonging to Abizum. The clear identification of Abizum the SANGA in the letter no. 1 makes it possible to identify Abizum SANGA in letter no. 2 as the same person, particularly since in this second letter, the head priest identifies himself as one "who before Kititum continuously prays for you". In TIM 2 7, a letter sent by Abizum SANGA to Belum-šagiš, Abizum similarly invoked Kititum in his salutation (11. 3-4): "May Kititum cause you to live (for) a long life (*ᵈKi-ti-tum da-ri-iš u₄-mi li-ba-al-li-iṭ-ka*)." In Ish. 34-T. 95, a letter sent by ⌜Ša⌝-lu-rum to Abizum, the writer mentions a task to be performed in the temple of Kititum; this reference and the fact that the tablet, like no. 1, was found at Ishchali in the temple building, make the identification of Abizum plausible. Abizum SANGA is also the sender of the letter TIM 2 4.

There are a number of letters sent by Abizum which make no mention of his title or of the temple of Kititum; they are: TIM 2 46, 47, 56, 122 and are all addressed *ana bēlija*. In TIM 2 52, the name of the sender is missing; however, the addressee is also *ana bēlija*; and since TIM 2 52 was part of the same group of purchased texts as TIM 2 46, 47, 56, it is possible that Abizum was the sender of that letter as well. TIM 2 31 is a letter sent by Abizum to the GAL.MAR.TU; and TIM 2 43 is a letter sent to Abizum by Sin-bel-ili[14].

In addition to the documents relating to Abizum, there is another group of texts which mention his brother Inbuša, who at one time also served as SANGA of the Kititum temple: nos. 90-92, 131-132, and 231. Inbuša seems to have preceded Abizum; all of the dated documents mentioning his name

---

[13] The PN is written *A-bi-zum* in TIM 2 46-47, 56, 122; in all other places it is written *A-bi-zu-um*.

[14] There is an *A-bi-zum* NIMGIR(?) mentioned in TIM 4 34:27 (ref. courtesy of M. Stol); this text may come from the Diyala region as well since an oath is sworn by Tišpak (1.34). Van Dijk, *AfO* 23 (1970) 64, also ponders the connection and concludes that a connection is difficult to demonstrate. TIM 4 34 contains seals of persons who are ARAD Kuduzuluš, *sukkalmaḫ* of Elam; Van Dijk thinks that this text comes from Malgium.

come from the reign of Daduša and the first part of the reign of Ibalpiel II[15], while the dated texts of Abizum mention only the succeeding regnal years of Ibalpiel II[16]. Igmil-Sin, their father, also served as SANGA of the Kititum temple, to judge from the seal impression which appears on the unpublished Ishchali text Ish. 34-T.85: Ig-mil-^{dr}EN.ZU^1 SANGA ^{d}INNIN Ki-ti-tum DUMU ^{dr}x^1[   ] .... The office of SANGA at Ishchali was thus apparently passed on through a hereditary succession[17].

A number of documents mention SANGA or SANGA ^{d}Kitītum without giving the names of the respective deity or person. SANGA ^{d}Kitītum is found in 110:5 while SANGA, unidentified, occurs as the sender of letters 3, TIM 2 8, and as the addressee in 4 (a-na ša-gi-im), TIM 2 42, and apparently also in Ish. 34-T. 93, which also mentions É ^{d}INNIN. An unidentified SANGA is also mentioned in 164:1, 3, 5, 7, 9.

In the Ishchali texts there are yet other persons who bear the title SANGA but their sovereign deity and the family connections are not stated: Sin-iddinam šaggûm, in Lutz 75:8 and 79:8[18]; Sin-abum SANGA in Szlechter Tablettes

---

[15] Nos. 90 and 91 are dated to MU Da-du-ša LUGAL (year formula 17 — see index); 92 bears year date formula 28 — also of Daduša. Inbuša is identified as ARAD Daduša on seal impressions in 132 and 231 which are fragmentary. The seal impression in 131 identifies Inbuša as ARAD Ibalpiel; and the text is dated to MU ^{d}UTU-ši-^{d}IM BA.UG$_x$(BAD), year date formula 59, which, according to the Harmal Date Lists, belongs to the first part of the reign of Ibalpiel II.

[16] Nos. 114 and 117 are dated to variants of year date formula 17, which also appears on the Harmal Date Lists among the years of Ibalpiel II, as does year date formula 25, which is found in no. 115. According to the Date Lists, year formulas 17 and 25 come after year formula 59, which is the sole Ibalpiel date for Inbuša. Abizum is consistently identified as ARAD Ibalpiel in the seals.

[17] Cf. Renger, ZA 59 (1969) 119f., who outlines a similar situation at Sippar in the Old Babylonian period. Note that the priests of Kititum are styled servants of the king and not of the deity they serve; they were probably appointed by the king (cf. Renger, loc. cit.) and may have functioned as the civil rulers of Ishchali. Birot, RA 61 (1967) 85, suggests that Igmil-Sin in the letters TIM 2 12 and 15 might be the father of Abizum SANGA. Letter TIM 2 14 mentions Šamši-Adad (of Assyria).

[18] For Sin-iddinam consider also no. 17, a letter addressed ana bēlija sent by Sin-iddinam. It apparently deals with the clearing of obstructed canals: (7) [up-ta-ši-i]q-ma i-na ša-ni-im u$_4$-mi-im (8) [pu-uš]-šu-qí-im ba-ta-qí-im (9) [qa]-ti aš-ku-un (10) [mu-ú š]a i-na bi-it-qí-im (11) [a-na ša-qí]-im 30 pa-ta-tim iṣ-ṣú "...(7) got clogged up and so on the second day (8) I set my hand to (9) opening up the obstructed area; (10) but the water (coming) through the sluice (11) is too meagre to feed 30 irrigation canals." The letter goes on to ask for workers: (16) [ERÍN].^{r}ḪI.A^1 a-na ab-ni LUGAL (17) [li-iš-š]a-ap-pa-ru-ú "(16) let them send workers (17) (to fetch) the king's stones." One may compare this letter to TIM 2 4, a letter written by Abizum SANGA, which also deals with the clearing of silted canals ((5) a-na na-am-ka-ri ḫe- < re > -^{r}e-em^1 (6) qa-tam aš-ta-ka-an) and likewise asks for workers ((7) šum-ma i-na ki-na-tim ta-ra-ma-an-ni (8) 10 GURUŠ.MEŠ (9) ṭú-ru-ud-ma). TIM 2 6 may also be a letter sent to a SANGA — this is really a conjecture since the addressee is not preserved — by his lord (cf. line 2: ^{r}um-ma^1 be-el-ka-ma); the letter goes on to mention oils belonging to the goddess and to the temple of the goddess (cf. ll. 4-7, 17-18).

pl. XXII MAH 16163A:3; and perhaps also Išme-Irra ʿSANGAʾ(?), 189:2[19]. Of these persons, only Sin-abum appears in a dated document — MU GUD.GIŠ.APIN KÙ.GI (which is formula 33 in the index). This year date is often found in association with the phrase *warki mīšar Dūr-Rimuš iššaknu*[19a]; this *mīšarum* may have taken place near the end of the reign of Ibalpiel II or in the reign of his successors. One could thus place the career of Sin-abum somewhat subsequent to the attested years of Abizum's career; it is, however, of course also possible that Sin-abum was SANGA of a temple other than that of Inanna Kititum[20] or that the *mīšarum* took place much earlier, in the reign of Daduša.

B. The Archive of Ilšu-naṣir

This largest single archive among the Ishchali tablets encompasses some 73 documents, all of which come from purchased collections. Most of the documents are part of the University of California collection published by Lutz[21]; four were published elsewhere[22]; and nine new texts are in this volume[23].

In two seal impressions[23a], Ilšu-naṣir identifies himself as ARAD ᵈʿGÌR. UNUG.GALʾ; could this title signify a role in one of the temple bureacracies[24]? There exists, however, no further information about the worship of Nergal at Ishchali. It is clear that there were temples at Ishchali which

---

[19]   In Lutz 110:ii 25 one should read: *Ip-qu-ša* DUMU *Ú-bar*(!)-ᵈUTU rather then SANGA ᵈUTU (collation).

[19a]   So in Lutz 1, 16-18, 20, 34, 55, 104, Szlechter Tablettes MAH 16163A; the only exception is Lutz 9 where it occurs with year date formula 55. These texts all belong to the archive of Ilšu-naṣir, which spans the reigns of Daduša and Ibalpiel. Year date formula 33 is not included among the early years of Ibalpiel II which are preserved in the Harmal Date Lists.

[20]   For other temples, see index of place names *sub* É DN.

[21]   Lutz 1, 4-9, 11, 13-25, 28-31, 34, 37-40, 42, 44-46, 50, 52, 55, 58-59, 63, 68-69, 74, 78, 81, 85, 89-90, 93, 95, 103-104, 106-107, 110. Additional, unpublished, tablets in the California collection are: UCLMA 9/2826, 2858+2863, 2860, 2862, 2895, 3019 (all *ḫubuttātum* loans for barley except 3019, which is a sale of property); Ilšu-naṣir is also mentioned in UCLMA 9/2958 and 3030.

[22]   TIM 3 126-127, TIM 5 21, Szlechter Tablettes MAH 16163A.

[23]   See index *sub* Ilšu-naṣir, entries 2) and 4) — eleven texts in all; but texts no. 94 and 218 are probably not part of the archives; Ilšu-naṣir is only mentioned incidentally in these documents.

[23a]   The seal impressions are 217 and UCLMA 9/2957.

[24]   The designation of a person as ARAD DN is not, incontrovertably, evidence that the person was a member of a temple bureaucracy, but it is probably the best reason for a person so to be designated on a cylinder seal. Other deities which appear in the designation ARAD (ša) DN are: ᵈIM (296, Lutz 11, 19, 52, 58, 107); ᵈMAR.TU (UCLMA 9/2863, OIP 72 no. 912); ᵈNIN.ŠUBUR (25, OIP 72 no. 920, TIM 5 21); ᵈNIN.LÍL (Lutz 11, 52, 107); ᵈŠul-pa-è-a (34). The SANGA ᵈKititum, who was a royal appointee (see above note 17), acknowledged the ruler who empowered him on his seal — thus ARAD RN.

were devoted to the worship of deities other than Ištar Kititum; there are a number of references to storehouses as well as to sanctuaries belonging to other deities; attested are Sin[25], Šamaš[26], Nana[27], and Išarkidisu[28]. In the early Old Babylonian god list, TCL 15 pl. xxxi 422, the name of Išarkidisu appears shortly after that of Nergal (line 418) in the enumeration of deities; one may thus assume some relationship between the deities[29] and thereby see in the title ARAD Nergal some role for Ilšu-naṣir in the known temple of Išarkidisu. Such connection is, of course, largely a conjecture in view of the limited evidence available. However, there are a few supporting items. In Lutz 78, large quantities of barley were given out from the storehouse of Išarkidisu (1.2: É.DUB É ^{d}I-šar(!)-ki-di-s[u]); Ilšu-naṣir was in charge (1.5 ṭup(?)-pa-tim DINGIR-šu-na-ṣir ma-aḫ-ru)[30]. Another priestly connection is found in Lutz 89; a large quantity of barley is disbursed (ZI.GA) under the authority of Ilšu-naṣir; the grain comes from the storehouse of the temple of Mišar in Dur-Rimuš (É.DUB É $^{d\ulcorner}Mi$-šar$^\urcorner$ (collated) ša BÀD-Ri-muš NÍG.ŠU DINGIR-šu-na-ṣir). Ilšu-naṣir also appears as an authorizing official in Lutz 31:8-9, again apparently in conjunction with a temple storehouse (a-na É.DUB ru-ug-bi NÍG.ŠU DINGIR-šu-na-ṣir ša-pí-ik). He is also an authorizing official in 214:2 but the institution which he serves in not mentioned by name. His seal impression appears on an administrative order (217) authorizing a transfer of institutional property (lard); he himself appears as recipient of institutional goods (barley, oil) in 145, 218, Lutz 37, 110[31] and as a recipient of silver for service in the militia of Neribtum in Lutz 106:11[32].

Most of the documents in the archive are loan records; 51 tablets are *ḫubuttātum* loans[33] while another 5 are loans of other types[34]. There are eleven administrative

---

[25] 27:9; 233:2; 247:8.

[26] 78:1-2; 79:3; 86:2-3; 182:2.

[27] 234:3-4.

[28] 237:4; Lutz 47:5; 78:2. There are still other deities attested at Ishchali (see index) but it is not certain whether any of them had a separate temple; cf., e.g., 27:3'-5' for Belgašir; 85:5 for Laqipum and Wir; and 80:12, 124:1 for Adad.

[29] De Genouillac *RA* 20 (1923) 95, following Deimel Pantheon 1474, took Išarkidisu to be an alternate name for Nergal himself. More recently, Leemans SLB 1/1 25f has re-affirmed this identification; he also discusses a possible relationship between Išarkidisu and the cult of Ištar.

[30] The first sign in line 5 is not *ša* (collation) but could be UM/DUB; the *šar*(!) in line 2 is somewhat as Lutz copied it except that there are only 3 (not 4) non-parallel horizontal wedges followed by three oblique (not 4 as Lutz copied) wedges before the GIŠ (collation).

[31] The mention of Ilšu-naṣir in Lutz 110 depends upon the restoration of his name in line 4 there.

[32] Lutz 106:30f: [   ] +8 5/6 MA.NA 1 1/3 GÍN $^\ulcorner$ma-za-áš$^\urcorner$-ti Ne-ri-ib-tim^{KI}; cf. Lutz 43:2, 4.

[33] Nos. 68-71, Lutz 1, 5-9, 13-21, 23-29, 34, 38-40, 42, 44-45, 50, 55, 59, 63, 69, 74, 81, 85, 93, 95, 103-104, UCLMA 9/2826, 2858+2863, 2860, 2862, 2895, TIM 3 126-127, Szlechter Tablettes MAH 16163A.

[34] Nos. 53, 82, Lutz 4, 46, 68.

texts, emanating apparently from various temples, that mention his name[35]. In addition, there are five sales contracts[36], a hire contract (Lutz 58), and a court record (Lutz 107).

Ilšu-naṣir often functioned with a co-creditor, Nanna.arḫuš[37]. The name of this associate has been a source of uncertainty to readers in the past, being written in several ways: most commonly ᵈŠEŠ.KI.ARḪUŠ (É x SAL!); sometimes with phonetic complement — ᵈŠEŠ.KI.ARḪUŠʰᵘ⁻ᵘˢ (Lutz 7:3, 42:4, 50:3, 95:3); and sometimes "defectively" written with AD in place of ARḪUŠ[38]. Nanna.arḫuš appears alone in one loan transaction and is mentioned, apart from Ilšu-naṣir, in two other administrative texts[39].

C. Administrative Archives

The circumstances of excavation and discovery suggest the existence of still other archives at Ishchali in that groups of tablets were found together in the same find spots. These find spots may very well have been disturbed and ransacked in antiquity; yet the tablets within the group often display similar formats or subject matter, confirming that they originally were part of the same archive.

The excavations at Ishchali uncovered a city wall and a road leading from a gateway in the wall into the interior of the town. There were three major building areas situated along the road (see figure 2): (1) immediately at the gateway and abutting the city wall, a small Šamaš temple surrounded by suites of administrative offices built up along the three outside walls of the temple, which faced into the town (2) on the same (north) side of of road as the Šamaš temple, but separated from it by a large street — a larger Kititum temple with its long axis situated along the main road (3) the Serai building — the only area excavated on the south side of the main road opposite the Kititum temple; it consisted of small suites and appears to have been used for administrative offices.

The largest group of tablets come from 3 V 30, a room in the Šamaš temple area. Thirty four tablets were found in all, 26 dealing with commodity outlays; 18 of these

---

[35]   These have been listed in the previous discussion; no. 94 should be added to this group. The administrative texts, properly speaking, are probably not part of the Ilšu-naṣir archive since they may not have been held in his keeping.

[36]   Lutz 11, 22, 52, 90, UCLMA 9/3019.

[37]   Ilšu-nàṣir appears with other associates as well: Belšunu in Lutz 107 and Kabta-illassu in no. 94.

[38]   "Defective" writings, where the sign appears to be AD instead of ÉXSAL, occur in Lutz 42:4 (sign does not appear on tablet as in Lutz's copy), 46:5, 95:3; and, in the present corpus, 68:4.

[39]   The loan text is Lutz 77; Nanna.arḫuš also is mentioned in nos. 95, 108, and UCLMA 9/2866.

tablets are so similar in format that they form a single group within the present volume — nos. 182-199[40]. Six legal documents of various types were found at 5 V 31, also in the Šamaš temple area; but these documents, almost everyone broken, do not reveal who their custodian might have been.

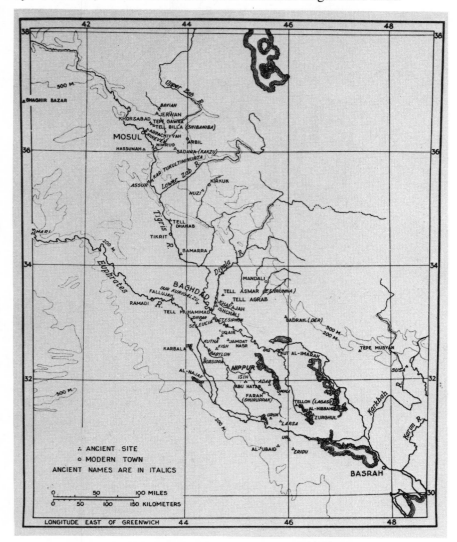

Fig. 1. Map of the Diyala Region [= OIP 78 no. 1].

[40] The balance of 26 texts, dealing with commodities, are 156-157, 161, 171-175. No. 141 also deals with grain but is a memo of receipt rather than of outlay. In many of the tablets the commodity is unspecified but is probably barley, which is mentioned in several of the tablets. The other tablets found at 3 V 30 are 50, 86, 165, 165A, 271, 296, 300, Ish. 35-T. 62; in addition, there were a number of envelope fragments : 245, 296, and a jeweler's weight (A 17667).

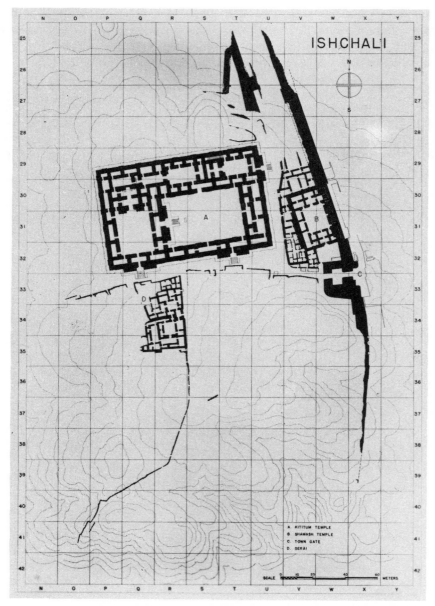

Fig. 2.   Contour Map of Excavated Area at Ishchali. Scale 1:2000 [= OIP 72 pl. 96]*

* The published plans of Ishchali do not include room numbers for the Šamaš Temple or the Serai buildings. Details of room numbers for the Kititum Temple appear in fig. 3. Additional details on the rooms in the Serai building are available from unpublished field plans; but we

In the Serai building, at 3 R 34, another group of related tablets were uncovered — 18 tablets. Six deal with delivery of fowl; nine with grain transfers; but the balance are mixed, including legal records and a school tablet[41].

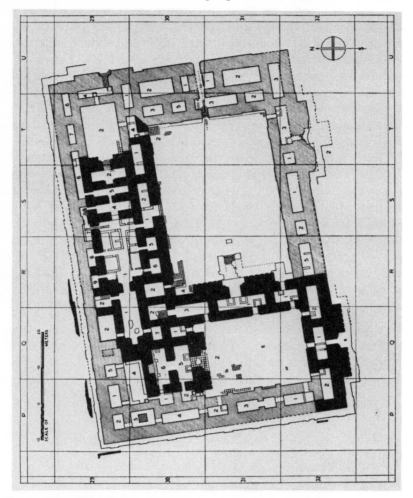

Fig. 3. Plan of Temple Complex at Ishchali. Scale 1:800 [= OIC 20 p. 77 fig. 60]**

can supply no further information on the rooms in the Šamaš Temple; that plan unfortunately was not available. In the Serai buildings, room 3 R 34, which is mentioned in the Introduction (II C), is the small square room with two doorways at the S. E. corner of R 34.

** See notes 44, 54 to the Introduction, II C, for additional information on minor variations in room numbering between recorded tablet find spots, unpublished plans, and the earlier published plan reproduced here.

---

[41] The tablets dealing with fowl are: 118, 121, 124-126; those dealing with grain are: 170, 177, 178, 180, Ish. 34-T. 26, 27, 30, 33, 38. The legal records are 87-88; and the school text is 284. Ish. 34-

12 INTRODUCTION

The Kititum temple, in rooms 1 S 29, 3 S 29, and 4 S 29, has yielded several groups of tablets which record the lending and use of tools and implements by various individuals; in one case, the recipient is identified as an *ikkarum* (261). These tools and implements include plows, plowshares, plow handles, metal rings, harness fittings, chains, shovels, spades, hoes, baskets, brick molds, and many other items, some of which are not identified, being poorly attested in the available secondary literature. Six of these records were found in room 1 S 29[42], some fourteen were unearthed in the adjoining room 4 S 29[43]; and five more came from the nearby (but unconnected) room 3 S 29[44]. The Oriental Institute Museum has a large collection of over 100 bronze implements which Henri Frankfort purchased from a dealer in Baghdad in 1930, which were said to have been found at Ishchali. These bronze objects include hooks, chisels, nails, spoons, sickles, large rings, hoes, needles, adzes, bowls, platters, tweezers, mirrors, razors, daggers, pins, spatulas, and similar objects reminiscent of the tools and implements mentioned in the Ishchali texts[45]. A recent study by P. R. S. Moorey[46] describes a similar hoard of Old Babylonian period tools found by Loftus at Tell Sifr in a public edifice in close proximity to a tablet archive. Moorey suggests that these tools were originally part of a storehouse of agricultural tools, housed in the administrative complex of the local temple and lent out by the temple for the season. It is tempting to reconstruct a similar situation in Ishchali; and to to suggest that the records recovered pertain to the lending out and use of these very tools and implements in the bronze hoard purchased by Frankfort.

The western sanctuary of the Kititum temple was the largest of the three sanctuaries in the Kititum temple complex; because of its size, Frankfort believed it to be the main sanctuary, the one actually dedicated to the worship of Ištar Kititum. The tablet finds bear out his judgement; letters belonging to the archive of the

---

T. 19 is a tag similar to nos. 118, etc. but its context is unclear. 177 probably belongs with this group as perhaps also does 297.

[42] Nos. 249, 251, 254, 265, Ish. 34-T. 83, 85.

[43] Nos. 250, 256-260, 262, Ish. 34-T. 129, 130, 132, 133-136; and perhaps also 101-102.

[44] Nos. 248, 255, 261, 266, Ish. 34-T. 105. Lutz 35 and 70 should also be compared; they are texts very similar in character to the excavated tablets. Because most of its area lies in square T 29, Room 3 S 29 was re-labelled 2 T 29 in the plan published by Frankfort in OIC 20 p. 77; our present numbering comes from the unpublished field drawings in the possession of the Oriental Institute; the tablets likewise follow this numbering. Room 2 T 29 is part of one of the subsidiary sanctuaries and leads into the cella, 2 S 29.

[45] In the Oriental Institute Museum these objects are accessioned under the numbers A 9382-9455, 9466-9505.

[46] P.R.S. Moorey, "The Loftus Hoard of Old Babylonian Tools from Tell Sifr in Iraq" *Iraq* 33 (1971) 61-86.

SANGA of Kititum were found in 6 Q 30 and 2 Q 31[47]. Frankfort remarked on the door securing Room 4 Q 30; the long, low clay shelves around this room are typical features of temple archive rooms[48] and Frankfort believed that this secured area of the temple also served as repository for treasure and precious materials. Account records relating to such valuables were found in 1 P 29, 6 Q 30, 2 Q 31[49]. Physical clues to the existence of the ancient treasures were also found: seals[50], beads[51], an amulet, a pendant, and fragments of carved stone vessels[52]. To quote Frankfort, "We could not hope, of course, to recover more than an infinitesmal fraction of the ancient treasure; in fact, we obtained none but broken bits which, when the temple fell into disuse, had not been considered worth the trouble of removal..."[53].

Tablets relating to valuables were also found in 1 S 29, a room behind the cella of the northeast sanctuary[54].

[47] No. 1 and Ish. 34-T. 74 (a letter from Abizum) were found in 6 Q 30; no. 4 and Ish. 34-T. 95, a letter to Abizum from ⌜Ša⌝-lu-ru-um, were found in 2 Q 31.

[48] Ernst Posner, *Archives in the Ancient World* (Harvard University Press, Cambridge Mass.: 1972) pp. 36 (Boghazkoi), 44 (Pylos), 54 (Telloh), 56-58 (Nippur, Šemšara); Mogens Weitmeyer "Archive and Library Techniques in Ancient Mesopotamia" *Libri* 6 (1956) 220-222.

[49] In 1 P 29, no. 107, Ish. 34-T. 88, 90; in 6 Q 30, no. 98; in 2 Q 31, Ish. 34-T. 87. Other records were stored in this area as well; in 1 P 29, no. 242; in 4 Q 30, no. 119 and a school text, Ish. 34-T. 92; in 1 P 30, nos. 18, 31, 41, Ish. 34-T. 106, 108 (sales of fields), Ish. 34-T. 68; in 6 Q 30, nos. 120, 264, 276, Ish. 34-T. 73; in 5 Q 30, no. 219; in 2 Q 31, Ish. 34-T. 93 (letter).

[50] The seals are as follows: in 1 P 29, A 16970 (=OIP 72 no. 915), 1671 (=OIP 72 no. 914); in 4 Q 30, A 17007, 17008, OIP 72 nos. 910 (Ish. 34:48), 923 (Ish. 34:39), 925 (Ish. 34:49); in 1 P 30, OIP 72 no. 916 (Ish. 34:121); in 6 Q 30, OIP 72 no. 917 (Ish. 34:45); in 5 Q 30, A 16975 (=OIP 72 no. 901), 16982, OIP 72 nos. 911 (Ish. 34:72), 912 (Ish. 34:69), p. 61 — Ish. 34:47.

[51] Beads: in 4 Q 30, A 16969; in 1 P 30, A17006; in 6 Q 30, A 21206.

[52] Amulet: in 4 Q 30, A 17005; pendant: in 6 Q 30, A 16974; fragments of carved stone vessels: in 2 P 30, A 21192 and in 4 Q 30, according to Frankfort OIC 20 85. A large number of small stone weights, made of semi-precious stones, which were found scattered in various places at the site, as well as some purchased (said to come from Ishchali), also testify to the weighing of precious materials.

[53] Frankort, *loc. cit.*

[54] This room was labelled as 5 S 29 in fig. 60, OIC 20 p. 77; cf. note 44 above; the tablets involved are nos. 104-106.

[55] Year date formula 54. This ruler is also mentioned in TIM 3 5:20ff, in a text belonging to the archive of Nur-Šamaš (see Reschid *Nuršamaš* 9) and in a literary letter, IM 54005, published by van Dijk in *Sumer* 13 (1957) 109 pl. 21 and treated by him in *AfO* 23 (1970) 65-71. At Eshnunna, Rubum is found as an addressee in three unpublished letters, T.A. 1930-96, 261, and 325; references to these tablets are by courtesy of Dr. Robert Whiting of the Oriental Institute, who is preparing a study of a collection of royal letters found at Eshnunna. There is some question as to whether Rubum is a royal name or a title "prince"; van Dijk, *op. cit.* 68, leans to the former opinion but notes that Rubum is grammatically declined in IM 54005 (as it is in the Tell Asmar letters). The matter will require further evidence. On the basis of epigraphic and other evidence, Whiting would place the time of this ruler prior to that of Ibalpiel I.

III. History and Chronology

According to the evidence, the following kings ruled over Ishchali: Rubum[55], Ipiq-Adad[56], Naram-Sin[57], Daduša[58], Ibalpiel[59], Dannum-taḫaz[60], Iqiš-Tišpak[61], and Ṣilli-Sin[62] are rulers who ruled over Eshnunna as well as over Ishchali[63]; whereas Ḫadati[64], Ḫammi-dušur[65], Ibbi-Sin[66], Sin-abušu[67], Sumu-abi-iarim[68], Sumu-Amnanim[69] are rulers who, to our knowledge, did not rule at Eshnunna but who may have ruled over other cities in addition to Ishchali[70]. The kings who ruled over both Eshnunna and Ishchali represent the imperial extension of the former city's power over the Diyala region. The other rulers would represent either the rise of local dynasts during periods of weakness at Eshnunna or conquest by other foreign powers.

The first group to be considered are the rulers of Eshnunna and Ishchali. The stratigraphic evidence from Eshnunna argues for the sequence: Ibalpiel I — Ipiq-

---

[56] Year date formulas 4 (see note there), 29 (see also note there), 40, 43.

[57] Year date formulas 50, 51; an oath is sworn by Naram-Sin in 25:25.

[58] Year date formulas 8, 17, 28 (see note there), 32, 47, 52.

[59] Year date formulas 1, 19, 21, 22, 23, 25, 27, 30, 36, 37, 46, 59.

[60] Year date formulas 9, 15.

[61] Year date formulas 44, 45. Year date formula 44, which states that Iqiš-Tišpak entered his father's palace (as king), suggests that Ibni-Irra, father of Iqiš-Tišpak, also ruled at Ishchali and Eshnunna; cf. Jacobsen OIP 43 121[19a]. A formula of Ibni-Irra's was found at Tell Harmal; see Simmons JCS 13 (1959) 118, no. 41:19f.(t).

[62] Year date formula 57.

[63] The evidence for rule at Eshnunna comes from tablets and inscriptions unearthed at Tell Asmar, the ancient site of Eshnunna; see the discussion of T. Jacobsen OIP 43 116-200. For Rubum see note 55 above; and for Dannum-taḫaz see ARM 5 59:7ff, 6 37:5ff, and 14 104:5, where he is mentioned in association with Eshnunna and its armies. See also TIM 5 19:14.

[64] Year date formula 34.

[65] He is mentioned in text no. 326, the treaty.

[66] Year date formula 41.

[67] Year date formulas 5, 13, 18 (see note there), 38, 60, 61 (see note there).

[68] No. 27:8', which is a tablet excavated at Ishchali. R. al Hashimi, Sumer 28 (1972) 32, records the existence of a tablet bearing the oath by Sin and Sumu-abi-arium (sic), found in Level II at Tell Dhiba'i. These are apparently the same rulers.

[69] See note 6 above.

[70] Specific information is available for Hammi-dušur, who ruled at Šaduppum (Tell Harmal), Tutub (Khafaje), Ṣilli-Adad, Dur-Rimuš, and the site now called Tell Dhiba'i; see Simmons JCS 13 (1959) 78f sub (w); see now also YOS 14 p. 3. Al Hashimi, Sumer 28 (1972) 30f. states that Hammi-dušur also controlled Zaralulu and Šadlaš; but his sources are not given. Sin-abušu reigned at Šaduppum, Tutub, Dur-Rimuš, Šulgi-Nanna, Dur-Sin-abušu, and Aškuzum; see Reschid Nuršamaš 6-9 and Al Hashimi, loc. cit.. Rubum ruled at Šaduppum (see note 55). Sumu-Amnanim called himself king of Šadlaš; his inscriptions have been found at Ishchali and Dhiba'i (see notes 6, 106).

Adad II — Naram-Sin — Daduša — Ibalpiel II[71]; there is no interruption between the reigns of Daduša and Ibalpiel II[72]; and there is very likely no break between Ibalpiel I and Ipiq-Adad II[73]. Naram-Sin son of Ipiq-Adad and Daduša son of Ipiq-Adad are placed together after Ipiq-Adad II because of their patronymics and because bricks bearing the names of Naram-Sin and Ibalpiel son of Daduša were found together in a context later in time than Ipiq-Adad II[74]. But there is no absolute certainty that Ipiq-Adad II, Naram-Sin, and Daduša ruled consecutively without a break, i.e., that no other king ruled during that period of time[75].

Both Daduša and Ibalpiel II are known to have been contemporaries of Šamši-Adad I of Assyria; this is based (1) on year data formula 59 which is the fifth year of Ibalpiel II according the Harmel Date Lists[76]; and (2) a text fragment from Mari published by Dossin, which links Šamši-Adad, Daduša, and Iaḫdun-Lim[77]. Dannum-taḫaz is also mentioned in the Mari correspondence; he occurs both in letters of Iasmaḫ-Adad and of Zimri-Lim[78]. But he could not have ruled during all of that time since Ibalpiel II was king at Eshnunna during the time of Iasmaḫ-Adad (son of Šamši-Adad) and likewise continued to rule during the reign of Zimri-Lim[79]. Dannum-taḫaz apparently did not have a long reign; there are only two year dates attested and another king of Eshnunna, Ṣilli-Sin, also reigned as a contemporary to Zimri-Lim[80].

[71] Jacobsen OIP 43 116f., 119.
[72] The so-called Harmal Date List 2 (IM 53955), published by T. Baqir *Sumer* 5 (1949) 45f, 84, shows that year date formula 52 directly preceeded Ibalpiel II's first regnal year.
[73] Jacobsen OIP 43 118.
[74] Jacobsen OIP 43 117.
[75] Simmons *JCS* 13 (1959) 78 suggests that Iqiš-Tišpak and Ibni-Irra ruled between Naram-Sin and Daduša; and that Ibni-Irra was a brother of Daduša and Naram-Sin. Simmons was moved towards this suggestion because of the "spread" of rulers in the Gidanum archive; on this problem, see the discussion presently below.
[76] T. Baqir *Sumer* 5 (1949) pp. 37, 45-46, 83-84.
[77] Dossin *Syria* 20 (1939) 99.
[78] See note 63; that Dannum-taḫaz actually reigned can be seen from (1) his year date formulas (nos. 9, 15); (2) TIM 5 19:14-16 where an oath is taken by Tišpak and by Dannum-taḫaz (see van Dijk *AfO* 23 (1970) 64f.); (3) seal legends where persons call themselves ARAD Dannum-taḫaz (no. 34, TIM 5 19, Simmons *JCS* 15 (1961) 83 no. 140).
[79] Dossin, *Syria* 19 (1938) 117f; this is the famous letter to Zimri-Lim which mentions Hammurapi, Rim-Sin of Larsa, Ibalpiel II, Amutpiel of Qaṭanum, and Iarim-Lim of Iamḫad.
[80] Bottéro ARM 15 157, based on ARM 2 45: rev. 2. It is possible that year date formula 15, which refers to Dannum-taḫaz's fortress of (royal) sonship, is not actually a formula of his own reign but one of his father's. Van Dijk, *AfO* 23 (1970) 65, was the first to offer the reconstruction of the sequence: Ibalpiel II — Dannum-taḫaz — Ṣilli-Sin.

There is a question of where to place the reigns of Iqiš-Tišpak and his father Ibni-Irra[81]. The Gidanum archive, published by Simmons, contains year date formulas of Ipiq-Adad, Naram-Sin, Dannum-taḫaz, Ibni-Irra and Iqiš-Tišpak[82]. Simmons was troubled by the omission in that archive of any year formulas belonging to Ibalpiel II and was therefore moved to insert the reigns of Ibni-Irra and Iqiš-Tišpak into the period before Daduša and Ibalpiel II. But this is no longer a compelling reason; since Dannum-taḫaz must have ruled after Ibalpiel II, the omission of Ibalpiel II year dates is therefore simply an accident of discovery or preservation; and the years of his reign as well as that of Daduša must be assumed in the life of Gidanum.

Accordingly, at least seven kings — the five mentioned plus Daduša and Ibal-piel II — must have reigned during the public career of Gidanum. Minimal estimates based on known year date formulas add up to no less than 34 years[83]. This necessary compression of time has important implications for the overall chronology. For if the death of Šamši-Adad I occurred between the 10th and 12th year of Hammurapi[84],

---

[81]   See note 61.

[82]   Simmons *JCS* 13 (1959) 76-78, incorporating his years (k) through (u).

[83]   In adding up the years of Gidanum, it makes little difference whether one places Ibni-Irra and Iqiš-Tišpak after Naram-Sin as Simmons or after Dannum-taḫaz as given here. In either case, the same years are counted. The figures are: $1+5+9+14+2+1+2$. Ipiq-Adad II ruled for at least one year (Simmons *JCS* 13 (1959) 74ff. (k)), allowing for the possibility that this could have been the last year of Ipiq-Adad II (for other formulas see note 56 and Jacobsen OIP 43 126f). Naram-Sin ruled for at least five years: Simmons (l), (m), (o), formula 50 (disregarding 51 as perhaps overlapping one of the other year date formulas), T. Baqir *Sumer* 5 (1949) 52, 77, no. 3, 55, 77, no. 7 (possibly the same year as Simmons (m)). Daduša ruled for at least nine years — cf. Simmons *JCS* 13(1959) 80, dates 1-8, 10; date 9 belongs to Sin-abušu; see note to year date formula 38. Ibalpiel II has at least 14 year date formulas: Harmal Date List 1:1, formula 27 (= Harmal Date List 1:2), formula 46 (= Harmal Date List 1:3), formula 48 (= Harmal Date List 1:4), formula 59 (= Harmal Date List 1:5), Harmal Date List 1:6 (cf. formula no. 24), formula 1 (= Harmal Date List 1:7), formula 19 (= Harmal Date List 1:8), formula 53 (= Harmal Date List 1:9), formula 25 (= Harmal Date List 1:10), formula 30 (= Harmal Date List 1:11), formula 23 (= Harmal Date List 2:14 and assuming the possibility that formula 23 can be merged with 24 — see note to year date formula 24), formulas 21, 37 (see note there). Dannum-taḫaz reigned for at least two years: cf. formulas 9, 15; formula 10 may be the same as 9. There is a possibility that formula 15 reflects a time before Dannum-taḫaz was king; in that case, one could assign it to Ipalpiel II and leave Dannum-taḫaz with a one year reign. The number of total years (34) would not, however, change. There is a possibility that there is one additional year to be added to the reign of Dannum-taḫaz or Ibalpiel II; see note 41 to year date formula 29. This additional year would raise the total from 34 to 35 years. Another year, possibly to be added to the total and to be assigned to the reign of Daduša or later, is the enigmatic YOS 14 74:12f: MU BÀD *Da-du-ša* (?) *ša ka-a-ri*, "The year Fort Daduša of the quays". Ibni-Irra has one — Simmons (t); and Iqis-Tišpak has two formulas: no. 44 (= Simmons (s)) and 45.

[84]   Rowton CAH³ 1/1 209f; Jacobsen OIP 43 125.

then the last years of Ipiq-Adad II would fall as late as in the middle of the reign of Sin-muballiṭ, the immediate predecessor of Hammurapi[85].

Hammurapi seems to have won a decisive victory over Eshnunna in his 37th year[86]; while no actual evidence of his occupation has been found at Eshnunna, the forces of Babylon do seem to have penetrated into the Diyala area. Year formulas of Samsu-iluna (regnal years 10 and 27) have been found at Khafaje, Mound B, where that king built a fort, Dur-Samsu-iluna[87]. It is however possible that local rulers continued to govern Eshnunna. The city was not permanently destroyed; soldiers of Samsu-iluna were stationed there according to the military rolls from

[85] See the previous note. If one begins with the fifth year of Ibalpiel II, which commemorates the death of Šamši-Adad, then one, counting backwards in time, arrives at the figures 5+9+5+1 or 21. If one goes back in time from Hammurapi 10/12, then one arrives at Sin-muballit 10/12 for the earliest possible synchronism date for the last year of Ipiq-Adad II. This placement of rulers would rule out the view that identifies Naram-Sin of Assyria, the second king prior to Šamši-Adad I with Naram-Sin of Eshnunna. Šamši-Adad ruled for 33 years according to the Assyrian King List (Gelb, *JNES* 4 (1954) 209-230); the beginning of his reign would thus fall around Apil-Sin 15. If one allows some time for his predecessor Erišum II, then Naram-Sin of Assyria must have ruled near the beginning of the reign of Apil-Sin (cf. Edzard ZZB 164). It is impossible to reconcile this chronology with the chronological implications of the Gidanum archive.

[86] Ungnad "Datenlisten" RLA 2 180-181.

[87] See year date formulas 70-72. Samsu-iluna's year date formulae for his 24th year and his inscriptions attest to the building of Dur-Samsu-iluna on the shores of the Turan (Poebel, *AfO* 9 (1933/34) 247 (see also p. 244) col. iii, 3-5). Cf. further 311: obv. 7' which records PN [*wa-ši*]-*ib* BÀD *Sa-am-su-i-lu-na*[KI] *ša* GÚ ÍD *Dur*-ʿÚLʾ. The ÍD *Dur*-ÙL is the river Diyala or Turan (also Turnat); on this identification see Jacobsen *Sumer* 14 (1958) 83 and, more recently, the discussion of Borger, *AfO* 23 (1970) 1. The line in Diri III 200, which Falkenstein, *ZA* 45 (1939) 69f, based on ZA 42 (1934) 151, 200, wished to read [na-r]a-an = ÍD.DUR.KIB, was subsequently read by Landsberger as [Tu]-ra-an = ÍD.DUR.UL$_x$ = *Tu-ra-an* (reference to ms. courtesy of Prof. I. J. Gelb). The Ṭaban, mentioned in 314: rev. 3, is the other great water system of the Diyala region and is probably to be identified with the precourser to the Mahrudh canal system, and continuing southward via the Asmar-Ajrab canal into what was later to be the lower Nahrwan; see figure 3 in Adams, *Land Behind Baghdad* (University of Chicago Press: 1965). This identification requires slight modification of the reconstruction earlier put forward by Jacobsen in *Sumer* 14 (1958) 83 and represents his current opinion (private communication). Khafaje has been identified as the site of Dur-Samsu-iluna for the following reasons: (1) a duplicate of Poebel's inscription was found at the site — Mounds B+C (OIP 43 123[26]), (2) a fortress structure, probably dating to before the time of Samsu-iluna, was found on Mound D (Frankfort *AJSL* 52 (1935-35) 210), (3) texts no. 305-325, which deal with military personnel and which date to the time of Samsu-iluna, are said to come from Mounds B+C (OIP 43 123[26]). If Khafaje is Dur-Samsu-iluna, then the Diyala, which now runs close by, should be the Turan. The Ṭaban, on the other hand, is associated with Eshnunna (Tell Asmar) and other cities east of the Tigris like Der. Tablets from Tell Asmar mention the Ṭaban close by (Jacobsen OIP 43 181 in note to formula 77); and in the "Lipšur"-litanies of later periods, Tišpak, the god of Eshnunna, is referred to as the *gugallum* of the Ṭaban (Reiner *JNES* 15 (1956) 134 line 53). The proximity of the Ṭaban to Der, further to the south, is seen in King BBSt no. II 11. 2 and 8. The Turan, according to tradition, is "the mother of rivers" (Reiner *op. cit.* line 52) and the Ṭaban is its major tributary system.

Khafaje[88]; and the king had to fight Anni (or Iluni), a king of Eshnunna, in about his 23rd year[89].

Ibalpiel II, Dannum-taḫaz, Iqiš-Tišpak, and Ibni-Irra all reigned as contemporaries to Zimri-Lim of Mari[90]. According to the preserved evidence, Iasmaḫ-Adad must have reigned for at least one year at Mari after the death of Šamši-Adad[91]; and Zimri-Lim for at least some 22 to 24 years thereafter, before the conquest of Mari by Hammurapi[92]. According to available sources, the four Eshnunna rulers must account for at least 14 of the years after the death of Šamši-Adad[93]; if Eshnunna was totally vanquished in Hammurapi's 37th year, then that would leave a minimum of 11/13 years[94] which could be assigned to the known rulers of Eshnunna or to other kings who are as yet unknown. If native rule was not abolished at Eshnunna after the conquest by Hammurapi, then there would be even more years left to account for[95].

---

[88]   See Index of Place Names. The military rolls of Khafaje also mention soldiers stationed at Neribtum, Tutub, and Dur-Rimuš (see Index). The pessimistic picture of the effects of Babylon's conquest of the Diyala area given in Adams, *Land Behind Baghdad* (University of Chicago Press: 1965) 46-49 can be a little brightened. See Table 12, page 47 there; under 3, sites largely or wholly abandoned..., one can remove from the list of large towns nos. 244 (Tell Asmar), 421 (Khafaje B + C), 442 (Ishchali), and the as yet unidentified site of Dur-Rimuš.

[89]   Jacobsen OIP 43 200. No inscriptions or year date formulas of this ruler have survived.

[90]   For Ibalpiel II and Dannum-taḫaz, see above, in conjunction with notes 78-80. Iqiš-Tišpak and Ibni-Irra are not expressly mentioned as contemporaries of Zimri-Lim; they did, however, reign later than the time of Naram-Sin as shown by stratigraphic evidence at Tell Asmar (OIP 43 100, 121). If, as it seems, there were no other rulers who ruled between the time of Naram-Sin and Daduša, then Ibni-Irra and Iqiš-Tišpak must be placed after Ibalpiel II and Dannum-taḫaz, presumably contemporary with Zimri-Lim.

[91]   ARM 4 20 demonstrates that Iasmaḫ-Adad was ruler of Mari (cf. especially 11. 13ff); Dossin Studia Mariana 53 no. 3 is a year date formula of his.

[92]   Dossin, *Studia Mariana* 54-59, records 32 year date formulas for Zimri-Lim; nos. 6, 12, 15, 17, 24 are named after the events of previous years so they could be duplicates of other formulas of Zimri-Lim. This is also the case with the formula published in ARM 11 149:9-12, which is named after the events of Dossin's year date formula 21. Formulas 2 and 3 could be merged as well, leaving 26 year date formulas. But even this may be too many years if one counts from Hammurapi 10/12, which was when Šamši-Adad was still alive. If one allows but one year to Iasmaḫ-Adad, then there are but 22/24 years left for Zimri-Lim up to Hammurapi 35 when Hammurapi destroyed the walls of Mari (cf. Edzard ZZB 164f). But the reign of Zimri-Lim at Mari could even be shorter; Hammurapi 33 already celebrates the defeat of Mari and a tablet bearing his year formula 32 was found at Mari (Dossin, *Studia Mariana* 59).

[93]   Samsi-Adad's death is commemorated as Ibalpiel year 5 (year date formula 59); this leaves (cf. note 83) at least nine more years for Ibalpiel II, two for Dannum-taḫaz, one for Ibni-Irra, and two for Iqiš-Tišpak.

[94]   Hammurapi 10/12 = Ibalpiel 5; if one adds the 14 years, one arrives at Hammurapi 24/26, leaving some 13/11 years.

[95]   Van Dijk, *AfO* 23 (1970) 63ff, raises the question of Elamite rule at Eshnunna. He notes that the Diyala tablet TIM 4 34:35 has an oath by ᵈTišpak *u* SUKKAL.M[AḪ]; even if the

B.C.	Babylon	Aššur	Eshnunna	Mari	Ishchali	Khafaje	Harmal [2]	Dhiba·i [3]	Elsewhere [4]
1894	Sumu-abum (14)		Ipiq-Adad I						*Ašdum-labum
			Šiqlanum [1]						*Abi-bitim
			Abdi-erah						*Ahsakrum
1880									*Bali-apuh
						*Abdi-erah	*Waqrum		*Adaki
						*Tattanum	*Šumahum		*Ili-dahad
					*Hadati	*Iaqim-El	*Ištašni...		Immerum
					*Išme-Bali	*Išme-Bali	Immerum		Iarim-Lim
						*Abi-madar			Sumu-numhim
	Sumu-la-El (36)		*Abi-madar			*Sumu-narim			
					Hammi-dušur	Hammi-dušur	Ammi-dušur	Ammi-dušur	
					*Sin-abušu	*Sin-abušu	*Sin-abušu	Iadkur-El	
					*Ikun-pi-Sin	*Ikun-pi-Sin			
1844	Sabium (14)		*Belakum						
					*Rubum	*Warassa	*Taram-Urim		*Rim-Dagan
			*Warassa						*Iahzir-Il
									*Iamini
			*Rubum						
1830	Apil-Sin (18)								
1812	Sin-muballit (20)		Ibalpiel I						
			Ipiq-Adad II	Iaggid-Lim	Ipiq-Adad II				
			Naram-Sin		Naram-Sin				
			Daduša	Iahdun-Lim	Daduša				
1792		Šamši-Adad I (33)		*Sumu-iamam					
			Ibalpiel II	Iasmah-Adad	Ibalpiel II				
1782									
	Hammurapi (43)	Išme-Dagan (40)	Dannum-tahaz	Zimri-Lim	Dannum-tahaz				
			*Šilli-Sin		*Šilli-Sin				
			*Ibni-Irra		*Ibni-Irra				
					*Iqiš-Tišpak				
			*Iqiš-Tišpak		*Sumu-Amnanim			*Sumu-Amnanim	Kuduzuluš I
					*Sumu-abi-iarim			*Sumu-abi-arium	
1749					*Ibbišu-Malik				
	Samsu-iluna (31)				*Ibbi-Sin				
1726			Anni						

(1) For the synchronism of Šiqlanum and Sumu-abum, see Jacobsen OIP 43 191.
(2) For Harmal, see note 103. Waqrum, Šumahum, Ištašni..., Immerum are attested in documents of Level IV; Sin-abušu and Ammi-dušur are attested in texts of Levels III and IV. Taram-Urim is attested in Level III.
(3) See note 103. Ammi-dušur is attested in documents of Level V at Dhiba·i; Iadkur-El is mentioned in an oath formula from Level IV; Sumu-abi-arium(sic) is mentioned in an oath formula from Level II. Sumu-Amnanim is mentioned in an inscription found at Dhiba·i (see note 6).
(4) Sumu-numhim apparently also ruled at Marad (see note 97); Immerum was king of Sippar. We have provisionally assumed that all kings who are mentioned in the formula MU RN BA.UG$_x$ may not in fact have ruled in the place from which the commemoration originated. This is certainly true for Šamši-Adad of Assyria whose death is commemorated among the year formulae of Ibalpiel II (cf. year date formula 59). The same is very likely true for Iarim-Lim (cf. year date formula 35). For this reason, we have separated all of the rulers cited in death commemoration year date formulae. Ašdum-labum, Abi(Abu)-bitim, Ahsakrum, Ili-dahad(dihad) come from sources in Level V of Dhiba·i; the last named king is also commemorated in the archive of the Sin temple at Khafaje along with Bali-apuh and Adaki. The death of Belakum, king of Eshnunna, is similarly commemorated at Khafaje. From Harmal Level III comes mention of the deaths of Rim-Dagan(sic), Iahzir-Il, and Iamini.

* means that the position of the ruler within the column is not certain.

The search for hiatuses in the chronological scheme is prompted by the need to place the many local rulers, who ruled over Ishchali and other cities in the Diyala area but who apparently were not ever rulers of Eshnunna. Out of the six local rulers listed above, only three are really known to have ruled elsewhere, outside of Ishchali: Ḥammi-dušur, Sin-abušu, and Sumu-Amnanim[96]. Text no. 326 is a treaty between Ḥammi-dušur (written Ammi-dušur) and Sumu-numḫim, kings of Neribtum and Šadlaš; a king named Sumu-numḫim was ruler of Marad up to the 20th year of Sumulael of Babylon, who apparently conquered the city of Marad at that time[97].

The stratigraphic evidence from Eshnunna shows a gap between Ipiq-Adad I, son of Ur-Ninmar, and Ipiq-Adad II, son of Ibalpiel I; during this interval, a number of other persons ruled at Eshnunna: Warassa, Belakum, Šarrija, Abdi-eraḫ, and Šiqlanum. The first three are placed by stratigraphy; the latter two by prosopographic considerations[98]. The clustering of these rulers during the period between Ipiq-Adad I and Ibalpiel I, father of Ipiq-Adad II, is supported by the appearance of year date formulas mentioning Abdi-eraḫ, Belakum, Warassa, and Ḥammi-dušur in the administrative archive of the Sin temple at Khafaje[99]. The tablets were all discovered at the same time in adjoining rooms of the Sin temple; the tablets thus do not span more than a generation or so of time[100]. It therefore seems that Ḥammi-dušur and the other local rulers who ruled at Khafaje came to power because Eshnunna was in a period of decline and that this decline indeed did take place between the reigns of Ipiq-Adad I and Ipiq-Adad II[101].

reading of this line is not beyond question, seals of the judges in TIM 4 33 and 34 identify them as ARAD Kuduzuluš, who was ruler of Elam. TIM 4 34 and 35 do support the fact of some Elamite penetration into the Diyala area; but it is not enough evidence to support the assumption· of Elamite rule at Eshnunna itself.

[96]   See note 70 above. One would like very much to identify the ruler Iarim-Lim, who is mentioned in the date to the treaty, text no. 326 (year date formula 35). This royal name is reminiscent of names used for kings at Aleppo and Alalakh; but, of course, as Harris, *JCS* 9 (1955) 49[32] already notes, the king in the treaty must be earlier.

[97]   Jacobsen OIP 43 124 and note 29; cf. also Edzard ZZB 125 and Kupper *Les Nomades* 199f. The argument for taking the reigns of Hammi-dušur and Sumu-la-El to be proximate in time is a little furthered by the fact that oaths sworn by Immerum (a contemporary of Sumu-la-El — see Edzard ZZB 129) and year date formulae of Ammi-dušur are found in Harmal documents from Level IV (the latter also in Level III). See R. al Hashimi, *Sumer* 28 (1972) 30f.

[98]   Jacobsen OIP 43 119f. In connecting Abdi-eraḫ and Šiqlanum with Ipiq-Adad I, Jacobsen makes the important point that the successors of Ipiq-Adad II are known while those of Ipiq-Adad I are not.

[99]   R. Harris, *JCS* 9 (1955) 46-47, date formulas 10, 13, 17, 22.

[100]   Harris, *JCS* 9 (1955) 35-37.

[101]   Additional support for the placing of Ḥammi-dušur comes from Simmons JCS 13 (1959) 78-79, where he discusses the year date formulas of archive C; this archive records the names

The synchronism between Sumu-numḫim and Sumulael on the one hand and the setting of the reign of Ipiq-Adad II at the very latest to the middle of the reign of Sin-muballiṭ on the other would allow an interval of some fifty years between Ḥammi-dušur and Ipiq-Adad II[102]. Into this period one could assign the numerous local dynasts who ruled at Ishchali and elsewhere[103].

This must be the period in which Sin-abušu ruled. He is a well attested king who ruled for no less than 14 years[104]. Tablets from his reign have been found at Ishchali, Khafaje, and Harmal[105]; and according to the year date formulas, he controlled the ancient towns of Neribtum, Dur-Rimuš, Šulgi-Nanna, Aškuzum, besieging but not capturing Šadlaš. As far as the ancient sites can be identified[106], he seems to have confined his political activities around the mouth

of Belakum and Ḥammi-dušur only. Moreover, the selection of year date formulae found on tablets from Tell Dhiba'i, Level V, include mention of the death of Belakum along with year dates of Ammi-dušur; these are given by al Hashimi, *Sumer* 28 (1972) 31.

[102] According to note 85, the latest date for the last year of Ipiq-Adad II would fall at Sin-muballiṭ 10/12. According to the present evidence, Ipiq-Adad II ruled for at least four years; cf. year date formulas 4, 29, 40 and 43 (and cf. Simmons (k), (z)). This would mean that he came to the throne no later than Sin-muballiṭ 6/8. If at the other end, one assumes that Sumu-numḫim did not rule beyond Sumulael 20, then one arrives at 54/56 years between Ḥammi-dušur (same time as Sumu-numḫim) and the accession year of Ipiq-Adad II (i.e. 6/8 for Sin-muballiṭ, + 18 for Apil-Sin, + 14 for Sabium, + 16 years of Sumulael — up to his year 20). This figure would of course represent the maximum; discovery of more year dates in the reigns of the period Ipiq-Adad II — Ibalpiel II would reduce this gap.

[103] The local rulers of Ishchali are listed above. One should perhaps add Ikun-pi-Sin, who ruled at Khafaje (Harris *JCS* 9 (1955) 47 no. 25 and p. 55); there are two seal impressions on Ishchali tablets which style the bearer as ARAD Ikun-pi-Sin (see Index). Another possible local ruler is Ibbišu-Malik, who is mentioned on a seal impression in no. 130. Note also the third line of the seal impression in no. 29. For the local rulers at Khafaje (and some at Eshnunna) see the important discussion of Harris *JCS* 9 (1955) 46-58; for Harmal, see Simmons, *JCS* 13 (1959) 78-82, and al Hashimi, *Sumer* 28 (1972) 29-33. For Tell Dhiba'i, see T. Baqir *Sumer* 5 (1949) 140-143 and al Hashimi, *op. cit.*

[104] See Reschid *Nuršamaš* 2-6. The year dates listed can be reduced by (1) the numerous ús.sa formulas: aa-ac, ae are variants of ad; g is a variant of f; z is a variant of n (2) duplication: s and u; ka and kb; h, i, r, w, and y; ag and gf; n, o, t, and ab. This reduction yields 13 unique formulas, to which one can add year date formula 13 from Ishchali. Date formulas 5, 18, 38, 59, and 60 are duplicates of those in Reschid's collection.

[105] For Ishchali and Harmal see the previous notes. Khafaje year date formulas (Harris *JCS* 9 (1955) 46-47) nos. 15 and 24 must be assigned to Sin-abušu; cf. Ishchali year date formulas 13 and 60.

[106] Neribtum and Dur-Rimuš are Ishchali and vicinity; and Šulgi-Nanna cannot be far since it is mentioned along with Tutub as the destination for a loan of implements in 253. The location of Aškuzum is uncertain; while Šadlaš has been identified as Tell Dhiba'i by Reschid, *Sumer* 23 (1967) 177-182, on the basis of the inscription cited above in note 6. But inscriptions of that ruler, Sumu-Amnanim king of Šadlaš, have also been found at Ishchali (see note 6); accordingly, one can only argue for Dhiba'i = Šadlaš on the basis of the deity ᵈ[INNIN] NIN *Ša-ad-la-á*[*s*ᴷᴵ], assuming that her centre was in fact Tell Dhiba'i where the inscription was found. If Dhiba'i = Šadlaš, then some new

of the Diyala, never conquering Eshnunna, which his formulas never mention and where no trace of him has been found [107].

The Nur-Šamaš archive, in which most of the Sin-abušu year dates appear, also contains formulas for Rubum and Sin-iqišam of Larsa [108]. This synchronism helps place the span of the archive in the period between Ipiq-Adad I and Ibalpiel I, supporting the conclusion reached here and suggested earlier by van Dijk [109].

problems emerge. First, the treaty between Šadlaš and Neribtum (no. 326); Hammi-dušur is attested as ruler at Dhiba'i (see note 70); if Dhiba'i = Šadlaš, then we must ask (1) when did Hammi-dušur become king of Šadlaš? (2) was Sumu-numḫim, at the time of the treaty, king of Šadlaš or Neribtum? Sumu-numḫim has been associated with a king of the same name from Marad (see discussion above in connection with note 97); he is not attested in the Diyala while Hammi-dušur is attested at several other Diyala sites (see note 70). Most scholars have thus taken him (i.e., Hammi-dušur) to be ruler at Neribtum, which is more frequently named in the OB Diyala tablets and have assigned Šadlaš, less commonly mentioned, to Sumu-numḫim.

[107]   Still to be identified is the anonymous builder of the palace at Eshnunna which stood between the levels of Ipiq-Adad I and Ibalpiel I, father of Ipiq-Adad II (see Jacobsen OIP 43 119). Perhaps Rubum, whose political power was well established (cf. van Dijk *AfO* 23 (1970) 70), is the person to whom this building should be assigned.

[108]   Reschid *Nuršamaš* 3, year date m belongs to Rubum; and the fragmentary formula p Reschid (pp. 9 f) assigns to Sin-iqišam of Larsa (see, too, van Dijk *AfO* 23 (1970) 70), who is a contemporary of Sabium of Babylon.

[109]   See the previous note.

YEAR DATE FORMULAS

Ishchali year date formulas

1 MU A.LAM$_x$(LUM) K[Ù.G]I[1]   Lutz 59:15
   "The year the golden statue"[2]

2 MU ALAM KÙ.GI *a-na* É.GAL-lim *i-ru-bu*[3]   137:16-17
   "The year the golden statue entered the palace"

3 ⸢MU A.LAM$_x$(LUM)⸣ KÙ.GI É ᵈEN.ZU ⸢Ù É ᵈEN.LÍL⸣
   BA.DÍM[4]   Lutz 29:13f
   ⸢MU ALAM⸣ KÙ.GI É ᵈEN.⸢LÍL Ù⸣ ᵈ*É-a* BA.⸢DÍM⸣[5]   Lutz 93:16f
       "The year he built the golden statue and the temples of
       Sin (var. Ea) and Enlil"

4 MU ALAM KÙ.GI ⸢X⸣ *Ši-ma-ḫa-tu*   134:7f
   MU ALAM KÙ.GI ⸢*Ši*⸣-*ma-ḫa-tu*[6]   123:5f
       "The year the golden statue (and) Šimaḫatu"

5 MU(!) URUDU ALAM.MEŠ *a-na* É EŠ$_4$.DAR *i-ru-bu-ú*   43:21f
   "The year the copper statues entered the temple of Ištar"

---

[1] Collation. Cf. MU ALAM KÙ.GI, IM 53955:8 (Harmal Date List 2) T. Baqir *Sumer* 5(1949) 84; the corresponding line in Harmal Date List 1, IM 52962:7, (pp. 45 and 83) is MU ALAM KI.GUB KÙ.GI. According to T. Baqir, *op. cit.* 66 *sub* no. 27, this formula also occurs in IM 53931, 51621, and in IM 52561 (see p. 58 there). MU ALAM KÙ.GI also occurs in UCLMA 9/2943.

[2] It may be possible to take A.LUM as UDU.A.LUM "sheep"; cf. CAD A/1 374b. However, variants in ALAM (in formula 3) suggest the present reading.

[3] Similar but as yet unrelated formulas are: MU I-ba-al-pí-el ALAM KÙ.GI *a-na e-šèr-tim ú-še-lu-ú* Simmons (d), *JCS* 13 (1959) 106, no. 5:14-17; MU ALAM KÙ.GI *a-na i-šer-tim i-ru-bu*, MU ALAM KÙ.GI ZAG.GAR.RA BA.AN.KU$_4$.KU$_4$ Harmal No. 15, discussed by T. Baqir *Sumer* 5 (1949) 59f and 79 — IM 52929 and 52275; MU ALAM ŠUD$_x$(KAxŠU)(!) KÙ.GI ZAG ᵈ⸢X X⸣ BA.DÍM, IM 52276, 52416, *op. cit.* 60 and 79 *sub* no. 16. A possible relationship between these and formula 2 is yet to be determined.

[4] For a doubtful augment to this formula see note 34 below.

[5] See formulas 19 and 20 below; formula 3 may serve as a "bridge" uniting formulas 3, 19, and 20 into one. It has been suggested that formulas 23 and 24 are also related formulas; on this see note 29 below.

[6] Text no. 123 bears a seal of PN ARAD Ipiq-Adad; the formula is reminiscent of MU BÀD *Ši-ma-ḫa-at-tu i-na pa-šum* BA.DÙ, which occurs in TIM 4 39:47f. That tablet is clearly from the reign of Ipiq-Adad, as can be seen from 11. 6, 9f, which record an oath by Tišpak and Ipiq-Adad.

MU ꞌALAM.MEŠ *a-na* É ^{<d>}INNINꞌ [¹30-*a-bu-šu ú(?)-še(?)-*   44:20-21
ri-bu-ú(?))][7]

"The year Sin-abušu brought in the statues into the temple
of Ištar"

6   MU 1 ALAM NA₄.AŠ.NU$_x$(ŠIR).GAL 2 ALAM UD.KA.BAR   147:11

"The year 1 alabaster statue, 2 bronze statues"

7   MU ALAM ŠUD$_x$(KAxŠU) KÙ.GI[8]   93:10

"The year the golden statue in a prayerful attitude"

8   MU ALAM ŠUD$_x$(!) (KAxŠU) *ša Da-du-ša*   TIM 3 127:20

"The year Daduša the statue in a prayerful attitude"

      MU [A]LAM ŠUD$_x$(?) UD.ꞌKA.BARꞌ(?)[9]   Lutz 109:33

"The year the bronze statue in a prayerful attitude"

9   M[U] ALAM ꞌŠI.TAꞌ UD.KA.BAR [*Da-nu-um*]-*ta-ḫa-ꞌaz*ꞌ [*a-na*
E] ꞌᵈTIŠPAK(?)ꞌ *ú-ꞌše*ꞌ-[*ri-bu*][10]   65:17

"The year Dannum-taḫaz brought in the bronze statue in a
prayerful attitude into the temple of Tišpak"

10a ꞌMU 1 ALAM UD.KA.ꞌ[BAR]   103:13

"The year 1 bronze statue"

10b MU ALAM UD.KA.BAR *ma-ḫi-ṣum*[11]   79:25; 96:7

"The year the hammered(?) bronze statue"

---

[7]   Feigin was apparently able to read text no. 44 in a state of preservation more fully intact than
represented on the present copy (drawn by Prof. Jacobsen). This copy is all that is now available,
since the original tablet and envelope are now missing from the Oriental Institute Collection. Feigin
transliterated as follows: MU ALAM.MEŠ *a-na* KISAL INANNA ¹30-*a-bu-šu ik*(?)-*ri-bu*(?)-*šu*(?).
F. Reschid *Nuršamaš* 2 cites an unpublished Tell Harmal date (*b) IM 63163 supplied to him by
A. Goetze: MU ALAM.MEŠ Sin-*a-bu-šu a-na* É ᵈTIŠPAK *ú-še-ri-bu*; Goetze's reading of ᵈTIŠPAK
is of course possible; but we have read ^{<d>}INNIN in our formula on the basis of Prof. Jacobsen's
copy, S. Feigin's notes, and text 43:21f. *Cf.* also F. Reschid *Nuršamaš* 5 IM 55374 (*af), also
supplied by Goetze: MU [ALAM.MEŠ] *a-na* É ᵈSin(?) ᵈSin-*a-bu-šu ú*-[*še-ri-bu*], as well as IM 55157
(*ag) [MU ALAM.MEŠ] X X É ᵈAdad Sin-*a-bu-šu* x[   ].

[8]   Cf. formula 9 and MU ALAM KÙ.GI *ka-ri-bu ša Da-nu-um-ta-ḫa-az a-na* É ᵈTIŠPAK *i-ru-bu-ú*
Simmons (ff), *JCS* 14 (1960) 53, no. 84:13-17. For ŠUD$_x$ = *karābu* see CAD K 193a, 197.
Cf. also MU ALAM ŠUD$_x$(!), IM 51201, cited by T. Baqir, *Sumer* 5(1949) 59, no. 14.

[9]   Collation. Lutz 109 belongs to the period of Daduša, by whose name an oath is sworn in l. 16.

[10]   See note 8. For ŠI.TA = *kāribu* see CAD K 216a and cf. MU ALAM ŠI.TA(?) ŠUD$_x$(?)
UD.ꞌKAꞌ.BAR Simmons (j), *JCS* 13 (1959) 105 no. 2:15. Cf. also the obscure formula MU ALAM
KI.GUB KÙ.GI, T. Baqir *Sumer* 5 (1949) 45 Harmal Date List 1:7 which is, however, apparently
a year date formula of Ibalpiel II; see also, on this last formula, note 1 above.

[11]   For *maḫāṣum* said of metals cf. GIM ALAM *ma-ḫi-ṣi*, BRM 4 13 69, 71 (hammered gold
statues); *Sumer* 9 24 (hammered gold). For this year date formula cf. MU ALAM URUDU
UD.KA.BAR *ma-ḫi-ṣi* ¹*Da-nu-ta-ḫa-az a-na* É ᵈTIŠPAK, Simmons (9), *JCS* 13 (1959) 117, no. 36:22f;
could one perhaps read ŠITA₅ (for ŠITA, ŠITA₄ = *karābu, ikribu*) in place of URUDU, which
the case there omits? Year formulas 9 and 10 may prove to be the same year.

11 MU 2 ALAM [   ]¹²   62:19
    "The year 2 statues ..."

12 MU ʾBÀDʾ.AN^{K[I]} ¹³   55:18
    "The year Der"

13 MU BÀD *Bi-is-ki-la*^{KI}¹⁴ ¹*30-a-bu-šu i-pu-šu*   UCLMA 9/2831
    "The year Sin-abušu built the wall of Biskila"

14 MU BÀD ʾ*Ḫu-ri-ib*ʾ-[*šum*^{KI}]   234:10
    "The year the wall of Ḫuribšum"
    ʾMUʾ *Ḫu-ri-ib-šum*^{KI} [MU.U]N.DÙ ¹⁵   31:rev. 17f
    "The year he built Ḫuribšum"

15 MU BÀD *ma-ru-ti-šu* ¹ʾ*Daʾ-an-nu-um-ta-ḫa-az i-pu-šu-ú* ¹⁶   47:25f; 66:14-16
    "The year Dannum-taḫaz built the fortress of his (royal)
    sonship"

16 MU ʾBÀD Xʾ [   ]   72:13
    "The year the wall ..."

17 MU *Da-du-ša* LUGAL ¹⁷   90:16, 91:21
    "The year Daduša (became) king"

18 MU DUMU.SAL LUGAL *a-na Ra-pí-qí-im i-ḫu-zu* ¹⁸   Lutz 61:10
    "The year he took the daughter of the king to Rapiqum
    (to be married)"

19 MU É ^dEN.LÍL.(LÁ) ¹⁹   57:15; 117:6
    "The year the temple of Enlil"

¹² Cf. MU 2 ALAM KÙ.GI 2 ALAM UD.KA.BAR *a-na* É, BIN 7 81:22, which is discussed by
Simmons *JCS* 13 (1959) 76 (n).
¹³ This mention of Der is unfortunately too brief to permit historical speculation. Text 55 is a
ḫubullu; the creditor Anum-pi-Šamaš son of Bur-^dEN.ZU also occurs in text 73:3f, date formula
no. 41, and in 56:4-5, date formula 46.
¹⁴ Cf. MU BÀD *Bi-is-ki-*ʾ*x*ʾ^{KI} *i-pu-šu*, R. Harris *JCS* 9 (1955) 31-120 (henceforth cited as Khafaje)
no. 15. Cf. further MU BÀD *Bi-is-ki-la*(?)^{KI} *Am-mi-da-šur*, IM 55400, unpublished year date formula
recorded by Ṭ. Baqir (in transliteration only — reference courtesy of T. Jacobsen and Maria DeJ. Ellis).
¹⁵ Cf. MU BÀD *Ḫu-ri-ib-šum*^{KI} (BA.DÍM), Khafaje no. 4. and MU SIG₄ *Ḫu-ri-ib-šum il-bi-nu*,
Khafaje no. 7.
¹⁶ Cf. MU BÀD NAM.DUMU.A.NI BA.DÙ, BIN 7 85:20 — Simmons (a); variants are MU BÀD
NAM.DUMU.A.NI.ŠÈ BA.DÙ, BIN 7 86:21f and Simmons JCS 13 (1959) 105, no. 1:16, and MU
BÀD DUMU.(A.)NI, Ṭ. Baqir *Sumer* 5 (1949) 54, no. 6 (IM 52264), Simmons *JCS* 15 (1961)
83, no. 140:rev. 5'. The variant formula with ŠÈ is not correctly translated by Edzard ZZB 74³⁵⁷
"The year the fortress was built for the crown-prince(?);" we suggest "The year he built (the
fortress) for his (royal) sonship." M. Stol has supplied another unpublished example of this year
date: MU BÀD.NAM.DUMU.A.NI.ŠÈ, IM 52928; this tablet was identified in a catalogue (p. 100
no. 174) describing an exhibit "Trésors du Musée de Bagdad des origines à l'Islam" held at the
Musée du Louvre, Galerie Mollien, 28 janvier – 28 mars 1966.
¹⁷ Cf. Ṭ. Baqir *Sumer* 5 (1949) 56 no. 9 MU *Da-du-ša a-na* É *a-bi-šu i-ru-bu*.
¹⁸ Cf. MU [¹*30-a*]-ʾ*bu-šu maʾ-ra-su a-na Ra-pí-qí*<^{KI}> *i-di-nu* TIM 3 30:13-15.
¹⁹ Cf. MU É ^dEN.LÍL.ʾLAʾ, Harmal Date List 1:8, Ṭ. Baqir *Sumer* 5 (1949) 66 and 83;

MU É ᵈEN.LÍL BA.DÍM [20]   114:6; Lutz 85:12
   "The year he built the temple of Enlil"

ʿMU É ᵈENʾ.LÍL(?) *in-ne-ep-*ʿ*šu*ʾ   225: rev. 4-5
   "The year the temple of Enlil was built"

MU É ᵈEN.LÍL BA.DÍM Ù A.LAMₓ(LUM) KÙ.GI   Lutz 13:14f
   "The year he built the temple of Enlil; and the golden statue"

MU É ᵈEN.LÍL ʿÙʾ A.LAMₓ(LUM) KÙ.GI ʿ*I*ʾ-*ba-al-pí-*[*el*
BA.DÍM] [21]   Lutz 44:15-17
   "The year Ibalpiel built the temple of Enlil and (fashioned)
   the golden statue"

20 MU É ᵈEN.Z[U]   60:17
   "The year the temple of Sin"

MU É ᵈEN.ZU BA.DÍM [22]   Lutz 24:15
   "The year he built the temple of Sin"

21 MU É EŠ₄.DA[R] [23]   214:6
   "The year the temple of Ištar"

MU É EŠ₄.DAR BA.DÍM [24]   69:18; 70:14; 71:14;
   "The year he built the temple of Ištar"   82:11; Ish. 34-T. 3;
Lutz 14:15; 15:5; 21:
14; 26:7 [25]; 28:18; 30:
6 [25]; 39:15; 40:14; 66:
8; 67:4; 69:17; 81:13;
89:43; UCLMA 9/-
2826; 9/2862; 9/2892;
2895

MU É EŠ₄.DAR ʿ*I*ʾ-[*ba*]-ʿ*al*ʾ-*pi-el i-pu-šu* [26]   Lutz 25:15-17
   "The year Ibalpiel built the temple of Ištar"

---

this reading, which appears in text 57:15, follows Simmons *JCS* 13 (1959) 75³¹; cf. also the occurrence of this form in Simmons (e), *JCS* 13(1959) 106 no. 6:19.

[20] Cf. IM 51178 cited by T. Baqir *Sumer* 5 (1949) 73; and cf. also the formulas collected by him on p. 66 under no. 28a (2) (the copies are on p. 81), which appear to read É ᵈEN.LÍL(!) BA.DÍM/BA.DÙ. É ᵈEN.ZU is apparently mentioned in only one of the forms listed on p. 81: MU É ᵈEN.ZU BA RU MA(?); but this enigmatic formula is not separately discussed by T. Baqir on p. 66 since he read ᵈEN.ZU throughout. For MU É ᵈEN.ZU BA.DÍM see now our formula no. 20. Simmons (y), JCS 13 (1959) 79 (= YOS 14 48:15), may also have [MU É ᵈEN.LÍ]L BA.DÍM.

[21] Cf. MU É ᵈEN.LÍL BA.DÍM ʿ*I-ba-al-pí*ʾ-*el*, IM 51472 cited by T. Baqir *Sumer* 5 (1949) 66 *sub* no. 28a (2).

[22] The reading ᵈEN.ZU is based on collation. The problem between reading ᵈEN.ZU or ᵈEN.LÍL in formulas 19-20 may be lessened in view of the discussion in note 5 above.

[23] Cf. MU É EŠ₄.DAR, IM 53913, cited by T. Baqir *Sumer* 5 (1949) 72 *sub* no. 32.

[24] Cf. UCLMA 9/1905 MU É EŠ₄.DAR BA.DÙ.A; this tablet is said to come form Abou Gawan.

[25] For a possible augment to this year formula see the discussion under note 34 below.

[26] Collation. Cf. also MU É EŠ₄.DAR ¹*I-ba-al-pi-el*, IM 54022, T. Baqir *Sumer* 5 (1949) 72 *sub* no. 32.

22 MU É ᵈINNIN BA.DÙ   272:15
    "The year he built the temple of Ištar"²⁷
23 MU É SÁ.GAR ᵈEN.LÍL²⁸   233:7
    "The year the House of Deliberation (of) Enlil"
    MU É ʼSÁʼ.G[AR.RA.N]I É ᵈEN.LÍL.LÁ[MU.UN].ʼNAʼ.[DÙ]²⁹ 112:14
    "The year he built his House of Deliberation, the temple
    of Enlil (for Enlil)"
24 MU É SÁ.GAR.NI É ᵈEN.ZU   152:8
    "The year his House of Deliberation, the temple of Sin"
    MU ʼÉʼ SÁ.GAR.RA.A.ʼNIʼ É ʼ ᵈEN.ZU BA.AN.ʼXʼ³⁰   Ish. 35-T. 53

²⁷ The sign INNIN is clear and cannot be read TIŠPAK (cf. MU É ᵈTIŠPAK BA.DÙ, IM
52946, cited by T. Baqir, *Sumer* 5 (1949) 65 no. 26; this formula also occurs on UCLMA 9/1876,
a tablet said to come from Khafaje. Formulas 21 and 22 are virtually the same and have been
kept separate only because of the varying writings for Ištar.
²⁸ Cf. MU É SÁ.GAR.RA.NI É ᵈEN.LÍL(!) IM 52179, 51316, T. Baqir *Sumer* 5 (1949) 67 and 81
sub. no. 28b. The latter tablet bears a seal PN ARAD Ibalpiel. The formula MU É SAG.GAR.RA.NI
(IM 52927), also cited, there, can either belong to formula 23 or be a variant to formula 24 following.
Simmons *JCS* 15 (1961) 82 no. 139:9 MU É SÁ.GAR.RA.NI.DÈ can be emended to read
ᵈEN.LÍL(!) or ᵈEN.ZU(!) in place of the DÈ (see now YOS 14 no. 80). Simmons (f), *JCS*
13 (1959) 7:12, MU É ʼSÁʼ.GAR.RA can belong either to formula 23 or 24.
²⁹ Cf. MU É SÁ.GAR.RA.NI É ᵈEN.LÍL.LA MU.UN.NA.DÙ, T. Baqir *Sumer* 5 (1949) 8 IM
53955 (Date List 2): 14 and IM 51690 discussed by him on p. 73 *sub* no. 33. Other variants
are MU É SÁ.GAR.RA.NI É ᵈEN.LÍL.LÁ MU.UN.DÙ Simmons (x), *JCS* 14 (1960) 28, no. 59:12f;
MU É SÁ.GAR.RA.NI BA.DÍM, IM 52182, cited by T. Baqir, *Sumer* 5 (1949) 73 *sub* no. 33; and
MU É SÁ^SAG.GAR.RA ᵈEN.LÍL BA.DÍM, with variant É SAG.GAR.RA cited by him on pp. 67 and
81 (reading ᵈEN.LÍL for ᵈEN.ZU throughout). There is a possibility that our formulas 19 and 23
may be related; but there are also significant problems which make identity uncertain. Harmal
Date List 1, T. Baqir *Sumer* 5 (1949) 83, ll. 8-10 has the sequence: MU É ᵈEN.LÍL.ʼLÁʼ (see
note 19 above), MU *Ra-pí-qú-um* BA.GUL (cf. formula 53 below), and MU *um-ma-na-ti Šu-bar-ti ù*
Ḫé-na GIŠ.TUKUL BA.SÌG (formula 25 below). However, IM 53955 (so called Harmal Date List 2),
T. Baqir *op. cit.* 84, has MU É SÁ.GAR.RA.NI É ᵈEN.LÍL.LÁ MU.UN.NA.DÙ (in line 14) as a date
subsequent to MU Ra-pí-qumᴷᴵ BA.AN.GUL. It is possible to make a single year out of the two
É ᵈEN.LÍL.LÁ formulas by arguing, as does Simmons *JCS* 13 (1959) 75, that IM 52962 (Date List 1)
is in error by placing MU *Ra-pí-qú-um* BA.GUL ahead of MU É ᵈEN.LÍL.ʼLÁʼ. We, however,
hesitate to vitiate the evidence of IM 52962, our only true Diyala Date List, in order to equate
these two formulas. It is perhaps preferable to conjecture that Date List 1 is only an excerpted list
and therefore not fully sequential. Cf. the remarks of T. Baqir *Sumer* 5 (1949) 42f. At the same
time, however, it must be observed that Date Lists 1 and 2 agree on the sequence of 7 other year
dates preceeding the dates in question. For the suggested relationship of formulas 23 and 24
and for another argument relating formulas 19 and 23 see note 30 following.
³⁰ This text, cited by T. Jacobsen in OIP 43 129⁵⁴, shows that the year MU ʼÉʼSÁ.GAR.A.ʼNIʼÉʼ ᵈEN.ZU
BA.AN.ʼXʼ preceeded MU ERÍN SU.BIR₄ᴷᴵ GIŠ.TUKUL BA.AN.SÌG (no. formula 25 below). This
text also mentions MU *Ra-pí-qum*ᴷᴵ BA.GUL, which must likewise have preceeded MU ERÍN
SU.BIR₄ᴷᴵ BA.GUL since the tablet itself is dated to that same year, i.e. MU ERÍN SU.BIR₄ᴷᴵ etc.
(this information comes from Prof. Jacobsen's field notebook). IM 52962 (Date List 1), T. Baqir
Sumer 5 (1949) 45, lists nine years between MU *I-ba-al-pi-el* LUGAL (the king's first year) and

"The year he built his House of Deliberation, the temple of
Sin"

25 MU ERÍN ⌜SU⌝.BIR₄ [31]   115:6
    "The year the army of Subartu"
    ⌜MU⌝ ERÍN <SU>.⌜BIR₄(?)⌝KI BA.SÌG⌝(?)   81:16
    "The year he smote the army of Subartu"
    MU ERÍN SU.BIR₄KI GIŠ.TUKUL BA.(AN).SÌG [32]   236:7f;
    "The year he smote the army of Subartu with (his) weapon" Ish. 35-T. 53
    MU ERÍN SU.BIR₄ BA RA GIŠ KU BAR [33]   Lutz 23:18;
    "The year ... the army of Subartu"   UCLMA 9/2858
    [MU ERÍN SU.BI]R₄ BA RA GIŠ ⌜KU BAR⌝ URU Ki-maš
    É-kal-l⌜a-tim] [34]   UCLMA 9/2863
    "The year ... the army of Subartu (and) the cities Kimaš
    (and) Ekallatum"

MU um-ma-na-ti Su-bar-ti etc. (see note 35 to formula 25); this latter year date, of course, is identical
with MU ERÍN SU.BIR₄KI etc. of Ish 35-T. 53. IM 52962 includes MU ᵈEN.LÍL.⌜LÁ⌝ and MU
Ra-pí-qú-um BA.GUL among the nine intervening years but omits any mention of a year MU É
SÁ.GAR.RA.A.⌜NI É⌝ ᵈEN.ZU BA.AN.⌜X⌝. We have already seen how formulas 19 and 20, which
mention É ᵈEN.LÍL and É ᵈEN.ZU, might be merged into a single formula if one would
incorporate them with formula 3 (see note 5 above). In the previous note we have discussed the
possibility of uniting formulas 19 and 23. This last identification gains favor because it could
also provide a place for formula 24 among the year dates prior to MU um-ma-na-ti Šu-bar-ti etc.
that are listed in IM 52962 (Date List 1) by attaching it to formula 19. If so, then one arrives at
a "grand" reconstructed formula that would contain the elements of formulas 24, 23, 20, 19,
and 3!

[31] Cf. MU ERÍN SU.BIR₄KI in IM 51295, 51539, and 10681 cited by T. Baqir Sumer
5(1949) 69f sub no. 30b.

[32] The variant BA.AN.SÌG appears in Ish 35-T. 53; see already note 29 above. Cf. further MU
ERÍN SU.BIR₄KIGIŠ.TUKUL BA.SÌG, IM 52009, cited by T. Baqir Sumer 5 (1949) 70, 81 sub no. 30b
and the variant with BA.DÁB, IM 71196 pp. 69, 81 — perhaps also to be read BA.SÌG(!)?

[33] Both tablets have been collated and the signs are clear even if not understood. In UCLMA 9/2858
one is required to read MU ERÍN <SU>.BIR₄ etc.

[34] UCLMA 9/2863 is an envelope fragment that covered UCLMA 9/2858; it bears the same
witnesses, scribe and borrower (being a ḫubuttātum). The addition of URU Ki-maš and É-kal-l⌜a-tim]
opens the door to possible confusions. The names of these cities are also appended to the year
formula MU GUD.APIN KÙ.GI in Lutz 34:16 (see formula 33 below). URU Ki-maš É-ka[l-la-tim]
may also be read in Lutz 30:5 but proceeding MU É EŠ₄.DAR BA.DÍM (formula 21 above). Ekallatum
is likewise mentioned in IM 51258, MU um-ma-na-at É-kal-la-timKI ¹Da-du-ša is-ki-pu-ú, IM 51628, MU
ERÍN É-kál-la-timKI, IM 52979, MU UGNIM É.GAL[   ] cited by T. Baqir Sumer 5 (1949) 56, 78. Cf.
also MU UGNIM Ra-pi-qúKI(?) ⌜É.GAL⌝ ᵈDa-du-ša LUGAL im-ḫa-áṣ-ṣú(?), UCLMA 9/2828, and
MU É-kál(?)-la-tum BA.DAB₅, TIM 5 65: 14f. In a fashion similar to Lutz 30:5, URU.KI
Za-la-ḫu-um precedes MU É EŠ₄.DAR BA.DÍM in Lutz 26:6; but this GN must be part of the
body of the text as is [UR]U.KI Za-la-ḫu(!)KI in Lutz 29:12, despite the presence there of a
strongly ruled line separating line 12 from the preceeding line (collation). Zalaḫum appears as a
local GN in the vicinity of Ishchali in Lutz 49:7 and 96:15. One could read the GN in Lutz 30:5 as
URU.KI Maš-kán ⌜x⌝ [   ] and assume it to be a local site.

MU ERÍN *ma-at Šu-bar-tim* ¹*I-ba-al-pi-el i-ḫa-zu*³⁵   Lutz 58:20f
"The year Ibalpiel captured the army of the land of Subartu"

26   MU GIŠ.APIN [   ]³⁶   54:13
"The year the plow ..."

MU GIŠ.ʿAPINʾ KÙ.GI *a-na* É ᵈTIŠ[PAK]³⁷   76:13f
"The year the golden plow ox (entered) the temple of Tišpak"

27   MU GIŠ.GIGIRᴳᴵᴿ ᵈIM   Lutz 51:16
"The year the chariot of Adad"

MU GIŠ.GIGIRᴳᴵᴿ *ša* ᵈIM³⁸   Ish. 34-T. 109
"The year the chariot of Adad"

MU GIŠ.GIGIR KÙ.GI *a-na* É ᵈʿIMʾ³⁹   64:17
"The year (he brought in) the golden chariot into the temple of Adad"

28   [MU GIŠ.GIGIR NU].ʿSÁ KÙʾ.GI [   ] ᵈUTU   92:18
"The year the golden ... chariot of Šamaš"

MU GIŠ.GIGIR GAL NU.SÁ ᵈUTU⁴⁰   Ish. 34-T. 111
"The year the great ... golden chariot of Šamaš"

29   MU GIŠ.GU.ZA ʿBÁRAʾ.M[AḪ   ]ᵈIM [   ]⁴¹   Ish. 34-T. 90

³⁵ Cf. MU *um-ma-na-ti Šu-bar-ti ù Ḫe-na* GIŠ.TUKUL BA.SÌG IM 52962:10; T. Baqir *Sumer* 5 (1949) 83 and variations on p. 69 *sub* 30a : MU ERÍN SU.BIR₄ᴷᴵ *Ḫé-na*ᴷᴵ GIŠ.TUKUL BA.SÌG (IM 52626, 52599, 52686, 52306, 51617); and MU ERÍN SU.BIR₄ᴷᴵ (IM 51330); Simmons (g), YOS 14 8:12, 77:8f (SU.BAL.BIR₄ᴷᴵ).

³⁶ Cf. MU GIŠ.APIN KÙ.GI, T. Baqir *Sumer* 5 (1949) 73f, tablets cited *sub* no. 34 1(b); Simmons *JCS* 14 (1960) 51 no. 73:15 (bb).

³⁷ Cf. MU GIŠ.APIN KÙ.GI *a-na* É ᵈTIŠPAK *i-ru-bu*, T. Baqir *Sumer* 5 (1949) 73 IM 52911, cited under formula no. 34 there.

³⁸ Cf. MU GIŠ.GIGIRᴳᴵᴿ ʿᵈʾIM(?), T. Baqir *Sumer* 5 (1949) 140, IM 54569; MU GIŠ.GIGIᴳᴵᴿ.RA ᵈIM, IM 53955:3 *op. cit.* p. 84.

³⁹ T. Baqir, *Sumer* 5(1949) 62 and 79, cites the following variants : MU GIŠ.GIGIR KÙ.GI, IM 54206, 52918; MU GIŠ.GIGIR KÙ.ʿGIʾ É ᵈ[   ], IM 51528; MU GIŠ.GIGIR KÙ.GI ʿᵈIMʾ, IM 52962:2 (Harmal Date List 1 — see also p. 83); MU GIŠ.GIGIRᴳᴵᴿ É ᵈIM *I-ba-al-pí-el* ʿ*ú*ʾ-*še-ri-bu* IM 5406A; MU GIŠ.GIGIRᴳᴵᴿ ¹*I-ba-al-pi-el a-na* [É] ʿᵈIMʾ *ú-še-ri-[bu]*, IM 54452.

⁴⁰ Cf. MU GIŠ.GIGIR(!) KÙ.GI NU.SÁ ᵈUTU, T. Baqir *Sumer* 5 (1949) 75 IM 51422 *sub* no. 36; MU GIŠ.GIGIR NU.SÁ KÙ.GI ᵈUTU, *op. cit.* 57 IM 6943 *sub* no. 11. As T. Baqir notes (p. 57), this formula is related to MU GIŠ.GIGIR NU.SÁ.ᵈUTU É TEMEN.UR.SAG ᵈIM (IM 52028) and (IM 44147 = TIM 5 3:15) MU GIŠ.GIGIR NU.SÁ ᵈ[UTU] É TEMEN.UR.SAG ᵈ[IM] *Da-du-ša* [*ú-še-ri-bu*]. No 92 is probably to be dated to the reign of Daduša; the seal of Inbuša SANGA (see 92:14) found in 131 identifies him as ARAD Daduša.

⁴¹ This formula can be restored to MU GIŠ.GU.ZA ʿBÁRAʾ.M[AḪ ᵈEN.ZU ᵈI-pí-iq]-ᵈIM [BA.DÍM] on the basis of Simmons *JCS* 14(1960) 49 no. 67:21-23 (z) (tablet and case) MU ʿGIŠ.GU.ZAʾ KÙ.GI BÁRA.MAḪ *ša* ᵈEN.ZU *ša* DU₆.DUBᴷᴵ ᵈ*I-pí-iq*-ᵈIM *ú-še-lu-ú* (tablet variant omits RN and appends simply *in-né-ep-šu*). We see no reason to keep this formula separate from

"The year ... the throne, the exalted dais ..."

30	MU ꞌMAR.GÍD.DA KÙ.GIꞌ	149:11
	"The year the golden wagon"	
	MU GIŠ.MAR.GÍD.DA KÙ.GI[42]	Lutz 99:11
	"The year the golden wagon"	
	MU GIŠ.MAR.GÍD.DA KÙ.GI KÙ.BABBAR	Lutz 45:13f; 63:17f; 103:17f
	"The year the gold (and) silver wagon"	
31	MU ÚS MU GIŠ.MAR.GÍD.DA KÙ.GI	Lutz 106:33
	"The year after the year the golden wagon"	
32	MU GIŠ.TUKUL ᵈUTU ¹Da-du-ša ú-še-ri-bu[43]	Lutz 50:12-14
	"The year Daduša brought in the divine weapon of Šamaš"	
33	MU GUD.APIN KÙ.GI	74:10; 113:5; 179:13; 215:8; 219:5; Ish. 34-T. 110; Ish. 34-T. 152; Lutz 1:17; 16:15; 17:17; 18:25; 19:14; 87:19
	"The year the golden plow-ox"	
	MU GUD.GIŠ.APIN KÙ.GI	297:2; Szlechter TJBD MAH 16163A:19
	"The year the golden plow-ox"	

Simmons *JCS* 13 (1959) 109 no. 12:19-22 (k): MU GIŠ.GU.ZA KÙ.GI ᵈNANNA ¹ᵈI-pi-iq-ᵈIM BA.DÌM. UCLMA 9/1816 (said to come from Khafaje) is probably related: MU GU.ZA ᵈŠE[Š.KI]. Cf. probably also MU GU.ZA ᵈ... recorded by T. Baqir *Sumer* 5 (1949) 46, Date List 3 Frag. A line 1. However, there is another possibility here as well. Recently, collation of Simmons no. 140 by E. Kingsbury (YOS 14 p. 3) has uncovered another year date formula written within the text of no. 140: (2) ÍB.TAG₄ GÚ.UN PN (3) ꞌšaꞌ MU [GIŠ.G]U.ZA ꞌBÁRAꞌ.MAḪ ꞌᵈŠAḪAN(?)ꞌ. This year date must precede MU BÀD.NAM.DUMU.NI, which belongs to Dannum-taḫaz (see note to year date formula 15 and note 78 to the Introduction) by one or at the most, 2-3 years. Simmons (YOS 14 p. 3) is inclined to identify this formula with his year formula (z), which has already been discussed above. But there is no way to juxtapose the reigns of Dannum-taḫaz (mentioned in the seals to Simmons no. 140) and Ipiq-Adad II. One may, however, restore year date formula 29 on the basis of Simmons no. 140:3 and read ꞌᵈŠAḪANꞌ there in place of]ᵈIM[. One would then assign the formula to the reign of Dannum-taḫaz or Ibalpiel II; on this last point, see Introduction, notes 80, 83. No. 140:3 is perhaps also to be connected with Simmons(i), *JCS* 13 (1959) = YOS 14 10:13, MU GU.ZA ꞌBÁRA.MAḪꞌ [ᵈŠAḪ] ꞌANꞌ(?). Cf. further OIP 43 194, formula 121: MU GIŠ.GU.ZA BÁRA(?) MAḪ(?) AB.BA ME.LUḪ.ḪA KÙ.GI GAR.RA.

[42] For this formula cf. Simmons *JCS* 13 (1959) 108 no. 9:23 (h); cf. also T. Baqir *Sumer* 5 (1949) 70 and 83, IM 52962:11 (Harmal Date List 1), IM 51741, 51323, 52431, 52961, 52931 (see also p. 81); IM 51795 (see also p. 46) has a shortened form: MU GIŠ.MAR.GÍD.DA. T. Baqir, *op. cit.* 71 and 81, relates these formulas to MU GIŠ.MAR.GÍD.DA KÙ.GI É ᵈNIN.A.ZU BA.AN.KU₄, a formula which occurs in IM 51786, 52010, 51637, 52294, 52267 — cited under his no. 31b.

[43] This formula bears a possible resemblance to MU 2 GIŠ.TUKUL KÙ.GI BAR.RA in TIM 5 4:28; one of the witnesses there, however, has a seal designating him as ARAD Ibalpiel; if Ibalpiel II is meant, then the year formula there cannot be one of Daduša.

MU GUD.APIN KÙ.GI URU *Ša-nu-ḫu-(um)* [44]   Lutz 20:15; 55:16
"The year the golden plow-ox (and) the city Šanuḫum"

MU GUD.APIN KÙ.GI URU Ki-maš É-kal-la-tim [45]   Lutz 34:16, 104:15f
"The year the golden plow-ox (and) the cities Kimaš and Ekallatum

MU GUD.APIN KÙ.GI BA.DÍM URU.KI *Ša-nu-ḫu-um*   Lutz 64:6f
"The year he fashioned the golden plow-ox; (and the year) the city Šanuḫum"

34 ʿMUʾ *Ḫa-da-ti Maš-kán* GIŠ ʿXʾ [46]   50:14f
"The year Ḫadati ... Maškan ..."

35 MU ÚS.SA *Ia-ri-im-[i-i]m* BA.UG$_x$(BAD)   326:55
"The year after (the year) Jarim-Lim died"

36 MU *I-ba-al-pi-el* BA.UG$_x$(BAD) [47]   Ish. 35-T. 62
"The year Ibalpiel died"

37 MU *I-ba-al-pi-el* GU.ZA ZÚ.AM.SI KÙ.GI GAR.ʿRAʾ
ᵈTIŠPAK.ʿKAʾ BA.DÍM [48]   Lutz 36:22-24
"The year Ibalpiel fashioned the ivory throne inlaid with gold for (lit. of) Tišpak"

38 MU ÍD 30-*a-bu-šu iḫ-ru-ú* [49]   Lutz 2:21
"The year he dug the Sin-abušu canal"

39 [M]U ÍD *ša* URU^KI *[ip]-pí-tu-ú*   98: rev. 7ʾ
"The year the canal of the city was opened"

MU ÍD.DA *li-bi* URU^KI *ip-pí-tu-ú*   UCLMA 9/2827
"The year the canal was opened in the city"

40 MU *I-pí-iq*-ᵈIM BÀD ʿ*Me-tu-ra*ʾ-*an* IN.ʿDAB₅ʾ [50] 63:17-19
"The year Ipiq-Adad captured the fortress Meturan"

---

[44] Lutz 20:15 has URU *Ša-nu-ḫu*.

[45] See note 34 on formula 25 above. This year formula is often found in transactions that are described as having taken place *warki mišar Dūr-Rimuš*; cf. texts cited in Lutz UCP 10 and Kraus, *Edikt* 231. Year formula 55 is also associated with this event in Lutz 9:20.

[46] Cf. MU *Maš-ʿkán*-ᵈʿUTU ʿBA.DÍMʾ, IM 54482, T. BAQIR *Sumer* 5 (1949) 76 and 82 *sub* no. 37.

[47] Cf. As 30: T. 325 cited by T. Jacobsen, OIP 43 191 no. 112.

[48] MU ZU.AM.SI ..., IM 54569, cited by T. Baqir *Sumer* 5 (1949) 140; this formula appears on a tablet with four other formulas, all of which belong to Ibalpiel II. OIP 43 p. 190. no. 111, which is the same formula as here, may thus better belong to Ibalpiel II rather than to Ibalpiel I as Jacobsen has it.

[49] Cf. [MU ÍD] 30-*a-bu-um*(sic) *iḫ-ru-ú*, TIM 3 3:19; MU ÍD Sin-*a-bu-šu* BA.BAL, IM 63232, 63261; MU ÚS.SA Sin-*a-bu-šu iḫ-ru-ú*, IM 55385; *ša-ni-tum* MU *ša* 30-*a-bu-šu na-ra-am ú-še-eḫ-ru*, TIM 3 4:19ff; MU ÍD Sin-*a-bu-šu i-pé-tu*, IM 63230, 63231, 63276 — all texts cited by F. Reschid *Nuršamaš* 3-5. It is possible that formulas 38 and 39 are related; they both occur in the lifetime of Bur-Sin, father of Ilšu-naṣir.

[50] This formula was earlier read differently (Dūr-rutumme?) by T. Jacobsen, OIP 43 127[47].

41   MU *I-bi-*ᵈ⌈EN.ZU⌉ *a-na* ⌈É⌉ *a-bi-*⌈*šu*⌉ *i-*⌈*ru*⌉*-bu-*⌈*ú*⌉[51]   73:16-18
     "The year Ib(b)i Sin entered his father's palace (as king)"

42   [MU   ] ⌈LUGAL⌉(?) É AD.DA.NI.<ŠE> BA.AN.KU₄[52]   Lutz 91:35-36

43   ⌈MU X⌉ ᵈ*I-pi-iq-*⌈ᵈIM⌉ KALAM.⌈MA⌉ DI[   ] ᵈ*I-pí-iq-*ᵈIM
     BA.DÍM.DÍM.⌈MA⌉   29:15-17
           "The year Ipiq-Adad built the ... (called) "Ipiq-Adad of the
           country...""

44   [MU] *I-qí(!)-iš-*ᵈ⌈TIŠPAK⌉ [*a-na*] É *a-bi-šu* ⌈*i-ru*⌉*-bu-ú*[53]   33:13-15
     "The year Iqiš-Tišpak entered his father's palace (as king)"

45   [MU I]*-qí-iš-*ᵈTIŠPAK [   ] ⌈X⌉*ia-ku-un* [   ] ⌈X⌉ UB RA
     KÚR U   Ish. 34-T. 87

46   MU KÁ.GAL KI.KUR[54]   58:13; 132:7
           "The year the gate of the Chapel"
     ⌈MU KA⌉.GAL ⌈*Ki-ku-ur-ri*⌉   75:12
     MU KÁ.GAL *Ki-kur-ri*[55]   Lutz 49:11, 65:7
     MU KÁ.GAL *Ki-kur-ri-im*[56]   68:19
     MU KÁ.GAL *Ki-ku-ri-im*[57]   Lutz 38:11, 48:6
           "The year the gate of the Chapel"
     MU KÁ.GAL *Ki-kur-ri-im* ¹*I-ba-al-pi-el*   Lutz 84:7f
           "The year the gate of the Chapel, Ibalpiel"
     ⌈MU KÁ.GAL KI⌉.[KUR *I-b*]*a-al-pi-el* ⌈*i*⌉*-pu-*[*šu*][58]   56:19f
           "The year Ibalpiel made the gate of the Chapel"

47   MU *Ma-an-*⌈*ki-su*⌉ᴷᴵ *Da-du-ša iṣ-ba-tu*   Lutz 7:17f
     "The year Daduša captured Mankisu"

---

[51]   There is no way to read *I-pí-iq-*ᵈIM (repeated collations); the reading ᵈEN.ZU seems further
to be confirmed by UCLMA 9/2859: [MU *I-b*]*i-*30 LUGAL [*a-na* É *a-b*]*i-šu* [*i-ru*]*-bu*. The placement
of Ibbi-Sin after Ibalpiel II is based upon (1) the relative "solidarity" of the sequence of kings
from Ipiq-Adad II through Ibalpiel II and (2) the fact that Anum-pi-Šamaš s. of Bur-Sin is lender
in 73:3f and is also found as lender in 56:4-5, which is dated to Ibalpiel II (year date
formula 46).

[52]   Cf. formula 44 below and MU *Da-du-ša a-na* É *a-bi-šu i-ru-bu*, IM 51331, cited by T. Baqir,
Sumer 5 (1949) 56 no. 9; cf. also CE (IM 51059) 11.4-5 ... É.AD.DA.NI.ŠÈ [BA.AN.K]U₄.RA.AM...
and the remarks of Landsberger, *Symbolae David* II (1968) 65-67, connecting this formula to Daduša's
first regnal year.

[53]   Cf. MU *I-qí(!)-iš-*ᵈTIŠPAK [*a-na*] É *a-bi-šu i-ru-bu*, BIN 7 85:16-18 (Simmons (s)).

[54]   Cf. MU KÁ.GAL KI.KUR.RA, IM 53955:4, T. Baqir *Sumer* 5 (1949) 84.

[55]   Cf. variants with KI.KUR.RA, *Ki-kur-ru*, cited by T. Baqir *Sumer* 5 (1949) 63 sub bo. 23(a).

[56]   For additional formulas with the writing *Ki-kur-ri-im* cf. the formulas cited by T. Baqir *Sumer* 5
(1949) *loc. cit.*: IM 52653 and the variant *Ki-kur-re-e-em* IM 52101. Additional attestations of
Ki-kur-ri-im are in UCLMA 9/2938, TIM 3 128:15, and Simmons *JCS* 14(1960) 52 76:16 (cc).

[57]   Cf. IM 52962:3 *Ki-ku-ri-im* cited by T. Baqir *Sumer* 5 (1949) 63, 83.

[58]   Cf. MU KÁ.GAL *Ki-ku-ri en-ne-ep-šu*, IM 53921, 53927, 54207, 54210; MU KÁ.GAL *Ki-ku-re-e*
i-ni-ep-šu, IM 54205; ... *Ki-kur-ri in-ne-ep-šu* IM 54465, cited by T. Baqir *Sumer* 5 (1949) 63 and
80 *sub* no. 23.

48 MU *ma-at Ma-ḫa-zum*[59] 145:10
"The year the land (of) Maḫazum"

49 MU MA.DA *Aš-na-kum ù Tar-ʿniʾ-ip*KI BA.AN.DAB₅[60] Ish 35-T. 49
"The year he seized the land of Ašnakkum and Tarnip"

50 MU ᵈ*Na-ra-am*-ᵈEN.ZU *Ka-ku-la-tim*KI BA.AN.ʿDAB₅ʾ 45:25f
MU *Na-ra-am*-ᵈEN.ZU *Ka-ku-la-tim iṣ-ba-tu*[61] Ish. 34-T. 112
"The year Narām-Sin captured Kakulatum"

51 MU ÚS.SA *Ka-ku-la-tim iṣ-ba-tu* 129:5
"The year after (the year) he captured Kakulatum"

52 MU *Qa-ba-ra*KI *Da-du-ša iṣ-ba-tu*[62] Lutz 4:21f
"The year Daduša captured Qabara"

53 MU *Ra-pí-qum* 128:9; 130: rev. 3;
"The year Rapiqum" 136:17
MU *Ra-pí-qum*KI BA.GUL[63] Ish. 35-T. 53;
  Ish. 34-T. 144;
  TIM 3 126:19;
  Lutz 8:17; 47:7f

MU *Ra-pí-qum* BA.GULUL 138:14
"The year he laid waste Rapiqum"
MU *Ra-pí-qum* É ᵈNIN.A.ZU BA.AN.DAB₅[64] Lutz 68:18f
"The year he captured Rapiqum (and) the temple of Ninazu"

---

[59] Cf. MU *ma-at Ma-ḫa-zi* (Date List 1) IM 52962:4; MU *ma-at Ma-ḫa-zi*KI (Date List 2) IM 53955:5; MU MA.DA *Ma-ḫa-zi* IM 54008; *i-na ša-na-at ma-at Ma-ḫa-zi* IM 51254; MU *ma-at Ma-ḫa-zi*KI *I-ba-al-pi-el* BA.DÍB, IM 52162, 52163 — cited by T. Baqir *Sumer* 5 (1949) 64 and 80 *sub* no. 24.

[60] This formula appears on As. 30-T. 126, cited by T. Jacobsen OIP 43 192 no. 114; cf. also the variant MU *Aš-na-kum*KI cited there. BIN 7 37:21ff (Simmons (r)) has MU *Aš-na-ak-kum iṣ-ṣa-ba-tu*. It is possible that Date List 3 Frag. A: 2 and B: 4, cited by T. Baqir *Sumer* 5(1949)46, may read MU *Aš-na-ʿkuʾ-[um*KI].

[61] Cf. MU *Ka-ku-[la-tum*KI] *Na-ra-am*-[ᵈEN.ZU *iṣ-ba-tu*], IM 51449 cited by T. Baqir *Sumer* 4(1969) 52 and 77.

[62] Cf. MU *Qa-ba-ra*KI ¹*Da-du-ša* IN.DAB₅, IM 52284 and abbreviated variants MU *Qa-ba-ra*KI BA.DÍB, IM 53907; MU *Qa-ba-ra* BA.SÌG, IM 53910; MU *Qa-ba-ra*KI, IM 53955:1 (Date List 2), IM 52974; these are all cited by T. Baqir *Sumer* 5(1949) 58 and 78. Cf. also MU URUKI *Qà-ab-ra*, TCL 10 125 as read by W. F. Leemans *RA* 49(1955)202.

[63] For Ish. 35-T. 53 see note 30 above; the tablet is dated to year formula 25 and is thus to be dated to the reign of Ibalpiel II. MU *Ra-pí-qù-um* BA.GUL also appears on (Date List 1) IM 52962:9 and (Date List 2) IM 53955:8 with BA.AN.GUL; for literature and the problems of sequence in placing this year formula see notes 29-30 above. MU *Ra-pí-qum*KI BA.GUL also occurs on a number of other tablets cited by T. Baqir *Sumer* 5(1949) 68 *sub* no. 29; cf. also Simmons *JCS* 14(1960) 50 69:12 (aa). T. Baqir, *op. cit.* 140, also cites the variant BA.AN.GUL in IM 54659.

[64] Reading established by collation. Cf. also MU ʿ*Ra-pi-qum*ʾKI IN.DAB₅(!), TIM 3 123f. The formula MU *Ra-pí-qum*KI *I-pí-iq*-ᵈIM BA.DAB₅, BM 82498 LIH 3 239[72], is apparently a different formula and cannot be related to formula 53, which belongs to Ibalpiel II (see previous note and T. Jacobsen OIP 43 127). The mention of É ᵈNIN.A.ZU suggests that formula 53 was originally much longer. É ᵈNIN.A.ZU is also mentioned in variants to formula 30; see note 42 above.

54   MU *Ru-bu-um* DUMU.SAL *Ḫa-ab-ʿx xʾ i-ḫu-zu*[65]   61:16-18
     "The year Rubum married the daughter of Ḫab..."

55   MU SAḪAR *zi-ku-ra-at* ᵈUTU[66]   Lutz 9:20, 76:14
     MU SAḪAR *zi-ku-ra-tum* ᵈUTU   Lutz 12:16
     "The year the earth (for) the ziggurat of Šamaš"

56   MU *Ṣí-la-ʿxʾ* [   ] *a-na ki-di-im* ʿxʾ [   ][67]   271: rev. 6f
     "The year ... outside ..."

57   MU Ṣilli*ˡⁱ*-Sin LUGAL[68]   Ish. 35-T. 52
     "The year Ṣilli-Sin (became) king"

58   MU TÚG ᵈEN.LÍL BI.TA   78:12
     "The year the raiment of Enlil together with (the statue (?))"

59   MU ᵈUTU-*ši*-ᵈIM BA.UGₓ(BAD)[69]   53:13; 59:14; 95:10;
     "The year Šamši-Adad died"   131:7; 226:rev. 4;
                                                                  Lutz 5:15; 6:14; 74:
                                                                  15[70]

60   MU ᵈ*Šul-gi*-ᵈŠEŠ.KI *in-na-aq-ru*[71]   Ish. 34-T. 28;
     "The year Šulgi-nanna was destroyed"   Ish. 34-T. 68

     MU ᵈ*Šul-gi-na-na*ᴷᴵ *i-qí-ru-ú*   TIM 3 125:20
     "The year he destroyed Šulgi-nanna"

     MU *Šul-ʿgiʾ-[na-na*ᴷᴵ] ᴵ*30-a-bu-šu* ʿ*iq-qí-ru*ʾ[72]   UCLMA 9/2942
     "The year Sin-abûšu *destroyed* Šulgi-nanna"

61   MU ÚS.SA ʿᵈ*Šul-gi-na-na*ʾᴷᴵ[73]   Ish. 34-T. 41
     "The year after (the year) Šulgi-nanna"

---

[65]   Perhaps *Ḫa-ab-ʿdi-elʾ* can be read in line 17; but this RN is not otherwise known to us. For Rubum, see Introduction, part III.

[66]   Lutz 9:20 has an extraneous << DIŠ >> after ᵈUTU.

[67]   Cf. perhaps MU URU *Ṣil-[li*-ᵈIM(?)] *Am-mi-ʿduʾ-[šu-ur]* IN.[DAB₅], T. Baqir *Sumer* 5(1949) 143, Tell Harmal no. 6 following the restoration of Simmons *JCS* 13(1959)79. The putative relationship assumes a reading Ṣill-Adad for *Zi-la-ʿxʾ* [   ] in formula 56.

[68]   We are not clear about the Sumerogram underlying this RN; we assume GIŠ.MI or MI for Ṣilli and presumably ᵈEN.ZU for Sin. A ruler of Ešnunna by this name is evidenced by other data: building inscription no. 117 on a brick, As 33-T. 106, published by T. Jacobsen OIP 43 140; the reading there relies on Dossin, *Syria* 20(1939) 109.

[69]   Cf. T. Baqir, *Sumer* 5(1949) 64 and 83f, IM 52962:5 and IM 53965:6 (Date Lists 1-2), IM 54612; T. Baqir *op. cit.* 139f has the phonetic writing *Sa-am-si*-ᵈIM; similarly, TCL 11 222 (following W. F. Leemans *RA* 49 (1955) 202) and Simmons *JCS* 13 (1959) 106 4:20 *Sa-am-si-e*-ᵈIM (b). For this last writing see also T. Jacobsen OIP 43 129[51].

[70]   Lutz 74:15, by collation: MU ʿᵈUTU-*ši*-ᵈIMʾ [BA.UGₓ(BAD)].

[71]   This formula is cited by R. Harris *JCS* 9 (1955) 56.

[72]   This text is an envelope fragment recording a loan of 1/2 mina silver, at the interest rate of Šamaš, by Bur-Sin. Cf. further [MU] ʿ*Šul-gi*-ᵈŠEŠ.KI [30]-*a-bu-šu iṣ-ba-ʿtu*ʾ, TIM 3 35:11f and Lutz 80: rev. 1ʾf, whose traces could support reading (1ʾ) ʿMUʾ [   ] (2ʾ) ᴵ*30-a-b[u-šu]* (collation).

[73]   Cf. MU.2.KAM *ša* ᵈ*Šul-gi*-ᵈŠEŠ.KI, TIM 3 36:15f.

MU ÚS.SA ʳᵈŠuľ'-gi-na-na-ru(!) in-na-aq-ru-ú [74]   UCLMA 9/2864
"The year after (the year) Šulgi-nanna was destroyed"

Fragmentary formulas

62	ʿMU(?) A-li-e-ši(?)ʾ	106:39
63	ʿMU X Xʾ NA KI [75]	42:20
64	[MU] ʿXʾEŠ A ʿXʾ [ ] ʿX Xʾ	49:15f
65	MU ÚS ʿX X X ᵈ Xʾ	67:21
66	MU [ ] ʿX X KÙ.GIʾ(?)	116:6
67	MU ʿXʾ [ ] ʿXʾ	146:9
68	MU ʿDa(?)-x x ʿKU [U]R(?)	Lutz 97:12
69	[MU]BA.DÍM	UCLMA 9/2866
69a	[MU] ʿľʾ-ba-al-pí-e[ľ] [76]	Lutz 42:17f

Khafaje year date formulas

70 [MU] Sa-am-su-i-lu-na LUGAL [   ] ʿXʾGIŠʿXʾ [   ]
[UGNI]M I-da-ma-ra-aṣ TAB [   ]TA AL ʿXʾ [   ]   315: rev. 5'f
"The year Samsu-iluna the king ... the army of Idamaraṣ ..."

(Year 10)

71 MU Sa-am-su-ʿi-luʾ-na LUGAL.E ḪUR.SAG.GAL
KUR MAR.TU.A 1 1/2 GAR 4 KUŠ 10 Á(!).BI.ŠÈ   314:22-24
"The year Samsu-iluna the king (had them quarry a stone)
from the great mountain of Amurru, 1 1/2 rods, 4 cubits,
10 (inches) on a side"

(Year 27)

72 [MU Sa-am-su-i-lu]-ʿnaʾ LUGAL.E
[   ] ʿX Xʾ
[   ] ʿx šaʾ [   ] ʿxʾAN.ZA ʿXʾ [   ] ʿX X Xʾ [   ]
[   ] ʿx KI xʾ [   ] ʿX RUʾᴷᴵ ŠA ʿX Xʾ [   ]
ʿXʾ [   ] [77]   305:53-56
"The year Samsu-iluna the king ..."

---

[74] Cf. MU ÚS.SA ᵈŠul-gi-na-< na >ᴷᴵ 30-[a]-bu-šu iṣ-ba-ʿtuʾ(!), TIM 3 14:22ff; MU ÚS.SA Šul-gi-
n[a-na ᴷ]ᴵ IN.DAB₅, TIM 3 75 case; MU ÚS.SA Šul-gi-na-naᴷᴵ in-na-aq-ru, IM 63139 cited by
F. Reschid Nuršamaš 5 sub ac.
[75] One cannot read Ḫe-naᴷᴵ; [Šul-gi]-na(!)-naᴷᴵ is possible but not really supported by the traces.
[76] This formula should be compared with Lutz 84:7f, which is year date formula 46.
[77] For this formula, see p. 74 below.

CATALOGUE OF TEXTS

I. Letters*

* Texts 152 and 217 should also be noted when considering the letters at Ishchali. They have been placed among the administrative documents since they are dated as well as sealed; letters normally have no date and are addressed as well. Cf. further 120-121, which appear to be administrative texts but which are unusually discursive in tone. Text 28 should also be considered, particularly if one restores [*lu t*]*i*-[*di ša*] in line 2 there.

II. LEGAL DOCUMENTS*

25 Court Record : Divorce
26 Court Record
27 Court Record
28 Court Record
29 Court Record : Settlement of account by *kārum*
30 Sale of house
31 Sale of field
32 Sale of field
33 Sale of wagon
34 Sale of slave
35 Sale of slave
36 Sale of slave
37 Sale of slave
38 Sale of slave
39 Sale of slave
40 Sale
41 Sale
42 Rental of commercial premises
43 Silver loan with interest (MÁŠ ᵈUTU)
44 Silver loan with interest (MÁŠ ᵈUTU)
45 Silver loan with interest (MÁŠ ᵈUTU)
46 Silver loan with interest (MÁŠ ᵈUTU)
47 Silver loan with interest (MÁŠ ᵈUTU)
48 Silver loan with interest (MÁŠ ᵈUTU)
49 Silver loan with interest (MÁŠ ᵈUTU)
50 Silver loan with interest (MÁŠ ᵈUTU)
51 Silver loan with interest (MÁŠ ᵈUTU)
52 Barley loan with interest
53 Barley loan with interest
54 Barley loan with interest
55 *Ḫubullu* loan (barley)
56 *Ḫubullu* loan (barley)
57 *Ḫubullu* loan (barley)
58 *Ḫubullu* loan (barley)
59 *Ḫubullu* loan (barley)
60 *Ḫubullu* loan (barley)

*   Text no. 85 may also belong to the group of court records (nos. 25-29). No. 28 could conceivably also be a letter, particularly if one restores [*lu t*]*i*-[*di ša ki-a*]-*am la* ʿ*aq*ʾ -*bu-šum* in 11. 2-3.

61 *Ḫubullu* loan (barley)
62 *Ḫubullu* loan (barley)
63 *Ḫubullu* loan (barley)
64 *Ḫubullu* loan (barley)
65 *Ḫubullu* loan (barley)
66 *Ḫubuttātum* loan (silver)
67 *Ḫubuttātum* loan (silver)
68 *Ḫubuttātum* loan (barley)
69 *Ḫubuttātum* loan (barley)
70 *Ḫubuttātum* loan (barley)
71 *Ḫubuttātum* loan (barley)
72 *Ḫubuttātum* loan (barley)
73 *Ḫubuttātum* loan (barley)
74 *Ḫubuttātum* loan (barley)
75 *Ḫubuttātum* loan (barley)
76 *Ḫubuttātum* loan (barley)
77 Silver loan without interest
78 Barley loan from the storehouse of Šamaš
79 Barley loan from the storehouse of Dur-Išḫara
80 Barley loan from Ištar and ŠÀ.TAM.MEŠ
81 Barley loan from storehouse
82 Barley loan without interest
83 Guaranty for slave girl
84 Guaranty for debt
85 Record of a penalty
86 Assignment of responsibility for grain missing from a storehouse
87 Assignment of responsibility for error in land transaction
88 Administrative memo: assignment of responsibility for three men
89 Administrative memo: guaranty for outstanding barley

III. Administrative Documents*

90 Jewelry, ornaments, garments; record of income
91 Jewelry, ornaments, garments; record of income
92 Jewelry, silver, garments; record of income

* In organizing the texts, we have attempted, as a first principle, to be guided by internal documentary features rather than by our own judgements as to the transactions involved. When the documents are labelled, i.e., *ḫubullu*, sale, etc. or when the genre is clearly identifiable by style, e.g., a letter, there are no real questions or disputes. The problems arise mainly in classifying what Assyriologists term "administrative texts" i.e., documents and records emanating from the bureaucratically operated archives of larger economic units i.e., the palace and temple storehouses.

93 Silver; record of income
94 Silver; ŠU.TI.A
95 Silver; ŠU.TI.A
96 Silver; ŠU.TI.A
97 Gold ornament; memo of withdrawal
98 Gold; record of obligation
99 Silver; memo of obligation
100 Silver; memo of obligation
101 Implements; memo of amount, person, destination
102 Implements; memo of amount, person, destination
103 Garments; record with tally of wool rations
104 Silver and bronze; list of objects
105 Emblems; frag. list
106 Gems, jewelry, precious items; list of objects, some persons
107 Jewelry, ornaments, gems; list of objects and persons
108 Silver; list of amounts and persons
109 Silver; list of amounts and persons
110 Silver; list of amounts and persons
111 Silver; short list of amounts and persons
112 Cattle, sheep; record of income

We have assumed that the basic characteristic of legal documents are witnesses, that is to say, that these records were executed for evidentiary purposes and for potential use in helping prove a claim in a court of law. These texts notably deal with the rights of individual persons and describe transactions taking place between two or more named individuals.

Administrative texts, on the other hand, are usually anonymous and normally have no lists of witnesses attached. They record transactions and in place of witnesses, offer dates, authorizing officials (e.g. NÍG.ŠU, GÌR), and seals as the means of showing their binding force. In our presentation, we have termed documents like these "records." But there are many documents which are simpler in form, often little more than lists or a few lines noting that a transaction has taken place. We take these texts to be administrative in origin, based on the assumption that private individuals in the conduct of their lives had no ready access to scribes, while the larger households (notably temple and palace) certainly possessed and required the services of scribally kept accounts. Such "minor" documents are the product of "intermediate" record keeping, i.e., jottings and notes that ultimately were to be incorporated into more "official" or final records. When the final records where written, these memos would either be discarded or else kept in a file until their business was completed. We have labelled these "intermediate" or "minor" documents as "memos, lists, tallies," depending on the number of entries and the inclusion of totals. The term "memo" is used to describe a brief text of no more than two entries or transactions; it may state item, amount, person, and sometimes mention the occasion of the transaction but has no full date or authorization statement. A "list" is a large memo, sometimes containing abstracts of a series of transactions but still lacking a date or official authorization statement. A "tally" is a list with a total. The term "receipt" is used when the document explicitly states that a given party has received (*maḫāru*) the commodities involved. "Order" is a memo addressed to a second person, i.e., spoken to a second person in the fashion of a letter.

A number of administrative documents are "out of place" in terms of the text numbering sequence: nos. 101-102 (see nos. 247-265); 151 (see 267-275); 153 (231 ff.).

113 Sheep; memo on assignment for fattening
114 Sheep; record, with seal, of missing animals
115 Goats; record, with seal, of dead animals
116 Goat; record, with seal, of dead animals
117 Sheep; record, with seal, of dead animals
118 Fowl; perforated label, with seal, of birds removed from flock
119 Sheep; record of dead animals
120 Cattle; memo on loss
121 Fowl; record, with seal, of outlay
122 Sheep and Goats; tally of animals assigned for fattening
123 Cattle; record, with seal, of disposal
124 Fowl; list of offerings
125 Fowl; perforated label, with seal, bearing record of outlay
126 Fowl; perforated label, with seal, bearing record of outlay
127 Barley; administrative storehouse loan
128 Barley; ŠU.TI.A
129 Barley; ŠU.TI.A
130 Barley; ŠU.TI.A
131 Barley; ŠU.TI.A
132 Barley; ŠU.TI.A
133 Barley; record of receipt
134 Barley; record of withdrawal
135 Barley; record of withdrawal
136 Barley; record of withdrawal
137 Barley; record of withdrawal
138 Barley; record of rent collections
139 Barley; list of collections, outlays, and expenditures
140 Barley; record of receipt
141 Barley; memo of receipt
142 Barley; record of loan
143 Barley; partly tallied list of outlays
144 Barley; record of loan
145 Barley; record of transfer
146 Barley; record of outlay
147 Barley; record of outlays
148 Barley; record of outlays
149 Barley; record of outlays
150 Barley; tally of outlays
151 List of Overseers with note
152 Barley; administrative order
153 Pitch; tally of outlays

154 Unspec. commodity; memo of amount and person
155 Unspec. comm.; perforated label with amount and person
156 Unspec. comm.; list of amounts and persons
157 Unspec. comm.; short list of amounts and persons
158 Unspec. comm.; list of amounts and persons
159 Barley; perforated label with list of amounts and persons
160 Barley; perforated label with list of amounts and persons
161 Unspec. comm; memo of amount and person
162 Unspec. comm.; tally of amounts and persons
163 Barley; tally of amounts and persons
164 Barley; tally of collections from temple fields
165 Unspec. comm.; tally of amounts and persons
166 Barley; tally of figures
167 Barley; tally of outlays
168 Barley; list of outlays
169 Barley; tally of outlays
170 Barley; memo of amount, person, and place
171 Unspec. comm.; memo of amount, person, and place
172 Unspec. comm.; memo of amount, person, and place
173 Unspec. comm.; perforated label with amount, person, and place
174 Unspec. comm.; memo of amounts, persons, and place
175 Unspec. comm.; short list of amounts, persons, and place
176 Barley; memo of amount, person, and field
177 Barley; memo of amount, person, and field
178 Unspec. comm.; short list of amounts, persons, and field
179 Barley; tally of collections
180 Barley; memo of amount, person, and field
181 Barley; record of outlay
182 Barley; list of outlays
183 Unspec. comm.; memo of amount, person, and overseer
184 Unspec. comm.; memo of amount, person, and overseer
185 Unspec. comm.; memo of amount, person, and overseer
186 Unspec. comm.; memo of amount, person, and overseer
187 Barley; memo of amount, person, and overseer
188 Unspec. comm.; memo of amount, person, and overseer
189 Barley; memo of amount, person, and overseers
190 Unspec. comm.; memo of amount, person, and overseer
191 Barley; memo of amount, person, and overseer
192 Unspec. comm.; memo of amounts, persons, and overseers
193 Barley; memo of amount, person, and overseer
194 Unspec. comm.; memo of amount, person, and overseer

195 Barley; memo of amount, person, and overseer
196 Barley; memo of amounts, person, and overseers
197 Unspec. comm.; memo of amount, person, and overseer
198 Barley; memo of amount, person, and group
199 Unspec. comm.; memo of amount, person, station, and group
200 Unspec. comm.; perforated label with amount and person
201 Unspec. comm.; perforated label with amount and person
202 Unspec. comm.; perforated label with amount and person
203 Unspec. comm.; perforated label with amount and person
204 Unspec. comm.; perforated label with amount and person
205 Unspec. comm.; perforated label, with seal, stating amount and person
206 Unspec. comm.; perforated label, with seal, stating amount and person
207 Unspec. comm.; perforated label with amount and person
208 Unspec. comm.; perforated label with amount and person
209 Unspec. comm.; perforated label with amount and person
210 Unspec. comm.; perforated label with amount and person
211 Unspec. comm.; perforated label with amount and person
212 Unspec. comm.; perforated label with amount and person
213 Unspec. comm.; perforated label with amount and person
214 Oil; ŠU.TI.A
215 Oil; record of expenditure
216 Beans; tally of amounts and persons
217 Oil; administrative order
218 Oil; record of receipt
219 Flour; record of outlay
220 Flour; memo of amount and person
221 Flour; memo of amounts and persons
222 Oil; memo of amount and person
223 Bread; partially tallied list of amounts and persons
224 Flour; memo of amount and person
225 Oil; record of outlay
226 Oil; list of amounts and persons
227 Flour; list of amounts, persons, and dates
228 Peas and vessels; tally of expenditures and dates
229 Flour; tally of expenditures with amounts, persons, and place
230 Unknown comm.; list of amounts and persons
231 Wool; ŠU.TI.A
232 Oil; ŠU.TI.A
233 Utensil; ŠU.TI.A
234 Unknown comm.; ŠU.TI.A
235 Oxen; record of loan

236 Vessels : record of loan
237 Stone blank, flour; memo of outlay
238 Bricks; memo of outlay
239 Wooden beams; memo of outlay
240 List of items and persons
241 List of items and persons
242 List of items, persons, and overseers
243 List of items and persons
244 Perforated bulla with seal
245 Perforated bulla with seal
246 Perforated label with seal
247 Utensils; list of deposited items
248 Harness and wagon gear; list of borrowed items
249 Implements; tally of items given out
250 Implements; record of loan
251 Implements; list of items loaned
252 Implements; record of loan
253 Implements; memo on items sent out
254 Implements; memo on items returned and outstanding
255 Implements; list of items returned
256 Implements; memo on items given out
257 Implements; list of items given out
258 Implements; list of items given out
259 Implements; memo on items given out
260 Implements; memo on items given out
261 Implements; list of items given out
262 Implements; list of items, persons, destinations
263 Utensils and implements; list of items
264 Implements; list of items, persons
265 Implements; list of items, persons
266 Implements; list of items
267 List of persons
268 List of persons
269 List of persons and overseer
270 List of persons and station
271 Record of persons
272 Record of hired workers
273 Record of hired workers
274 Record of hired workers
275 Record of personnel
276 List of land parcels and persons

IV. School and Literary Texts*

277　OB Gilgameš fragment (previously published by Theo Bauer JNES 16 (1957) 254-262)
278　Liver omens
279　Lexical fragment
280　School tablet; list of names
281　School tablet; list of names
282　Exercise tablet; names
283　Exercise tablet; deities
284　Exercise tablet; leather items
285　Exercise tablet; birds
286　Exercise tablet; birds
287　Exercise tablet; fish
288　Exercise tablet; goats
289　Exercise tablet; wild animals
290　Exercise tablet; wagon parts
291　Exercise tablet
292　Table of area measures
293　Practice tablet

V. Miscellaneous and Unclassified

294　Literary text or letter fragment
296　Letter(?)
296　Envelope fragment and seal impression
297　Envelope fragment and seal impression
298　Clay fragment with seal impression
299　Scribal exercise(?)
300　Text fragment with seal impression
301　Exercise tablet(?)
302　Literary text(?)
303　Tablet fragment
304　Apparent forgery

---

* One may also consider nos. 13 and 20 (and 12?) as possible school texts; cf. 13:5-8 and 20:5-9. These passages are similar to passages which appear in four other letters discussed by Kraus, *JEOL* 16 (1959-1962) 20f. The occurrence of identical passages has led Kraus to conclude that such duplicates or near duplicates are in fact school exercises rather than letters actually sent.

VI. Texts from Khafaje

VII

TABLE OF TEXTS — MUSEUM NUMBERS — DIMENSIONS

Text No.	Museum No.	Dimensions (in mm.) $(L \times W \times H)$	Text No.	Museum No.	Dimensions (in mm.) $(L \times W \times H)$
1	A21917	$45 \times 39 \times 25$	30	A21952	$66 \times 49 \times 25$
2	7704	$66 \times 43 \times 28$	31	21912	$117 \times 48 \times 25$
3	7729	$44 \times 39 \times 29$	32	21961	$56 \times 42 \times 16$
4	21923	$62 \times 46 \times 25$	33	7713	$36 \times 32 \times 20$
5	7646	$55 \times 42 \times 23$	34	7634	$78 \times 43 \times 24$
6	7703	$49 \times 35 \times 21$	35	7694	$80 \times 48 \times 19$
7	7803	$39 \times 31 \times 21$	36	21893	$75 \times 54 \times 22$
8	7758	$44 \times 36 \times 23$	37	7857	$61 \times 45 \times 18$
9	7812	$58 \times 43 \times 27$	38	21958	$42 \times 45 \times 23$
10	7834	$24 \times 25 \times 20$	39	7890	$51 \times 47 \times 18$
11	7763	$54 \times 38 \times 25$	40	7889	$67 \times 49 \times 18$
12	7664	$58 \times 41 \times 18$	41	21908	$48 \times 41 \times 21$
13	7661	$62 \times 54 \times 20$	42	7867	$64 \times 45 \times 25$
14	7678	$70 \times 42 \times 31$	43	7628	$73 \times 50 \times 20$
15	7761	$58 \times 43 \times 23$	44	7633	
16	21901	$65 \times 50 \times 21$	45	7756	$67 \times 39 \times 23$
17	7870	$86 \times 44 \times 28$	46	7651	$55 \times 42 \times 23$
18	21933	$96 \times 48 \times 23$	47	7699	$57 \times 41 \times 24$
19	21905	$31 \times 30 \times 15$	48	7696	$67 \times 45 \times 22$
20	7672	$60 \times 41 \times 21$	49	7681	$36 \times 33 \times 18$
21	22003	$73 \times 41 \times 17$	50	21963	$44 \times 30 \times 15$
22	7759	$67 \times 45 \times 26$	51	7697	$78 \times 48 \times 25$
23	7705	$85 \times 54 \times 29$	52	7814	$65 \times 44 \times 23$
24	7695	$80 \times 46 \times 21$	53	7648	$44 \times 39 \times 20$
25	7757	$92 \times 55 \times 26$	54	7778	$40 \times 38 \times 28$
26	21957	$35 \times 49 \times 22$	55	7688	$38 \times 36 \times 24$
27	21886	$37 \times 48 \times 22$	56	21887	$49 \times 37 \times 23$
28	21956	$47 \times 42 \times 29$	57	7684	$48 \times 35 \times 24$
29	7716	$50 \times 44 \times 20$	58	7884	$35 \times 34 \times 23$

Text No.	Museum No.	Dimensions (in mm.) (L × W × H)	Text No.	Museum No.	Dimensions (in mm.) (L × W × H)
59	A7798	30 × 30 × 25	97	A7665	21 × 29 × 18
60	7723	34 × 30 × 20	98	21910	35 × 37 × 17
61	7702	53 × 37 × 18	99	21881	23 × 26 × 20
62	7685	48 × 41 × 11	100	7679	23 × 23 × 16
63	7692	44 × 38 × 19	101	21942	28 × 24 × 12
64	7760	35 × 33 × 24	102	21943	24 × 22 × 13
65	7732	39 × 35 × 24	103	21900	42 × 38 × 22
66	7727	32 × 33 × 25	104	21926	63 × 83 × 29
67	7709	56 × 39 × 22	105	21932	19 × 67 × 23
68	7680	68 × 52 × 25	106	21998	56 × 121 × 35
69	7637	53 × 41 × 26	107	21915	232 × 119 × 37
70	7718	47 × 39 × 27	108	7710	48 × 35 × 22
71	7687	42 × 37 × 25	109	21999	43 × 40 × 22
72	7638	42 × 35 × 20	110	7714	51 × 41 × 25
73	7712	34 × 33 × 22	111	7666	30 × 33 × 16
74	7632	35 × 35 × 21	112	21947	37 × 35 × 24
75	7790	33 × 30 × 23	113	7674	33 × 30 × 20
76	7715	38 × 35 × 25	114	7836	22 × 24 × 17
77	21953	56 × 42 × 21	115	7777	29 × 31 × 24
78	7711	57 × 45 × 26	116	7766	28 × 34 × 24
79	7650	68 × 45 × 23	117	7725	23 × 27 × 19
80	7728	50 × 40 × 27	118	21884	32 × 43 × 16
81	7730	51 × 37 × 25	119	21906	34 × 34 × 18
82	7720	37 × 35 × 23	120	21909	36 × 37 × 20
83	21960	67 × 40 × 20	121	21883	31 × 38 × 19
84	7690	57 × 42 × 19	122	7669	50 × 47 × 26
85	7891	57 × 43 × 20	123	7792	28 × 35 × 19
86	21964	49 × 39 × 19	124	21890	31 × 45 × 22
87	21888	59 × 50 × 23	125	21880	30 × 35 × 10
88	21889	44 × 45 × 18	126	21885	31 × 37 × 16
89	21930	30 × 23 × 14	127	7642	42 × 34 × 19
90	7667	72 × 42 × 22	128	7825	27 × 30 × 15
91	7698	71 × 41 × 23	129	7830	27 × 31 × 17
92	7706	55 × 41 × 26	130	7829	24 × 27 × 15
93	7668	40 × 36 × 24	131	7640	30 × 30 × 18
94	7647	64 × 43 × 24	132	7722	31 × 30 × 22
95	7649	43 × 36 × 18	133	21935	35 × 33 × 21
96	7643	33 × 31 × 19	134	7789	30 × 32 × 16

Text No.	Museum No.	Dimensions (in mm.) (L × W × H)	Text No.	Museum No.	Dimensions (in mm.) (L × W × H)
135	A7770	$38 \times 35 \times 17$	173	A21978	$24 \times 31 \times 13$
136	7701	$44 \times 39 \times 21$	174	21986	$25 \times 32 \times 13$
137	7636	$42 \times 35 \times 20$	175	21980	$29 \times 36 \times 14$
138	7686	$49 \times 40 \times 23$	176	21877	$18 \times 22 \times 14$
139	7810	$50 \times 37 \times 24$	177	21895	$25 \times 32 \times 15$
140	7717	$37 \times 34 \times 21$	178	21873	$11 \times 29 \times 14$
141	21973	$26 \times 35 \times 13$	179	21946	$46 \times 38 \times 23$
142	7645	$23 \times 22 \times 13$	180	21875	$32 \times 40 \times 15$
143	7689	$54 \times 47 \times 19$	181	7808	$24 \times 24 \times 15$
144	7655	$30 \times 37 \times 16$	182	21985	$33 \times 33 \times 12$
145	7691	$40 \times 37 \times 22$	183	21969	$25 \times 35 \times 15$
146	7793	$33 \times 33 \times 23$	184	21982	$24 \times 34 \times 12$
147	7682	$57 \times 41 \times 22$	185	21993	$21 \times 36 \times 12$
148	7731	$26 \times 25 \times 16$	186	21984	$22 \times 31 \times 12$
149	7708	$38 \times 36 \times 25$	187	21991	$20 \times 33 \times 11$
150	7724	$30 \times 27 \times 17$	188	21988	$27 \times 34 \times 14$
151	21950	$93 \times 51 \times 24$	189	21971	$25 \times 33 \times 12$
152	7670	$32 \times 31 \times 20$	190	21977	$26 \times 38 \times 13$
153	7683	$33 \times 32 \times 21$	191	21996	$22 \times 32 \times 13$
154	21990	$24 \times 35 \times 14$	192	21981	$27 \times 39 \times 14$
155	7673	$19 \times 35 \times 18$	193	21989	$23 \times 30 \times 12$
156	21965	$43 \times 48 \times 21$	194	21970	$22 \times 45 \times 12$
157	21974	$27 \times 34 \times 12$	195	21972	$22 \times 28 \times 11$
158	7659	$76 \times 53 \times 23$	196	21983	$21 \times 29 \times 11$
159	7906	22×36	197	21987	$24 \times 28 \times 15$
160	7904	24×40	198	21994	$22 \times 30 \times 12$
161	21968	$21 \times 32 \times 12$	199	21979	$22 \times 32 \times 12$
162	7635	$55 \times 42 \times 23$	200	7899	$19 \times 25 \times 18$
163	7733	$36 \times 36 \times 20$	201	7901	$17 \times 25 \times 16$
164	7641	$46 \times 39 \times 23$	202	7918	$18 \times 26 \times 16$
165	21965A	$42 \times 51 \times 20$	203	7908	$19 \times 26 \times 16$
166	21945	$32 \times 31 \times 15$	204	7916	$18 \times 27 \times 16$
167	22002	$65 \times 41 \times 21$	205	7898	$22 \times 28 \times 15$
168	7843	$38 \times 34 \times 13$	206	7913	$19 \times 33 \times 15$
169	21902	$63 \times 50 \times 22$	207	7903	$21 \times 28 \times 19$
170	21876	$31 \times 33 \times 14$	208	7914	$17 \times 27 \times 18$
171	21992	$26 \times 34 \times 12$	209	7912	$12 \times 27 \times 17$
172	21995	$21 \times 32 \times 11$	210	7911	$17 \times 28 \times 18$

Text No.	Museum No.	Dimensions (in mm.) (L × W × H)	Text No.	Museum No.	Dimensions (in mm.) (L × W × H)
211	A7909	17 × 26 × 16	249	A21920	43 × 31 × 13
212	7905	19 × 28 × 15	250	21937	30 × 35 × 19
213	7910	20 × 30 × 19	251	21921	52 × 35 × 19
214	7676	24 × 24 × 21	252	7801	28 × 29 × 19
215	21899	36 × 37 × 18	253	7654	32 × 58 × 15
216	7804	47 × 35 × 20	254	21919	35 × 27 × 16
217	7726	23 × 22 × 19	255	21929	36 × 27 × 15
218	7783	37 × 48 × 21	256	21940	35 × 28 × 18
219	21916	31 × 30 × 29	257	21934	50 × 34 × 15
220	7721	23 × 24 × 16	258	21938	29 × 25 × 14
221	7660	40 × 39 × 15	259	21936	32 × 27 × 19
222	21918	52 × 55 × 21	260	21939	30 × 26 × 14
223	7652	84 × 47 × 19	261	21931	41 × 31 × 15
224	7644	36 × 33 × 15	262	21941	38 × 28 × 12
225	21879	29 × 28 × 19	263	7693	67 × 43 × 23
226	21897	27 × 29 × 21	264	21911	35 × 36 × 15
227	21914	40 × 38 × 19	265	21924	78 × 41 × 19
228	7629	68 × 58 × 24		+ 21925	
229	7719	45 × 38 × 19	266	21928	78 × 42 × 23
230	7663	70 × 50 × 23	267	21904	38 × 36 × 19
231	7796	25 × 26 × 18	268	7871	134 × 91 × 36
232	7675	25 × 28 × 19	269	22000	45 × 40 × 20
233	7671	23 × 24 × 16	270	22008	71 × 47 × 24
234	21907	38 × 33 × 15	271	21967	36 × 39 × 18
235	7799	30 × 30 × 21	272	7776	43 × 37 × 20
236	7658	25 × 25 × 20	273	7817	43 × 40 × 20
237	7835	26 × 24 × 16	274	7838	31 × 32 × 17
238	22001	29 × 30 × 14	275	21949	60 × 40 × 25
239	21944	26 × 24 × 18	276	21913	40 × 38 × 20
240	21894	55 × 42 × 22	277	22007	118 × 61 × 30
241	7653	57 × 40 × 16	278	7893	93 × 174 × 35
242	21922	68 × 45 × 24	279	21891	53 × 46 × 30
243	7700	62 × 40 × 18	280	7631	69 × 51 × 24
244	7900	29 × 33 × 14	281	7630	73 × 47 × 21
245	21976	28 × 35 × 13	282	7662	71 diam. × 16
246	22010	34 × 42 × 14	283	21955	75 diam. × 26
247	7707	42 × 32 × 24	284	21874	70 diam. × 22
248	21927	46 × 36 × 16	285	21903	73 × 73 × 19

Text No.	Museum No.	Dimensions (in mm.) (L × W × H)	Text No.	Museum No.	Dimensions (in mm.) (L × W × H)
286	A21898	62 × 63 × 21	306	A7749	47 × 56 × 24
287	7656	89 diam. × 20	307	7734	101 × 64 × 33
288	21896	64 × 69 × 20	308	7742	67 × 56 × 27
289	21954	69 max. w. ×	309	7744	80 × 52 × 32
		75 max. h.	310	7750	38 × 49 × 19
290	21882	65 × 75 × 30	311	7746	59 × 55 × 30
291	21975	67 diam. × 23	312	7737	70 × 45 × 23
292	21948	142 × 59 × 28	313	7741	101 × 56 × 26
293	21892	55 × 69 × 16	314	7740	128 × 73 × 32
294	7850	37 × 70 × 19	315	7859	96 × 56 × 31
295	7768	39 × 34 × 5	316	7736	76 × 72 × 31
296	21997	24 × 34 × 7	317	7745	50 × 113 × 29
297	21878	51 × 23 × 10	318	7735	109 × 76 × 35
298	21962	50 × 8 × 45	319	7755	65 × 43 × 23
299	7826	44 × 50 × 7	320	7753	95 × 68 × 28
300	21966	51 × 26 × 24	321	7747	63 diam. × 15
301	21951	57 × 60 × 21	322	7751	58 × 41 × 21
302	21959	38 × 56 × 21	323	7775	35 × 34 × 17
303	7828	17 × 35 × 14	324	7748	46 × 42 × 25
304	22009	39 × 34 × 15	325	7743	72 × 67 × 32
305	7752	129 × 65 × 30	326	7894	172 × 74 × 36

TABLE OF MUSEUM NUMBERS — TEXT NUMBERS

Museum No.	Text No.	Museum No.	Text No.	Museum No.	Text No.
7628	43	7661	13	7693	263
7629	228	7662	282	7694	35
7630	281	7663	230	7695	24
7631	280	7664	12	7696	48
7632	74	7665	97	7697	51
7633	44	7666	111	7698	91
7634	34	7667	90	7699	47
7635	162	7668	93	7700	243
7636	137	7669	122	7701	136
7637	69	7670	152	7702	61
7638	72	7671	233	7703	6
7640	131	7672	20	7704	2
7641	164	7673	155	7705	23
7642	127	7674	113	7706	92
7643	96	7675	232	7707	247
7644	224	7676	214	7708	149
7645	142	7678	14	7709	67
7646	5	7679	100	7710	108
7647	94	7680	68	7711	78
7648	53	7681	49	7712	73
7649	95	7682	147	7713	33
7650	79	7683	153	7714	110
7651	46	7684	57	7715	76
7652	223	7685	62	7716	29
7653	241	7686	138	7717	140
7654	253	7687	71	7718	70
7655	144	7688	55	7719	229
7656	287	7689	143	7720	82
7658	236	7690	84	7721	220
7659	158	7691	145	7722	132
7660	221	7692	63	7723	60

Museum No.	Text No.	Museum No.	Text No.	Museum No.	Text No.
7724	150	7775	323	7891	85
7725	117	7776	272	7893	278
7726	217	7777	115	7894	326
7727	66	7778	54	7898	205
7728	80	7783	218	7899	200
7729	3	7789	134	7900	244
7730	81	7790	75	7901	201
7731	148	7792	123	7903	207
7732	65	7793	146	7904	160
7733	163	7796	231	7905	212
7734	307	7798	59	7906	159
7735	318	7799	235	7908	203
7736	316	7801	252	7909	211
7737	312	7803	7	7910	213
7740	314	7804	216	7911	210
7741	313	7808	181	7912	209
7742	308	7810	139	7913	206
7743	325	7812	9	7914	208
7744	309	7814	52	7916	204
7745	317	7817	273	7918	202
7746	311	7825	128		
7747	321	7826	299	21873	178
7748	324	7828	303	21874	284
7749	306	7829	130	21875	180
7750	310	7830	129	21876	170
7751	322	7834	10	21877	176
7752	305	7835	237	21878	297
7753	320	7836	114	21879	225
7755	319	7838	274	21880	125
7756	45	7843	168	21881	99
7757	25	7850	294	21882	290
7758	8	7857	37	21883	121
7759	22	7859	315	21884	118
7760	64	7867	42	21885	126
7761	15	7870	17	21886	27
7763	11	7871	268	21887	56
7766	116	7884	58	21888	87
7768	295	7889	40	21889	88
7770	135	7890	39	21890	124

Museum No.	Text No.	Museum No.	Text No.	Museum No.	Text No.
21891	279	21931	261	21970	194
21892	293	21932	105	21971	189
21893	36	21933	18	21972	195
21894	240	21934	257	21973	141
21895	177	21935	133	21974	157
21896	288	21936	259	21975	291
21897	226	21937	250	21976	245
21898	286	21938	258	21977	190
21899	215	21939	260	21978	173
21900	103	21940	256	21979	199
21901	16	21941	262	21980	175
21902	169	21942	101	21981	192
21903	285	21943	102	21982	184
21904	267	21944	239	21983	196
21905	19	21945	166	21984	186
21906	119	21946	179	21985	182
21907	234	21947	112	21986	174
21908	41	21948	292	21987	197
21909	120	21949	275	21988	188
21910	98	21950	151	21989	193
21911	264	21951	301	21990	154
21912	31	21952	30	21991	187
21913	276	21953	77	21992	171
21914	227	21954	289	21993	185
21915	107	21955	283	21994	198
21916	219	21956	28	21995	172
21917	1	21957	26	21996	191
21918	222	21958	38	21997	296
21919	254	21959	302	21998	106
21920	249	21960	83	21999	109
21921	251	21961	32	22000	269
21922	242	21962	298	22001	238
21923	4	21963	50	22002	167
21924		21964	86	22003	21
+21925	265	21965A	165	22007	277
21926	104	21965	156	22008	270
21927	248	21966	300	22009	304
21928	266	21967	271	22010	246
21929	255	21968	161		
21930	89	21969	183		

SUPPLEMENTAL DATA ON EXCAVATED TABLETS.

Text No.	Field No.	Find Spot			Date
1	Ish. 34-T. 74	6	Q	30	31-XII-34
4	Ish. 34-T. 94	2	Q	31	10-I-35
16	Ish. 34-T. 53	1	S	36	19-XII-34
18	Ish. 34-T. 107	1	P	30	29-XII-34
19	Ish. 34-T. 58	2	R	30	19-XII-34
21	Ish. 35-T. 109	3	T	30	5-I-36
26	Ish. 35-T. 14	5	V	31	4-XII-35
27	Ish. 35-T. 22	5	V	31	5-XII-35
28	Ish. 35-T. 12	5	V	31	4-XII-35
30	Ish. 35-T. 2	1	R	29	27-II-35
31	Ish. 34-T. 66	1	P	30	28-XII-34
32	Ish. 35-T. 21	5	V	31	5-XII-35
36	Ish. 34-T. 45	4	Q	35	15-XII-34
38	Ish. 35-T. 17	5	V	31	5-XII-35
41	Ish. 34-T. 61	1	P	30	28-XII-34
50	Ish. 35-T. 26	3	V	30	8-XII-35
56	Ish. 34-T. 23	2	R	34	10-XII-34
77	Ish. 35-T. 8	1	S	30	2-XII-35
83	Ish. 35-T. 20	5	V	31	5-XII-35
86	Ish. 35-T. 28	3	V	30	8-XII-35
87	Ish. 34-T. 25	3	R	34	10-XII-34
88	Ish. 34-T. 32	3	R	34	10-XII-34
89	Ish. 34-T. 102	3	S	29	11-I-35
98	Ish. 34-T. 64	6	Q	30	28-XII-34
99	Ish. 34-T. 12	1	R	35	9-XII-34
101	Ish. 34-T. 127	4	S	29	16-I-35
102	Ish. 34-T. 128	4	S	29	16-I-35
103	Ish. 34-T. 54	10	R	33	19-XII-34
104	Ish. 34-T. 98	2	S	29	10-I-35
105	Ish. 34-T. 104	2	S	29	10-I-35
106	Ish. 35-T. 99	2	S	29	15-XII-35

Text No.	Field No.	Find Spot	Date
107	Ish. 34-T. 69a	1 P 29	
109	Ish. 35-T. 102	Temple road at gate	19-XII-35
112	Ish. 34-T. 146	2 R 30	
118	Ish. 34-T. 15	3 R 34	9-XII-34
119	Ish. 34-T. 59	4 Q 30	27-XII-34
120	Ish. 34-T. 63	6 Q 30	28-XII-34
121	Ish. 34-T. 14	3 R 34	9-XII-34
124	Ish. 34-T. 35	3 R 34	12-XII-34
125	Ish. 34-T. 11	3 R 34	9-XII-34
126	Ish. 34-T. 16	3 R 34	9-XII-34
133	Ish. 34-T. 120	4 S 29	16-I-35
141	Ish. 35-T. 39	3 V 30	8-XII-35
151	Ish. 34-T. 153	City Gate	6-II-35
154	Ish. 35-T. 80	3 V 30	12-XII-35
156	Ish. 35-T. 31	3 V 30	8-XII-35
157	Ish. 35-T. 40	3 V 30	8-XII-35
161	Ish. 35-T. 34	3 V 30	8-XII-35
165			
166	Ish. 34-T. 143	4 S 29	7-I-35
167	Ish. 35-T. 106	12 V 32	31-XII-55
169	Ish. 34-T. 54	10 R 33	19-XII-34
170	Ish. 34-T. 7	3 R 34	9-XII-34
171	Ish. 35-T. 82	3 V 30	12-XII-35
172	Ish. 35-T. 85	3 V 30	12-XII-35
173	Ish. 35-T. 57	3 V 30	12-XII-35
174	Ish. 35-T. 66	3 V 30	12-XII-35
175	Ish. 35-T. 59	3 V 30	12-XII-35
176	Ish. 34-T. 8	3 R 35	9-XII-34
177	Ish. 34-T. 47	3 R 34	17-XII-34
178	Ish. 34-T. 2	3 R 34	9-XII-34
179	Ish. 34-T. 145	2 R 30	20-I-35
180	Ish. 34-T. 6	3 R 34	9-XII-34
182	Ish. 35-T. 65	3 V 30	12-XII-35
183	Ish. 35-T. 35	3 V 30	8-XII-35
184	Ish. 35-T. 61	3 V 30	12-XII-35
185	Ish. 35-T. 83	3 V 30	12-XII-35
186	Ish. 35-T. 64	3 V 30	12-XII-35
187	Ish. 35-T. 81	3 V 30	12-XII-35

Text No.	Field No.	Find Spot	Date
188	Ish. 35-T. 78	3 V 30	12-XII-35
189	Ish. 35-T. 37	3 V 30	8-XII-35
190	Ish. 35-T. 56	3 V 30	12-XII-35
191	Ish. 35-T. 86	3 V 30	12-XII-35
192	Ish. 35-T. 60	3 V 30	12-XII-35
193	Ish. 35-T. 79	3 V 30	12-XII-35
194	Ish. 35-T. 36	3 V 30	8-XII-35
195	Ish. 35-T. 38	3 V 30	8-XII-35
196	Ish. 35-T. 63	3 V 30	12-XII-35
197	Ish. 35-T. 77	3 V 30	12-XII-35
198	Ish. 35-T. 84	3 V 30	12-XII-35
199	Ish. 35-T. 58	3 V 30	12-XII-35
215	Ish. 34-T. 51	10 R 33	19-XII-34
219	Ish. 34-T. 70	5 Q 30	30-XII-34
222	Ish. 34-T. 75	1 Q 32	2-I-35
225	Ish. 34-T. 10	1 R 35	9-XII-34
226	Ish. 34-T. 49	Dump of R 35	17-XII-34
227	Ish. 34-T. 69	3 Q 30	30-XII-34
234	Ish. 34-T. 60	1 Q 30	27-XII-34
238	Ish. 35-T. 105	4 V 32	22-XII-35
239	Ish. 34-T. 141	Dump	17-I-35
240	Ish. 34-T. 46	8 R 35	16-XII-34
242	Ish. 34-T. 91	1 P 29	24-XII-34
245	Ish. 35-T. 50	3 V 30	11-XII-35
246	Ish. 35-T.120	1 V 32	27-I-35
248	Ish. 34-T. 99	3 S 29	11-I-35
249	Ish. 34-T. 78	1 S 29	4-I-35
250	Ish. 34-T. 122	4 S 29	16-I-35
251	Ish. 34-T. 80	1 S 29	4-I-35
254	Ish. 34-T. 76	1 S 29	4-I-25
255	Ish. 34-T. 101	3 S 29	11-I-35
256	Ish. 34-T. 125	4 S 29	16-I-35
257	Ish. 34-T. 119	4 S 29	16-I-35
258	Ish. 34-T. 123	4 S 29	16-I-35
259	Ish. 34-T.121	4 S 29	16-I-35
260	Ish. 34-T.124	4 S 29	16-I-35
261	Ish. 34-T.103	3 S 29	11-I-35
262	Ish. 34-T. 126	4 S 29	16-I-35
264	Ish. 34-T. 65	6 Q 30	

Text No.	Field No.	Find Spot	Date
265	Ish. 34-T. 96, 97	1 S 29	10-I-35
266	Ish. 34-T. 100	3 S 29	
267	Ish. 34-T. 57	2 Q 30	22-XII-34
269	Ish. 35-T. 103	5 V 32	21-XII-35
270	Ish. 35-T. 118	1 V 32	27-I-36
271	Ish. 35-T. 33	3 V 30	8-XII-35
275	Ish. 34-T. 150	1 T 31	20-I-35
276	Ish. 34-T. 67	6 Q 30	28-XII-34
277	Ish. 35-T. 117	4 V 30	12-XII-35
279	Ish. 34-T. 43	10 R 35	14-XII-34
283	Ish. 35-T. 11	1 R 29	2-XII
284	Ish. 34-T. 5	3 R 34	9-XII-34
285	Ish. 34-T. 55	2 R 30	23-XII-34
286	Ish. 34-T. 50	2 Q 30	19-XII-34
288	Ish. 34-T. 48	8 R 33	17-XII-34
289	Ish. 34-T. 9	2 S 30	2-XII
290	Ish. 34-T. 13	1 R 35	9-XII-34
291	Ish. 35-T. 47	2 Q 29	1-XII
292	Ish. 34-T. 149	City Gate	23-I-35
293	Ish. 34-T. 44	7 R 34	14-XII-34
296	Ish. 35-T. 98	Dump	13-XII-35
297	Ish. 35-T. 9	Dump in R 34-35	9-XII-34
298	Ish. 35-T. 25	2 S 29	6-XII-35
300	Ish. 35-T. 32	3 V 30	8-XII-35
301	Ish. 34- T. 154	6 T 29	8-II-35
302	Ish. 35-T. 18	6 S 29	5-XII
304	Ish. 35-T. 119	1 V 32	26-I-36

SELECTED DOCUMENTS IN TRANSLITERATION AND TRANSLATION*

No. 5

obv.	(1)	a-na É.GI₄.A É
	(2)	qí-bí-ma
	(3)	um-ma I-zi-Su-mu-ú-ma
	(4)	a-nu-um-ma 2 (PI) ŠE.GIŠ.Ì
	(5)	i-na-ad-di-nu-ki-im
	(6)	¹Na-am-si-e-ᵈIM
l.e.	(7)	pu-ru-um 2 1/2 SILA₃ Ì.NUN.NA
	(8)	šu-ud-di-ni-šu
	(9)	šum-ma it-ta-ad-na-ki
rev.	(10)	1/2 a-na GEMÉ-ᵈEN.ZU
	(11)	⌈šu⌉-li ⌈šum⌉-ma
	(12)	[pu-ru-u]m 2¹⁄₂ SILA₃ Ì.NUN.NA
	(13)	⌈la id⌉-di-na-ki la ta-ma-⌈ḫa-ri⌉-šu
	(14)	ù GUD.ḪI.A [ša] ⌈É⌉-tim
	(15)	⌈a⌉-na šu-ku-l[i(?)-im]
u.e.	(16)	⌈šu⌉-ki-li-šu-nu

obv.	(1)	To the daughter-in-law of the house
	(2)	speak;
	(3)	thus says Izi-Sumu :
	(4)	Behold, O.a.O kor of sesame
	(5)	they will give you.
	(6)	(As for) Namse-Adad,
l.e.	(7)	a stone vessel (and) 2¹⁄₂ quarts ghee
	(8)	collect from him.
	(9)	If it has (already) been given to you,
rev.	(10)	one half for Amat-Sin
	(11)	take out; if (however)
	(12)	the stone vessel (and) 2¹⁄₂ quarts ghee

* Single parenthesis in the numbering of translation lines (cf., e.g., No. 9:3-6, 12-14) indicates that the English wording is not in phase with the Akkadian.

(13)   he has not given to you, do not confront him.

(14)   And the cattle of the house —

(15)   for fattening

u.e.   (16)   let them be fed.

(1)   *Kallat bītim*, mentioned in this letter as well as in nos. 6:1 and 7:1, seems to have functioned as a kind of estate manager. For additional references see CAD K 79b and Gelb RA 66 (1972) 4, who discusses the possibility of her being the principal of a female religious community. Cf. further Kraus, *Vom mesopotamischen Menschen der altbabylonischen Zeit und seiner Welt* Mededelingen d. Kon. Nederland. Akad. v. Wetenschappen Amsterdam (1973) 53-54.

(5)   "They" must refer to the persons arriving with this letter for the addressee.

(7)   For *pūrum* cf. AHw 881b; note the nominative form.

(9)   Note -*ki* for expected -*ki-im*; cf. also 6:17.

(10)   One could also consider reading 1/2 <SILA$_3$>. Reading 1 (BÁN) seems to be excluded since the total amount of Ì.NUN.NA in question is less than 1 (BÁN). The 2 (PI) ŠE.GIŠ.Ì, the only other commodity mentioned in this text, was apparently delivered together with this letter.

(16)   The suffix -*šunu* is either an error for -*šu-nu-<ti>* or else it is an Assyrianism; cf. GAG §42g note 15, Hecker AnOr 44 §49a.

No. 9

obv.   (1)   a-na Ka-la-a qí-bí-ma

(2)   um-ma A-ḫi-ša-ki-mi-ma

(3)   ṭe₄-e-em ᵈEN.ZU-i-din-nam

(4)   DUMU ᵈUTU-˹su-mu-um DI.KU₅˺

(5)   ù Ma-nu-um DUMU ᵈEN.ZU-ri-me-ni

(6)   ga-am-ra-am ˹ṣú˺-ḫa-ru-ú

(7)   [ša] ˹il-qú-nim-ma˺

(8)   [la] ˹il-li-ku-nim˺

l.e.   (9)   [a]-wi-lum ¹Ṭa-ri-du-˹um˺(?)

(10)   aš-šum mi-ni-ma

(11)   ˹ka˺-li-i

rev.   (12)   GUD.ḪI.A ša a-na a-wi-˹li-e˺

(13)   ṭú-uḫ-ḫi-e-em

(14)   it-ru-nim-ma ni-mu-ru-šu-nu-ti

(15)   i-na pa-ni-šu-nu ˹la˺ i-zi-bu-nim

(16)   10 UDU.NITÁ 3 ˹ÁB.AL˺ [ša i]d-bu-bu

(17)   i-na pa-ni-šu-nu la <i>-zi-bu-nim

(18)   a-na wa-ar-ka-tim pa-ra-si-im

(19)   ˹a-di ki˺-ma ˹šu-mi˺ i-na ˹ši-id-di˺-im

(20)   ˹ù˺ ši-it-nu-ni-˹im˺

u.e.   (21)   ˹bi˺-tum i-ḫa-al-li-˹iq˺-ma

(22)   [w]a-ar-ka-tum

	(23)	la i-pa-ra-ás
edge	(24)	ar-ḫi-iš ṣu-ha-ru-ú
	(25)	˹a˺-la-kam li-pu-šu-nim

obv.	(1)	Unto Kalaja speak;
	(2)	Thus says Aḫi-ša-kimi:
	3)	The complete report of Sin-iddinam
	4)	son of Šamaš-sumum the judge
	5)	and Manum son of Sin-rimenni —
	6)	the young men
	(7)	who took (it)
	(8)	have not (yet) arrived here.
l.e.	(9)	The man, Ṭaridum,
	(10)	why
	(11)	has he been detained?
rev.	12)	The cattle which they led away (in order)
	13)	to deliver (them) to the men
	14)	(and which) we saw —
	(15)	they indeed did not leave in their charge.
	(16)	(Furthermore,) the 10 male sheep (and) 3 cows (of) which they spoke —
	(17)	they did not leave (these) in their charge (either)!
	(18)	(Is it desirable) to investigate the matter?
	(19)	As long as my name (is involved) in *pulling*
	(20)	and contention,
u.e.	(21)	the house will go to ruin!
	(22)	Let the matter (therefore)
	(23)	not be investigated.
	(24)	Quickly, let the young men
	(25)	make the journey here!

(4) Cf. ᵈUTU-*su*(!)-*mu-um* DI.KU₅ in CT 6 35c:4; the similarity of name and title is a coincidence since the above text is dated to Ammiṣaduqa 19.

(15) For *ezēbu* + ventive in OB letters, cf. CAD E 419b and 16:17.

(16) A reading, [*ša*] ˹MÁŠ.ŠU˺.GÍD.GÍD, may also be possible at at the end of this line.

(19) The translation is uncertain, assuming *šiddum* from *šadādum* "to pull, to tear out", AHw 1121b. Another possibility is *šiṭṭum* "tearing" from *šaṭāṭum* "to cut, slit:" cf. Bab. 12 p. 27:11, cited by CAD K 224a and Del. HW 651a.

No. 21

| obv. | (1) | a-na Ur-ᵈKab-ta |
| | (2) | qí-bí-ma |

	(3)	um-ma Sa-la-tum-ma
	(4)	aš-šum 5 GÍN KÙ.BABBAR
	(5)	ša NIN.DINGIR ša ᵈBe-el-ga-še-er
	(6)	ša pí-ia ad-di-nu
	(7)	am-ta-am it-ma
	(8)	i-na ša-la-at
	(9)	it-ba-lu-ši
	(10)	ᵈUTU gi-mi-il-ma
	(11)	10 GÍN KÙ.BABBAR šu-bi-lam-ma
	(12)	GEMÉ lu-ša-am
l.e.	(13)	ù ta-ad-mi-<iq>-ma
rev.	(14)	i-na da-ma-qí-ka
	(15)	ù-ul ad-<mi>-iq
	(16)	ú šum-ma-an
	(17)	šu-lu-mu-ka-ma
	(18)	ta-aš-pu-ra-am
	(19)	da-mi-iq DINGIR
	(20)	ṭe₄-em-ka da-am-qá-am
	(21)	i-na ku-nu-ki
	(22)	šu-ṭe₄-ra-ma
	(23)	šu-bi-lam
	(24)	ᵈUTU gi-mi-il-ma
	(25)	mi-ma ša e-li-ˈkaˀ(?)
	(26)	ṭà-bu-ú
u.e.	(27)	šu-bi-lam
edge	(28)	ˈùˀ 7 GUR ša i-na É NIN.DINGIR
	(29)	ta-aš-pu-ku BUR.ᵈEN.ZU it-ba(?)-al ù id-di(?)-nam

obv.	(1)	Unto Ur-Kabta
	(2)	speak;
	(3)	thus (says) Salatum:
	(4)	Concerning the five shekels silver
	(5)	of the high priestess of Belgašer
	(6)	(to) whom I gave my word;
	(7)	she had sworn (to devote) a slave girl
	(8)	(but the one she had) they carried her off
	(9)	as war booty.
	(10)	Please Šamaš and
	(11)	send me ten shekels silver so
	(12)	(that) I may buy a slave girl (for her).
l.e.	(13)	Moreover, (when) you became prosperous

rev.   14)   I did not share
              15)   in your prosperity.
             (16)   And if you were
              17)   to write me
              18)   about your well-being
             (19)   (I would have said): "(his) god is gracious!"
              20)   Write down
              21)   the good news (about) yourself
              22)   upon a tablet and
             (23)   send it to me.
             (24)   Please Šamaš and
              25)   send me
              26)   whatever seems
              27)   fair to you.
              28)   Also, the seven kors which you stored in the house of
              29)   the high priestess, Bur-Sin took (them) away and gave (them)
                    to me.

(11)   Salatum's request appears to be: "Send me the five shekels I already owe her and five more in addition."

(17)   *Šullumuka* appears to be a nominative form; but our translation requires an accusative.

(19)   Another possibility is to read: *da-mi-iq-<ma>-an* "it would have been nice."

(29)   Translation assumes that *u iddinnam* properly belongs to the end of line 29 and was placed above it for lack of space.

No. 23

                    Beginning broken
obv.   (1')   aš-šu[m   ] ʿxʾ [   ]
            (2')   i-na AGA.UŠ.MEŠ [   ]
            (3')   a-di tap-pu-ut be-el-ti-i[a al-li-ku]
            (4')   i-na AGA.UŠ.MEŠ in-na-ás
            (5')   a-ḫi ú-ul ad-di aṣ-ri-i[m]
            (6')   ṣi-bi-a-ti-ia ma-da-tim ad-di-i-ma
            (7')   a-na ṣi-ir GAL.MAR.TU ù ša ʿbiʾ-ti-im
            (8')   e-še-er ù ú-ša-am-ši
            (9')   ù ša la a-mu-ru ù la e-iš-mu-ú
           (10')   ad-bu-ub ki-ma [sa-r]a-ʿtuʾ-šu-nu ra-bi-a-ma
           (11')   qí-bi-tam ú-ša-am-ri-is-ʿsúʾ-nu-ši-im
           (12')   a-na La-ma-sà-ni be-el-tim [aš]-pu-ur
           (13')   ù šu-na-a-tim ù i-gi-ir-re-e
           (14')   ša a-mu-ru ù e-eš-mu-ú aš-pu-ur-ši

(15')   ù 1 MA.NA KÙ.BABBAR ú-ša-bi-il-ši-im-ma
        ú-ut-te-er-ra-am

l.e.   (16')   i-na ki-ma la ad-bu-bu-ú-ma

(17')   ù tap-pu-ut be-el-ti-ia
        la al-li-ku

rev.   (18')   ù šu-nu-ú-ti ša-al-ma

(19')   ki-ma aṣ-ri-mu ù uš-ta-am-ʾḫi-ṣuʾ

(20')   li-iq-bu-ni-ik-kum

(21')   mi-nu-um ʾ1LÚʾ Ia-am-nu-nu aš-šu-mi-šu

(22')   ki-ma iš-ti-iš-šu ša-la-ši-šu

(23')   aš-pu-ra-ak-kum ù aq-bi-kum

(24')   um-ma a-na-ku-ú-ma a-we-el Ia-am-nu-nu

(25')   iš-tu MU.30.KAM qí-ir-ba-am

(26')   aš-šu-mi-ia gi-mi-il-šu

(27')   ka-ar-ṣí-šu li-ku-lu-ni-ik-kum-ma

(28')   a-di ši-bu-šu a-na pa-ni-šu la iq-bu-ú

(29')   ka-ar-ṣi-šu la ta-ma-aḫ-ḫa-ar

(30')   i-na-an-na šum-ma i-na ʾkiʾ-na-a-tim

(31')   ta-ra-am-ma-an-ni Ia-am-nu-nu

(32')   iš-ti-ib um-ti-ik la ú-dʾa-ab-baʾ-bu-ú-šu

(33')   ʾa-na Ia-am x xʾ [   ]
                break in text of several lines

edge   (34')   [   ] ʾxʾ-nim ad-di-in-šu-nu-ši-im-ma

(35')   [   ] ʾxʾ-bi-nu-tum qí-bi-tam ʾdu-unʾ-ni-in-šu-nu-ši-im-ma

(36')   [ap-pa-š]u-nu li-il-bi-ʾnuʾ

obv.   (1')   Concerning ...

(2')   among the soldiers ...

(3')   Until I went to the assistance of my mistress,

(4')   she was looked at askance among the soldiers.

(5')   I was not neglectful; I tried hard.

(6')   I dropped my many affairs and

(7')   unto the general and the palace steward

(8')   I went morning and night

9')   and I stated that I had not seen or heard (what was being reported).

10')   As their lies were great, so

(11')   I made them sick with (my) rhetoric.

(12')   I wrote to mistress Lamassani

(13')   and the dreams and the (oracular) utterances

(14')   which I saw and heard, I wrote to her;

l.e.

rev.

edge

(15')   and I sent her one mina of silver but she returned (it) to me.

(16')   How (then) did I not speak

(17')   and not go (to) the assistance of my mistress?

(18')   Ask them;

(19')   how much I exerted myself and let myself be hurt

(20')   let them tell you.

(21')   What (now)about the Jamnunite? Concerning him

(22')   once — even three times—

(23')   I wrote you and I spoke to you (as well);

(24')   thus did I say : "The Jamnunite man

(25')   has been close to me for thirty years.

(26')   Be kind to him for my sake."

(27')   Even if they slander him,

(28')   as long as his witnesses (i.e. his slanderers) have not spoken to his face,

(29')   do not believe the slander about him.

(30')   Now, if in truth

(31')   you love me : the Jamnunite

(32')   has grown old and has become feeble; they should not pester him.

(33')   ...

                          break in text of several lines

(34')   ... I gave to them and

(35')   ... reprimand them and

(36')   let them act in a humble manner.

(18')   Note the unusual form of the separable and preceeding pronominal suffix.

(32')   Translation assumes Gt of *šiābum*, "to be gray haired," and Dt (passive) of *muqqum* (III, AHw 675a); cf. *itti šibūtim u muqqūtim*, VS 16 3:13, and *kī šibi muqqi*, Era I 43, cited by AHw 674-675.

(33')   Traces do not support reading *a-na ⌜Ia-am-nu-nu⌝*.

No. 25

obv.

(1)   [1ᵈEN.ZU-e-ri-ba-am]

(2)   [1] A-b[u-ṭà-bu-um]

(3)   ù ᵈEN.ZU-na-d[a]

(4)   i-na ⌜KÁ⌝ ᵈUTU i-di-⌜nu-ú⌝

(5)   DI.KU₅.MEŠ 10 GÍN KÙ.BABBAR ᵈEN.ZU-n[a-d]a

(6)   i-mu-du-ši-ma 10 GÍN KÚ.BABBAR

(7)   ša DI.KU₅.MEŠ i-mu-du-ši

(8)   a-na ᵈEN.ZU-e-ri-ba-am

(9)   iš-ta-qa-al

(10) li-ib-bi ^{d}EN.ZU-e-ri-ba-am

(11) ṭà-ab ú-ul i-ta-ar-ma

(12) ^{1d}EN.ZU-e-ri-ba-am

(13) a-na ^{d}EN.ZU-na-da a-na KÙ.BABBAR

(14) ú-ul i-ra-<ga>-am

(15) ù sí-sí-ik-ti

l.e.   (16) ^{1d}EN.ZU-na-da

(17) ba-at-qa-at

(18) ú-ul i-ta-ar-ma

rev.   (19) ^{1}A-bu-ṭà-bu-um

(20) a-na ^{d}EN.ZU-na-da a-na aš-šu-tim

(21) ú-ul i-ra-ga-am

(22) ù ^{d}EN.ZU-na-da

(23) a-na A-bu-ṭà-bi-im

(24) mu-ti at-ta ú-ul i-qa-ab-bi

(25) ni-iš $^{d⌜}$TIŠPAK⌝ ù Na-ra-am-^{d}EN.ZU ut(!)-ta-ma-am-mu

(26) ra-gi-im i-ra-ga-am

(27) ⌜1⌝ MA.NA KÙ.BABBAR Ì.LAL.E

(28) DI.KU$_5$.MEŠ URU Pí-⌜ḫu⌝-ra

(29) ^{1}⌜Šum-šu-im-ma-tim⌝

      remainder lost

Seal A ^{d}[UTU]-mu-uš-te-pí-iš

                  DUMU Ú-še-pí

                  ARAD ša $^{d⌜}$NIN⌝.ŠUBUR

Seal B ^{d}EN.ZU-⌜i⌝-[qí]-⌜ša-am⌝

                  DUMU A-⌜lu-bu-um⌝(?)

Seal C   ⌜Šum-šu-im⌝-[ma-tim]

                  DUMU ⌜Ib-bi(?)⌝ [   ]

Seal D(?)   [   ] ⌜ba⌝-ni [   ]

obv.   (1) Sin-eribam,

(2) Abu-ṭabum,

(3) and Sin-nada

(4) litigated at the Šamaš Gate.

(5) The judges fined Sin-nada ten shekels silver;

(6) and the ten shekels silver

(7) which the judges fined her

	(8)	unto Sin-eribam
	(9)	she paid.
	(10)	Sin-eribam is
	(11)	satisfied; he will not contest;
	(12)	nor will Sin-eribam raise claim
	(13)	against Sin-nada
	(14)	for silver.
	(15)	Moreover, the hem of
l.e.	(16)	Sin-nada's (garment)
	(17)	has been cut;
	(18)	she may not contest.
rev.	(19)	Abu-ṭabum
	(20)	against Sin-nada for marriage
	(21)	will not raise a claim.
	(22)	And Sin-nada
	(23)	unto Abu-ṭabum
	(24)	shall not say : "You are my husband."
	(25)	They were (all) besworn by an oath by Tišpak and Naram-Sin.
	(26)	Any party who raises a claim
	(27)	will pay one mina silver.
	(28)	The judges of Piḫura :
	(29)	(29) Šumšu-immatim remainder lost

Seal A	Šamaš-muštepiš
	son of Ušepi
	servant of Ilaprat

Seal B	Sin-iqišam
	son of Alubum(?)

Seal C	Šumšu-immatim
	son of Ibbi(?)- ...

Seal D(?)	... bani ...

(24) This formula has been discussed by the writer in JAOS 89 (1969) 517[57].

(25) Cf. *ni-iš I-pí-iq-*^dIM *ú-t*[*a-m*]*a-mu-ú* TIM 4 39:6f, *ni-iš* DN$_1$, DN$_2$, DN$_3$ *ut-ta-ma-mu-ú* IM 63305:7-10, treated by M. DeJ. Ellis in JCS 26 (1974) 151, 140-142. For a discussion of Rt verbal forms see the literature cited by von Soden in AnOr 47 §§95e, 105u.

(28) The signs are as copied; the GN Piḫura is not elsewhere attested.

Seal D   The traces could also be read : [^dEN.Z]U-*ni*-[   ].

No. 34

obv.   (1)   1 SAG ARAD Ìr-ra-ga-mil
        (2)   MU.NI.IM
        (3)   aš-šu-mi-šu ᵈUTU-ʼna⁾-aḫ-ʼra-ruʼ
        (4)   ša a-na 18 GÍN KÙ.BI ša-mu
        (5)   a-na Im-gur-ᵈEN.ZU DUMU I-túr-Aš-du-ma
        (6)   ¹ᵈŠEŠ.KI.ME.DÍM
        (7)   DUMU ᵈUTU-mu-uš-te(!)-pí-iš
        (8)   id-di-nu-ma ip-ṭú-ru-uš
        (9)   u₄-um Ìr-ra-ga-mil KÙ.BI
        (10)   i-lí-šu ub-ba-lam
        (11)   ¹Ìr-ra-ga-mil
rev.   (12)   pa-ga-ar-šu i-pa-ṭà-ar
        (13)   IGI Mu-na-wi-rum DUMU Sa-li-ma-nu-um   case : -ru-[um]
        (14)   ¹Ḫa-lí-ia DUMU Iš-bi-Ìr-ra
        (15)   ¹I-pí-iq-EŠ₄.DAR DUMU Ì-lí-we-de-ku
        (16)   ¹Be-el-šu-nu
        (17)   DUMU ᵈEN.ZU-qar-ra-ad
        (18)   ¹A-ḫu-wa-qar DUMU Šum-ma-AN
        (19)   ¹Bur(!)-ri-ia DUMU Ip-qú-ša
        (20)   ¹Ip-qú-ša DUMU DINGIR-lam-mi-lik
        (21)   ¹Šu-mi-a-ḫi-ia
        (22)   DUMU ᵈEN.ZU-še-me   case : -še-mi
        (23)   ¹An-KA-ᵈUTU
        (24)   DUMU Bur(!)-ᵈEN.ZU

Seal Legends
    A.   A-lí-ia
            DUMU Iš-bi-Ìr-ra
            ARAD Da-nu-um-ta-ḫa-az

    B.   Ì-lí-we-de-ku
            DUMU ᵈEN.ZU-ba-ni

    C.   Ip-qú-ša
            DUMU DINGIR-mi-li[k]
            ARAD ᵈʼŠul-pa⁾-è-ʼaʼ

Labels

            [KIŠIB Šu-m]i-a-ḫi-ia
            (seal impression destroyed)

            ʼKIŠIB Mu-naʼ-wi-rum
            (seal impression destroyed)

obv.   (1)   1 slave Irra-gamil
            (2)   by name
            (3)   on his behalf, Šamaš-naḥraru
            (4)   who was bought for 18 shekels — his value,
            (5)   unto Imgur-Sin son of Itur-Ašduma
            (6)   Nanna.medim
            (7)   son of Šamaš-muštepiš
            (8)   gave and released him.
             9)   On the day Irra-gamil will bring
            10)   the money of his "fortune" (lit. his god),
            (11)   Irra-gamil
rev.   (12)   will release himself (from servitude to Nanna. medim).
            (13)   Witnessed by Munawwirum son of Salimanum
            (14)   Ḫalija son of Išbi-Irra
            (15)   Ipiq-Ištar son of Ili-wedeku
            (16)   Belšunu
            (17)   son of Sin-qarrad
            (18)   Aḫu-waqar son of Šummanum
            (19)   Burija son of Ipquša
            (20)   Ipquša son of Ilam-milik
            (21)   Šumi-aḫija
            (22)   son of Sin-šemi
            (23)   Anum-pi-Šamaš
            (24)   son of Bur-Sin

Seal legends
    A.   Alija
                son of Išbi-Irra
                servant of Dannum-taḫaz

    B.   Ili-wedeku
                son of Sin-bani

    C.   Ipquša
                son of Ilam-milik
                servant of Šulpaea

Labels
                Seal of Šumi-aḫija

                Seal of Munawwirum

(3) For ᵈUTU-*na-aḫ-ra-ru*/*ri* as an OB PN cf. Stamm Namengebung 212⁴ (citing VS 9 81:5)
    and also no. 169: rev. 13'. For *naḫraru* = *nēraru*, cf. Stamm *loc. cit.* and AHw 779b.

(8) The sense of 11. 1-8 is as follows : Nanna.medim gave the slave Šamaš-naḫraru to Imgur-Sin in exchange for Irra-gamil, whom he redeemed. Irra-gamil now belongs to Nanna.medim; he has the right to buy himself out of this servitude when he can acquire the means to do so.

(9) M. Stol has kindly called attention to the following parallels : A 32113 (unpublished tablet from Kish, dated to the reign of Alium) (19) K[Ù].BABBAR *i-li-šu ú-ba-la-am-ma* (20) A.Š[A]-*šu i-pa-ṭá-[a]r* (witnesses follow); Gordon, Smith College Tablets 39 (also from Kish and dated to reign of Alium) (15) *ú-um* KÙ.BABBAR *i-li-šu*(!) (16) *ú-ba-la-ma* A.ŠÀ *i-pa-ṭ[à-a]r*. On the basis of these parallels, one should have expected KÙ.BABBAR in place of KÙ.BI in line 9; yet *ilišu* must be in the genitive and not the subject of the verb *ubbalam* and the parallel with KÙ.BABBAR *ilišu* points the way to understanding the phrase. KÙ.BI is likewise "awkward" in line 4 where KÙ.BABBAR would have been "smoother".

(14) Note the variant Alija in Seal legend A.

(15) Seal legend B reads : Ili-wedeku son of Sin-bani; the accompanying label is destroyed but it seems possible that this seal was used by the witness Ipiq-Ištar son of Ili-wedeku.

No. 91

obv.

(1)   1 ri-mu 1/2 GÍN KÙ.GI DAM ⸢Bur⸣-ᵈIM
(2)   1 ŠU.GUR ⸢5/6⸣ GÍN 15 ŠE KÙ.BABBAR ⸢DAM⸣ 30-mu-ba-lí-iṭ
(3)   1 ŠU.GUR 5/6 GÍN 20 ŠE Ra-ma-rum
(4)   [1] ŠU.[G]UR 5/6 GÍN Ri-iš-ᵈUTU
(5)   1 Š[U.GU]R [1/3 GÍ]N 20 Š[E] ⸢A⸣-ḫa-tum
(6)   1 [Š]U.GUR 1/3 GÍN ⸢10⸣ ŠE ⸢Sa⸣-am-ma-tum
(7)   [1] ŠU.GUR 1/3 GÍN ⸢Na-ra-am-tum⸣
(8)   1 ᵈLAMMA 5/6 GÍN 15 ŠE DUMU.SAL GU.ZA.LÁ(!)
(9)   1 ri-mu 20 ŠE A-lí-ia-tum
(10) ŠU.NIGÍN 1/2 GÍN KÙ.GI
(11) 4 5/6 GÍN 10 ŠE KÙ.BABBAR
(12) 1 TÚG.⸢SI⸣.SÁ   DAM Tu-⸢ta⸣-ra-ab-nu
(13) 1 TÚG.SÍG   E-til-KA-ᵈ⸢EN⸣.ZU
(14) 1 TÚG.⸢SU⸣.UL   DAM Ar-wu-um
(15) 15 TÚG.BAR.SI.MEŠ(!)
(16) MU.TÚM PUZUR₄-ᵈK[i-t]i-tum
(17) NÍG.ŠU In-bu-ša SANGA
(18) ù Ib-bi-tap-pí-šu
(19) ITU A-bi-i
(20) UD.30.KAM
(21) MU Da-du-ša LUGAL

obv.

(1)   1 bull figurine, 1/2 shekel gold, (from) the wife of ⸢Bur⸣-Adad
(2)   1 ring, 5/6 shekel 15 grains silver, (from) the wife of Sin-muballiṭ
(3)   1 ring, 5/6 shekel 20 grains, (from) Ramarum (?)
(4)   1 ring, 5/6 shekel, (from) Riš-Šamaš

(5)   1 ri[ng, 1/3 shek]el 20 grains, (from) Aḫatum
(6)   1 ring, 1/3 shekel 10 grains, (from) Sammatum
(7)   [1] ring, 1/3 shekel, (from) Naramtum
(8)   1 *lamassu* figure, 5/6 shekel 15 grains, (from) the daughter of the throne bearer
(9)   1 bull figurine, 20 grains, (from) Alijatum
(10) Total : 1/2 shekel gold,
(11) 4 5/6 shekels 10 grains silver.
rev. (12) 1 ... garment (from) the wife of Tutar-abnu
(13) 1 woolen garment (from) Etel-pi-Sin
(14) 1 ... garment (from) the wife of Arwum
(15) 15 head coverings
(16) Income (taken in by) Puzur-Kititum
(17) (under the) control of Inbuša, the head priest,
(18) and Ibbı-tappišu.
(19) The month of Abu,
(20) the 30th day,
(21) the year Daduša, the king.

No. 261

obv. (1)   10 pa-nu-ù
(2)   8 ma-az-ru-ù
(3)   2 ma-aš-la-ḫu
(4)   6 ra-ap-šu
(5)   8 mu-ša-am-qí-ta-tum
rev. (6)   17 bu-ba-tum
(7)   [1]30-i-din-nam
(8)   i-ka-ru-um
(9)   a-na Maš-kán-Ba-ar-mi

obv. (1)   10 grain baskets
(2)   8 winnowing baskets
(3)   2 ...
(4)   2 grain shovels
(5)   8 sieves
rev. (6)   17 chariot frame pieces (?)
(7)   Sin-iddinam
(8)   the farm official (took)
(9)   to Maškan-Barmi

(1) AHw 822b.

(2) Cf. gi.[gur.ri.r]i.ga = *pa-an liq-ta-ti* = *ma-az-ru-[tu]*, MSL 7 70, 46b, Hg to Hh IX.

(3) Cf. AHw 618b, quoting MSL 7 47 (Hh IX) 235 and corrections of MSL 9 183. CAD B 24, citing ARM 7 245 ii 6', translates "sprinkling pots". All of the above interpretations relate our form to *salāḫu* "sprinkle"; yet 255:9-11 indicates that *mašlaḫu* is part of a wagon (*eriqqu*).

(6) Related possibly to *bubūtu*, pl. *bubātu*, CAD B 302b.

No. 305

obv.	(1)	[ ] ˹x˺ [ ] Maš-kán-LUGAL^{KI}
	(2)	[ ]-bu-˹um˺^{KI}
	(3)	[ ] ˹x x x˺ [ ]-nu
	(4)	[i]-˹na(?)˺ GIŠ.TUKUL ša ^dAMAR.UTU GIŠ.TUKUL ša ^dUTU
	(5)	˹x˺BI ù(?) ^dA-wa-li-tum
	(6)	ERÍN Ne-ri-ib-tum ú-te-eb-bi-bu
	(7)	˹1 ERÍN˺ A-ḫu-ši-na TUR
	(8)	ša i-na É Ip-˹qá˺-tum LÚ(?) UD.KIB.NUN^{KI} wa-aš-bu
	(9)	1 ERÍN ARAD-Ku-bi DUMU In-bu-ša
	(10)	ša i-na É E-til-KA-ša MÁŠ.ŠU.GÍD.GÍD wa-aš-bu
	(11)	1 ERÍN Be-el-šu-nu DUMU Ú-túl-EŠ₄.DAR
	(12)	ša i-na É Be-[l]a-nu-um DUMU Wa-ar-di-im wa-aš-bu
	(13)	1 ERÍN Li-pí-it-^dTIŠPAK DUMU DUMU-DINGIR-tum
	(14)	¹KUR-Ḫi-it-ti-mu-uš-te-še-er ŠEŠ.NI
	(15)	¹Ku-ub-bu-rum DUMU É ṭup-pí ŠEŠ.NI
	(16)	ša KI Na-bi-^dEN.ZU iz-za-az-zu i-na ˹x˺-ul-˹li(?)˺-im
	(17)	wa-ši-ib
	(18)	1 DAM.QAR U-ba-rum TUR
	(19)	¹˹Pir˺-ḫu-um ŠEŠ.NI
	(20)	ša ÙZ.ḪI.A ša Dam-qí-ì-lí-šu i-ri-˹ú˺
	(21)	1 DAM.QAR A-wi-li-ia DUMU Be-el-šu-nu UGULA DAM.[Q]AR.M[EŠ]
	(22)	˹ša i˺-[na] ˹É˺ Ḫu-du-li-ib-bi wa-aš-b[u]
l.e.	(23)	˹1˺^dWi-ir-a-bu-šu TUR
	(24)	ša a-na ERÍN.ḪUN(?) i-na ˹x x ub˺-bi-im ša-˹aṭ˺-[ru]
	(25)	wa-ši-ib AN.ZA.QAR A-ḫi-ma-ra-aṣ
	(26)	[ ] ˹ILLAT˺-ti LÚ(?) BÀD Ša(?)-am(?)-˹ḫu˺-u[m^{KI}]
rev.	(27)	[¹] ˹Ip(?)-qá˺-tum DUMU ˹I-bi˺-EŠ₄.DAR
	(28)	˹1˺^dEN.˹LÍL˺-be-el-ì-lí ˹AB˺ tu-ur-˹^dEN˺ [ ] ˹x˺
	(29)	[wa-š]i-ib AN.ZA.QAR A-ḫi-ma-ra-a[ṣ]
	(30)	˹1˺A-lí-ELLAT-ti ˹LÚ] BÀD-˹Ša˺-am-ḫu-um˺^{KI}
	(31)	˹x x˺ ¹Mi-˹nam-e˺-pu-uš-˹šu˺(!) DUMU E-ri-ib-^dEN.ZU
	(32)	˹wa-ši-ib˺ Ḫu-ri-ib-šum^{KI} ša ˹it-ti Ka-li˺-DINGIR / in-n[am]-ma-ru

(33)   [ ] ⸢x⸣.GAB E-ṭi-rum DUMU U-bar-rum

(34)   ¹Ma-šum ŠEŠ.NI

(35)   LÚ ⸢x⸣ [   ] ⸢x⸣ ta ⸢x⸣ PA

(36)   ša i-na ⸢x-ku-x x x⸣^{KI} in-n[am-m]a-ru

(37)   ⸢x x x NI⸣-ir-a-lum(?) DUMU Zi-a-tum

(38)   [   ] ⸢x x⸣-a-tum^{KI}

(39)   [ša i-na] ⸢x ku⸣-ub-⸢x x⸣^{KI} in-nam-ma-ru

(40)   1 NU.KIRI₆ E-ṭi-rum DUMU Iš-me-ka-ra-ab

(41)   LÚ BÀD-Ri-mu-uš^{KI}

(42)   ša i-na É Ib-ni-^{d}MAR.TU ša ki-di-im in-nam-ma-ru

(43)   a-na ÈŠ.NUN.NA^{KI} it-ta-ás-ḫa-am

(44)   [1] NU.KIRI₆ ARAD.^{d}INNIN DUMU In-bu-ša

(45)   LÚ BÀD-Ri-mu-⸢uš⸣^{KI}

(46)   ša i-na É Ib-ni-^{d}MAR.TU ša ki-di-im in-nam-ma-ru

(47)   a-na ÈŠ.NUN.NA^{KI} it-ta-ás-ḫa-am

(48)   13 ERÍN.SAG

(49)   DUMU.ŠEŠ.NI

(50)   ⸢ša⸣ [i-na] La-su-mi^{KI} ù ⸢Ki⸣-is-⸢mar⸣^{KI} in-nam-ma-ru

(51) ^{d}ŠEŠ.KI-tum DUMU É ṭup-pí

u.e.   (52)   ⸢ITU ŠE.KIN⸣.KUD UD.17.KAM

(53)   [MU Sa-am-su-i-lu]-⸢na⸣ LUGAL.E

(54)   [   ] ⸢x x⸣

edge   (55)   [   ] ⸢x ša⸣ [   ] ⸢x⸣AN ZA⸢x⸣ [   ] ⸢x x x⸣ [   ]

(56)   [   ] ⸢x KI x⸣ [   ] ⸢x-ru⸣^{KI} ŠA⸢x x⸣ [   ] ⸢x⸣ [   ]

obv.   (1)   ... Maškan-Šarrim

(2)   ... um

(3)   ...

(4)   ... in the Marduk regiment (and) the Šamaš regiment

(5)   ... and Awalitum

(6)   regular soldiers of Neribtum (who) have been cleared (on the military rolls).

(7)   1 regular soldier, Aḫušina, a knave

(8)   who resides in the house of Ipqatum, a citizen of Sippar.

(9)   1 regular soldier, Warad-Kubi son of Inbuša

(10)   who resides in the house of Etel-piša the diviner

(11)   1 regular soldier, Belšunu son of Utul-Istar

(12)   who resides in the house of Belanum son of Wardum

(13)   1 regular soldier, Lipit-Tišpak son of Mar-iltum

(14)   Ḫitti-mušteššir his brother

(15)   Kubburum, the student scribe, his brother

16)   who is stationed with Nabi-Sin;
17)   he resides in ...
(18)   1 merchant, Ubarum, a knave
(19)   Pirḫum his brother
(20)   who tends the goats of Damqi-ilišu
(21)   1 merchant, Awilija son of Belšunu the chief of merchants
(22)   who dwells in the house of Ḫudu-libbi

l.e.   (23)   Wir-abušu, a knave
(24)   who is registered with the hired troops in ...ubbum
(25)   resident of Dimat-Aḫimaraṣ
(26)   ... illati, citizen of Dur-Šamḫum

rev.   (27)   Ipqatum son of Ibbi-Ištar
(28)   Enlil-bel-ili ...
(29)   resident of Dimat-Aḫimaras
(30)   Ali-illati, citizen of Dur-Šamḫum
(31)   ... Minam-epuššu son of Erib-Sin
(32)   resident of Ḫuribšum who was mustered with Kali-Ilum
(33)   ... Eṭirum son of Ubarum
(34)   Mašum his brother
(35)   citizen of ...
(36)   who turned up in ...
(37)   1 ... son of Zijatum
(38)   ... (of) ...
(39)   who was mustered in ...
(40)   1 gardener, Etirum son of Išme-karab
(41)   citizen of Dur-Rimuš
(42)   who was mustered in the outside-of-the-walls house of Ibni-Amurru;
(43)   he was transferred to Ešnunna
(44)   1 gardener, Warad-Ištar son of Inbuša
(45)   citizen of Dur-Rimuš
(46)   who was mustered in the outside-of-the-walls house of Ibni-Amurru;
(47)   he was transferred to Ešnunna.
(48)   (Total :) 13 regular soldiers of the first rank
(49)   (with) their son (or) brother (indicated)
(50)   who were mustered in Lasumi and Kismar
(51)   Nannatum the apprentice scribe.

u.e.   (52)   The month of Addaru, the 17th day,
(53)   [the year Samsu-ilu]na the king
(54)   ...

edge	(55)	...
	(56)	...

(4) For *kakku* as an OB term for a military grouping see CAD K 55b.

(7) For TUR, along with DAḤ, DIRI, and ŠU as classes of military personnel, cf. references collected in the Index.

(50) Kismar is mentioned in the Harmal Geog. List Col. v 163 (Baqir *Sumer* 3 (1947) 79 = MSL 11 58).

(51) Alternatively, "military scribe"; cf. Landsberger, JCS 9 (1955) 125²²; so, too, in line 15 above.

(53) We assume that our text, like the others of its group, is to be dated to the period of Samsu-iluna, as seen from 314: rev. 11ff. dated to S-i 27 and the passing references to Dur-Samsu-iluna in 311:7' and 320: rev. 3'. There is a possibility of restoring the fragmentary formula in lines 53-55 in accordance with parts of the attested formula for S-i 23, the year formula prior to the S-i 24 which officially celebrated the building of Dur-Samsu-iluna. Accordingly, line 55 would be restored to contain the city *Za-a[r-ḫ]a-ʼnam*ᴷᴵʼ(?); it would also be possible to read the end of a city name at the beginning of l. 30 followed perhaps by *P[u-u]t-ru*ᴷᴵ as a possible variant to the attested form *Pu-ut-ra*ᴷᴵ.

No. 326

obv.	(1)	Ṣ[i-i]m-[da-tum]
	(2)	ša ʼŠaʼ-[ad-la-ášᴷᴵ]
	(3)	ù ʼNe-ri-ib-timᴷᴵʼ
§1	(4)	ʼDUMU LÚ 2/3ʼ MA.NA KÙ.[BABBAR]
	(5)	ʼARAD LÚ 15ʼ GÍN KÙ.BABBAR
	(6)	ʼù(?) GEMÉ(?)ʼ 10 ʼGÍNʼ KÙ.BABBAR
	(7)	ʼAB.BA ùʼ SAL.AB.BA
	(8)	[ ] ʼki(?)-ma(?)ʼ DUMU DIŠ ma-ḫi-ʼruʼ-um
§2	(9)	ʼša ma-at Šaʼ-ad-la-áš[ᴷᴵ] ù na-wi-ša
	(10)	ʼša ma-at Neʼ-ri-ib-timᴷᴵ ù na-wi-ša
	(11)	ʼša iš-tu ni-kuʼ-ur-tim in-na-bi-tu-ʼmaʼ
	(12)	ʼù in-na-ka-suʼ be-ʼelʼ-šu ú-ul i-ṣa-ba-su
§3	(13)	šum-ma ḫu-ub-tum ú pil-la-tum
	(14)	ʼiš-ša-al-ma laʼ-a na-ka-ar i-la-ʼakʼ
	(15)	šum-ma ʼna-ka-arʼ i-ṣa-[ba-a]t
§4	(16)	ʼki-ma Éʼ a-ʼna Éʼ.ḤI.A ʼx xʼ nim
	(17)	ù ʼLÚʼ ni-tim [ ] ʼxʼ-im
	(18)	šum-ma DUMU LÚ DUMU ʼLÚʼ i -ta-arʼ
	(19)	1 MA.NA KÚ.BABBAR Ì.LAL.E
	(20)	šum-ma ʼARAD LÚ ARAD LÚ i-ta-arʼ
	(21)	1/2 MA.NA KÙ.BABBAR Ì.LAL.E
§5	(22)	šum-ma a-wa-at na-pí-iš-ti ʼišʼ-ku-un
	(23)	šum-ma ʼiš-te-enʼ-ma i-ma-at
	(24)	šum-ma [ši]-ʼna(?)-maʼ a-na 3 a-di 5-ʼmaʼ
	(25)	ʼùʼ ma-du-tim-ma i-na na-pí-iš-ti it-ta-aṣ-ba-tu

(26) ⸢iš-te⸣-en ša ⸢i-ka-nu⸣-šum i-ma-at

(27) [ù] ⸢x⸣ ka-lu-šu-nu 1 2/3 MA.NA Ì.LAL.⸢E⸣.MEŠ

§6   (28) [šu]m-ma pil-la-tum-ma na-ka-⸢ar⸣ i-ṣa-ba-su(?)

obv. (29) ⸢ki⸣-[ma] ⸢ṣi⸣-im-da-da-a[t]

§7   (30) DUMU Ša-ad-la-áš^KI ù na-wi-šu

(31) DUMU Ne-ri-ib-tim^KI ù na-wi-šu

(32) ⸢ša⸣ la-ma ni-ku-ur-tim a-na ku-ši-im

(33) [i]-⸢li-ku-ma⸣(?) ka-lu-ú

edge   i-ta-ša-ar

§8 rev. (34) ARAD LÚ ša la-ma ni-ku-ur-tim

(35) ù iš-tu UG im-ma-aḫ-ṣu

(36) i-ka-lu-ú i-ta-ar

§9   (37) šum-ma ḫu-bu-ut GUD.ḪI.A ù UDU.ḪI.A i-ta-ab-ši

(38) šum-ma ša DI.KU₅.MEŠ ka-ša-di ù šu-⸢ḫu-zi⸣ i-ta-ab-ši

(39) šum-ma DUMU Ne-ri-ib-tim^KI

(40) MU.DINGIR ša DUMU Ne-ri-ib-tim^KI

(41) [^dEN.ZU ša⸣ Ka-ma-ni-im

(42) ⸢MU⸣.DINGIR ša DUMU Ša-⸢ad⸣-la-áš^KI

(43) ^dEN.ZU ša Ur-^dIŠKUR.RA^KI

§10   (44) KÙ.BABBAR(?) DAM.QÀ[R GIB]IL(?) ù SUMUN i-ta-ar

(45) ma-ṣa-ar-tum ù na-aš-pa-ku ša LÚ

(46) ú-ul in-na-ka-al-šum a-ki-el i-ta-ar

§11   (47) AGA.UŠ Su-mu-nu-um-ḫi-im

(48) ¹Am-mi-du-šu-ur ú-ul i-ra-ši

(49) AGA.UŠ Am-mi-du-šu-ur ERASURE

(50) ¹Su-mu-nu-um-ḫi-im ú-[ul] i-ra-ši

Space, of several lines

(51) iš-tu ⸢x x⸣-tum i-te-qú

(52) i-na ⸢wa-ar-ki⸣-im ṣi-im-da-at

(53) ¹Su-mu-nu-[um]-ḫi-im ERASURE

(54) [ù   ] Am-mi-da-šur(?) ERASURE

Space

(55) ITU SIG₄.A UD.15.KAM MU.ÚS.SA Ia-ri-im-L[i-i]m BA.UG_x

Obv.   (1) A decree

(2) of Šadlaš

(3) and Neribtum.

§1   (4) The son of a free man — (his value) is 2/3 mina silver.

(5) The male slave of a free man — (his value) is 15 shekels silver

(6) and of a female slave — 10 shekels silver.

(7) An old man or an old woman

	(8)	... like one child in price.
§2	(9)	A (free) resident of the territory of Šadlaš and its environs
	(10)	(or) of the territory of Neribtum and its environs
	(11)	who has fled (the country) because of war
	(12)	and who has been cut off (from home); his lord shall not seize him.
§3	(13)	If (the removal be a result of) a kidnapping or *brigandage*,
	(14)	he shall be investigated; (if) the person was not (originally) a foreigner, he may go back;
	(15)	if he is a foreigner, he may be seized.
§4	(16)	As one household *unto* (other) households ...
	(17)	so a man ....
	(18)	If (the unlawfully removed person is) the son of a free man, he shall return the son of a free man
	(19)	(and) he will pay 1 mina silver.
	(20)	If a slave of a free man, he shall *return* a slave
	(21)	(and) he will pay 1/2 mina silver.
§5	(22)	If he determined it to be a crime involving persons' lives —
	(23)	if one person (did it), he must die;
	(24)	if (the crime involved from) as many as two, three, five,
	(25)	or more, they shall (all) be seized for capital crimes;
	(26)	any one whom *they convict* shall die
	(27)	and ... all of them shall pay 1 2/3 mina.
§6	(28)	If (it was a matter of) *brigandage*, and an enemy had seized him,
	(29)	it is as the decree (has already stated in connection with kidnapping).
§7	(30)	A son of Šadlaš and its environs
	(31)	(or) a son of Neribtum and its environs
	(32)	who, prior to a war, for purposes of profit
	(33)	had gone (obroad) and was captured; he should *be set free*.
§8 rev.	(34)	A slave of a free man who prior to a war (had gone abroad)
	(35)	or who was smitten by a lion —
	(36)	they shall hold him captive and he shall return (home).
§9	(37)	If a robbery of cattle or sheep has taken place,
	(38)	(and) if the case falls within the reach and authority of the judges,
	(39)	(then) if (the shepherd) be a son of Neribtum,
	(40)	the oath of a son of Neribtum (he will swear):
	(41)	(namely) by Sin of Kamanum;
	(42)	the oath of a son of Šadlaš
	(43)	(will be) by Sin of Ur-Iškur.

§10   (44)   Silver (belonging) to a merchant — new or old (debts) — shall go back (to its owner).

(45)   The magazine or granary (supplies) of a free man

(46)   should not be consumed at his expense; (if) consumed, it must go back (to its owner).

§11   (47)   A soldier of Sumu-numḫim

(48)   Ammi-dušur shall not enlist;

(49)   a soldier of Ammi-dušur

(50)   Sumu-numḫim shall not enlist.
Space of several lines

(51)   When ... has passed,

(52)   ever after, this decree of

(53)   Sumu-numḫim

(54)   and Ammi-dašur (sic) (will be binding).
Space

(55)   The month of Simanum, the 15th day, the year after Jarim-Lim died.

This text is the oldest known Akkadian treaty, antedating the Alalakh treaties by some two centuries or more. (For the dating of Alalakh IV see Rowton, CAH³ 1/1 230f). The year date formula in line 55 is no. 35 in our list. The treaty bears no seals, although space was left open between 11. 54-55. No oath is sworn; perhaps this text was a draft document and thus both seals and oaths were omitted.

(1)   The reading of Ṣimdatum is conjectural. One might as readily expect R[i-ik-sum] "(Treaty) contract", yet ṣimdatum is mentioned in 11. 29, 52.

(13)   The translation "brigandage" is essentially contextual: but the meaning "stolen goods" seems also to fit in other contexts as well: cf. UET 7 3:4, 7 (cited by CAD Ḫ 60b as UET 6) and 43:18ff. (references courtesy of M. Stol).

(20)   For our translation, the form ú-ta-ar would have been preferred; cf. notes to forms in ll. 26 and 33 below for similar problems with G and D forms.

(26)   For our translation a form ú-ka-nu-šu would have been preferable; the form as given seems to say "anyone against whom (-šum) they are set", i.e., whom the body declare to be the leader responsible"(?).

(33)   Translation assumes i-ta-ša-ar written in error(?) (cf. CAD A/2 422 ašāru C) for ú-ta-ša-ar. Another possibility is to read i-ta-<<ša>>-ar "he shall return", conforming to line 36.

(38)   Note the omission of mimation in the forms kašādi and šūḫuzi.

(41)   For DN cf. 26:4f.

(54)   Note the writing Am-mi-da-šur for more usual Am-mi-du-šu-ur, despite Harris, JCS 9 (1955) 49²⁷. This writing is also found in an unpublished year date formula MU BÀD Bi-is-ki-la(?)ᴷᴵ Am-mi-da-šur, which is discussed infra in connection with year date formula 13.

(54)   Erasure reads: [LU]GAL BA.UGₓ(TIL).

INDEXES

I. INDEX OF PERSONAL NAMES*

In order to render the Akkadian names in a more familiar fashion, the following conventions have been used: ᵈAdad = ᵈIM, ⁽ᵈ⁾Amurrum = ⁽ᵈ⁾MAR.TU, Akšak = ÚḪᴷᴵ, Awīl = LÚ, ᵈEnlil = ᵈEN.LÍL, ᵈIlaprat = ᵈNIN.ŠUBUR, Ilum, Ìl = DINGIR, ᵈIštar = ᵈINNIN, Ištar = EŠ₄.DAR, mār = DUMU, mārtum = DUMU.SAL, ᵈNanna, ᵈNANNA = ᵈŠEŠ.KI, Puzur = PUZUR₄, ᵈSin = ᵈEN.ZU, Sin = 30, ᵈŠamaš = ᵈUTU, ᵈTišpak = ᵈTIŠPAK. In addition, the following symols are employed: s. = son, d. = daughter, f. = father, w. = wife, h. = husband, (w) = witness, (R) = royal name, (Y) = year date formulas, (s) = seal.

A ..., ᵈA...*
   1) 51:14 (w); 81:14 (w); 107:i 11*; 313:2

A-a-...   265:29

Ab-ʳdiʾ ...   156: rev. 3'

ʳAb-du-e-ra-aḫʾ   113:2.

A-bi ...
   1) s. of Sa-si-ia, 61:10 (w).
   2) f. of I-ʳxʾ-za, 152 (s).
   3) 230:6.

A-b[i]-ʳxʾ-rum   268 :i 7.

A-bi-la-ma-sí   268 :ii 9.

A-bi-li-bu-ʳra-amʾ   169 rev. 12'

ʳA-bi-ma-ra-aṣʾ   s. of ..., 36:17 (w)

A-bi-ʳna-da(?)ʾ   f. of Bur-ʳAdadʾ, 144:3

A-bi-sa-ma-su   143:4

A-bi-tum   240:4

A-bi-ʳumʾ-mi   320:12'

A-bi-zu-um
   1) s. of Ig-mil-ᵈSin, 1 (s); 114 (s); 115 (s); 116 (s) 117 (s); 131 (s); 132 (s)
   2) 1:3; 2:3

Abu(AD)-ma-ra-aṣ
   1) s. of ..., 36:17 (w)
   2) 85:8 (w); 179:6

A-bu-um-ilum   s. of ᵈSin-e-ri-ba-am, ᵈSin-eri₄-baʾ, 68:5; 71:9* (w)

A-bu-um-wa-qar
   1) s. of ʳEʾ-ri-ba-nim, 68:12 (w)
   2) s. of Nu-úr-ᵈŠamaš, 311: obv. 6'

A-bu-ṭà-bu-um
   1) h. of ᵈSin-na-da, 25:2, 19, 23
   2) 127:5, 7

A-bu-wa-qar
1) f. of Šu-mi-ʳkiʾ, 306:6
   2) b. of E-ri-ba-am, 20:3
   3) 167:9; 216:3

ᵈAdad-be-el-ì-lí   f. of [Be-e]l-šu-nu, 311: obv. 8'

ᵈAdad-ra-bi   31:3; 223:4

ᵈAdad-ʳumʾ-ma-t[i]   322:3

A-da-a-a, A-da-ia*
   1) s. of ʳTàʾ-ab-ṣil-ʳla-šuʾ, 31:4
   2) f. of PN (not given), 24:21
   3) f. of Ìl-šu-ba-ni, 31: rev. 12
   4) f. of Im-gur-rum, 79:20*
   5) f. of ᵈSin-ba-ni, 31:4f

A-da-rum   f. of ᵈŠamaš-ʳilumʾ, 79:22

A-du-lu-ʳx xʾ   308:3

Ad-m[a-a]t-i-lí   85:6

---

* The PNs listed in texts no. 280-81, 283 have not been included in the index; they are scribal school exercise tablets. For other texts of this genre, cf. Chiera PBS 11/2 101 ff; 11/3 pls. lxxiv, lxxxvif, xci, xcvii, nos. 14-15, 32, 34, 41, 48-49, 63; Çig and Kizilyay AS 16 41 ff; Gemser Persoonsnamen (1924) 10 ff.

A-ga-ša-a 266:17
A-gi-gu-ur? 78:3
Aḫam-arši (ŠEŠ.PA.TUK) 241:14
A-ḫa-am-nu-ta
  1) s. of Awat-ᵈEnlil (INIM.ᵈEN.LÍL.LA),
     31: rev. 9 (w)
  2) 226:3
A-ḫa-ta-ni 241:4
A-ḫa-tum
  1) w. of I-ˈša-biˈ, 229:10
  2) w. of Li-w[i-ra-šum], 139:5
  3) 91:5; 137:8; 139:11; 158:4; 268:ii 12
A-ḫa-at-wa-aq-ra-at 15:3
A-ḫi-a-ia-bi 268:i 15
A-ḫi-ia 94:28
A-ḫi-li- ... 268:ii 15
A-ḫi-ma-ra-aṣ 305:25
A-ḫi-ša-gi-iš b.(?) of Tar-mi-ia 308:15ˈ
A-ḫi-ša-ki-mi 8:1; 9:2
A-ḫi-um-mi-šu s. of Ia-aḫ-mi-iṣ-ˈIlumˈ, 79:
  17 (w)
ˈA-ḫu(?)-ga(?)-mil(?)ˈ 272:6
A-ḫu-ki-nu-um
  1) f. of Ìl-šu-na-ṣir, 33:11
     2) 267:3
A-ḫu-la-ap-ˈᵈˈ-Šamaš s. of ᵈSin-na-ˈṣirˈ, 40:
  rev. 7 (w)
ˈA-ḫu-umˈ(?) f. of Ḫu-..., 51:11
A-ḫu-ni
  1) s. of Sin- ..., 188:2
  2) s. of ˈÚˈ-mu-ta-mar, 154:2
  3) f. of Ga-mi-ilum, 195:3
  4) 156: rev. 1ˈ
A-ḫu-ši-na
  1) s. of ˈᵈˈAmmu[ru]-..., b. of Ši-ˈnaˈ-
     nu and ˈIaˈ-ar-ˈzaˈ(?), f. of Ṣil-lí-ᵈIštar,
     309:8
  2) 38: rev. 6ˈ; 267:4; 273:6; 305:7
A-ˈḫuˈ-ṭà-bu-um f. of Sa-ri-qum, 62:16
A-ḫu-ta-li-mi-im s. of Ì-lí-a-wi-lim, 320:5ˈ
A-ḫu-wa-qar
  1) s. of Su-ka-ˈliˈ-ia, 63:5
  2) s. of Šum-ma-AN, 34:18 (w)
  3) f. of ˈI-luˈ(?)-ka(?), 64:12
  4) 182:3
A-ḫu-wa-qa[r-r]u s. of In-bu-ša, 320:5ˈ
ᵈA-ia-be-li-ˈiṭˈ-ma-ˈtim(?)ˈ d.(!) of Puzur-
  ᵈŠamaš, 77:7
A-ia-e-ni-iš-i-lí 281:1

A-ia-ˈḫaˈ-... s. of ˈZuˈ-ba-..., 214 (s)
A-ia-ḫa-mu-ú h. of Nu-ṭú-up-tum, 53:8
A-ia-ˈḫu-umˈ 74:3
A-ia-a 103:11
A-ia-am-mu
  1) s. of Ak-ˈba-rumˈ, b. of ˈÌˈ-lí-ti-la-ti,
     309:2
  2) 314:20
A-ia-[ru-u]m 139:8
Ak-ˈba-rumˈ f. of [A]-ia-am-mu, b. of ˈÌˈ-lí-
  ti-la-ti, 309:2
Ak-ša-... f. of PN (not given), 167:13
Akšak-...
  1) s. of Na-bi-..., 67:3
  2) 242:13
Akšak-i-ˈdinˈ-nam 242:18
Akšak-ˈi(?)ˈ-di(?)-i 242:20
Akšak-ra-bi, Akšak-ra-bíˈ 83:1ˈ; 223:17;
  242:17
Akšak-še-me, Akšak-še-míˈ 93:5ˈ; 110:1,
  12
A-la-ni-tum 148:8
A-lí-... s. of Li-..., 72:12 (w)
A-lí-a-bu-ša 270:9
A-lí-a-ḫa-ti 270:11
A-lí-ba-ni-šu 95:4; 272:7
A-li-e-ši(?) 106:39 (Y)
A-lí-ḫaṭ(PA)-ili(DINGIR) 191:2
A-lí-illat (KASKAL.KUR)-ti 200:1; 201:
  1; 305:30
A-lí-ia
  1) s. of Iš-bi-Ir-ra, 34 (s) (also written
     Ḫa-lí-ia 34:14)
  2) s. of ˈᵈˈSinˈ-ga-mil, 76:8 (w)
  3) 96:4
A-lí-ia-tum 91:9; 148:5
ˈAˈ-lí-ˈwa-qarˈ(?) f. of Sin-še-mi, 127:11
A-lí-wa-aq-ru[m] 270:12
A-ˈlu-bu-umˈ f. of ᵈSin-ˈiˈ-[qí]-ˈša-amˈ(?), 25
  (s)
[A(?)]-ˈlum(?)ˈ-wa-qar b. of ... šu, 307:rev.
  i 4ˈ
Am-ˈx-umˈ 31:2
Amat(GEMÉ)-ᵈSin 5:10
Amat(GEMÉ)-Šamaš 45:4
Am-ˈmar(?)ˈ x x xˈ 59:13 (w)
Am-mi-du-šu-ur, Am-mi-da-šur(?)ˈ 326:
  48, 49, 54ˈ (R)

A-ʼmurʼ-na-ar-bi-[šu] f. of Anum(AN)-pî-
(KA)-..., 123 (s); 205 (s); 206 (s);

ᵈAmur[ru-...] f. of Ši-ʼnaʼ-nu, ʼIa-ar-ʼzaʼ,
A-ḫu-ši-na, 309:6-8

ᵈAmurru-na-ṣi-ʼirʼ, ᵈAmurru-na-ṣir*
1) f. of PN (not preserved), 311:rev. 3ʼ*
2) 249:6

[A-na-DN-t]a-ak-ʼlaʼ-[ku] 38:rev. 2ʼ

A-na-ᵈŠamaš-ták-la-ku
1) s. of ʼMu-taʼ-a-ʼaʼ, 31:rev. 5
2) 275:8

A-na-šar 223:15

A-na-ša-ʼruʼ-ᵈI[M] 248:9

A-na-ᵈTišpak-ta-ak-la-ak 102:2

Anum(AN)-pî(KA)-...
1) s. of A-mur-na-ar-b[i-šu], 123 (s); 205
(s); 206 (s); 244 (s)
2) s. of Im-gu-ia, 73:12, env. (w) [cf.
Anum-pî-ša s. of Im-gu-ia]

AN-um-pî(KA)-ᵈEnlil h. of ᶠPN (not (given), 92:6

Anum(AN)-pî(KA)-Ḫa-[am-m]u 190:2

Anum(AN)-pî(KA)-Ištar
1) b. A-pil-ᵈEN.ZU, b. of ...-ᵈEN.ZU,
18:2
2) h. of ᶠPN (not given), 107:ii: 19

Anum(AN)-pî(KA)-ᵈSin 322:10

Anum(AN)-pî(KA)-ša s. of Im-gu-ia, 66:
10 (w)

An-um-pî(KA)-ᵈŠamaš, Anum (AN)-pî-
(KA)-ᵈŠamaš*
1) s. of Bur(!)-ᵈSin, 34:23* (w); 55:4;
56:4*; 73:3
2) s. of Im-gur-ia, 56:12* (w)
3) 57:4; 94:14; 108:4*

<A>-pil-ᵈAdad 168:5

ʼA-píl-ᵈENʼ.[ ](?) s. of ...-ni, 52:5

A-pil-i-lí-šu
1) s. of I-ku-pí(?)-ʼšuʼ, 110:4
2) s. of In-bu-ša, 320:6
3) s. of ᵈSin-i-din-nam, 67:18
4) f. of [Sin-i]-ʼdinʼ-nam, 265:21
5) 110:3; 233:5; 241:7

A-pil-Ku-bi
1) f. of Ša-ma-ja, 62:18
2) 139:13; 229:8; 254:3; 257:10

A-pil-ᵈSin, A-pil-Sin*
1) s. of ... -ta-nim, 85:24 (w)

2) b. of [AN]-ʼKAʼ-EŠ₄.DAR, b. of ...-
ᵈEN.ZU, 18:4
3) b. of PN (not given), 30:5
4) 19:3*; 174:2*; 178:2*; 202:1*; 226:5*

ʼA-pilʼ-ᵈŠamaš s. of ..., 309:15

A-pil-ʼŠeʼ-rum 240:1

Aplum(DUMU.NITÁ)-ʼi-diʼ 275:13

Ap-pa-an-ilim
1) s. of Ṣíl-lí-ᵈIM, 64:13 (w)
2) 164:6

A-ʼqáʼ-ab-ʼbi-líʼ 321:4

A-ra(?)-šu-um-ilum 165:4ʼ

ʼArʼ-ki-Ilum-ma s. of Ḫa-ab-du-Ilu[m],
151:8ʼ

Ar-ši-ʼtumʼ f. of Sin-ki-i-lí-ia, 30:17

Ar-wi-im (Arwum) w. of PN (not given),
91:14

A-sa-la-kum 85:20 (w)

A-sa-šum 1:6

A-su-um s. of Nu-úr-ᵈIštar, 45:16 (w)

Aš-du-di-in 87:9

A-ṣu-šum(?) s. of [I]b-ni-ᵈIštar, 73:5

Aš-ʼqúʼ-du f. of Šu-ᵈAmurrim, 306:4

Aš-šur.ʼᴷᴵ-enʼ-nam s. of Da ..., 67:5

[A]-ʼtaʼ-kal-ši s. of PN (not preserved),
b. of ...ra-at, 312:9

A-ta-ka-al-ʼšuʼ 249:8

A-te-šu-mi-i 136:2

A-ti-ta 272:9

Awat(INIM)-ᵈEnlil
1) s. of ʼNu-úr-ìʼ-lí-šu, 44:4
2) f. of A-ḫa-am-nu-ta, 31:rev.:10

Awat(INIM)-Ilim 243:12

Awīl- see also under LÚ

Awīl-... 107 i:3; 243:5

Awīl-ᵈAdad
1) s. of Ì-lí-a-wi-lim, 320:9ʼ
2) 307:rev. ii:19ʼ

Awīl-ᵈAmurrim, Awīl-Amurrim*
1) f. of ʼLi-pí-it-Ištarʼ, 46:14
2) 26:1, 226:4*

ʼAwīlamʼ(?)-mu-ba-lí-iṭ f. of ʼI-bi(?)ʼ-Sin,
225:rev. 2

A-wi-li-ia
1) s. of Be-el-šu-nu, 305:21
2) s. of Zi-kir-ᵈʼŠamašʼ, b. of Warad-Sin,
306:rev. 8f
3) 307:rev. ii:20ʼ

ˊIaˋ-aḫ-su-uk-Ilum   s. of [ᵈS]in-en-nam, 151:
    10ˊ
Ia-ak-ni-Ilum   246:2
Ia-am-ˊziˋ-Ilum   f. of Ib-ni-ᵈŠamaš, 296 (s)
Ia-an-...-nu   f. of [W]arad-ᵈˊIštarˋ, 67:3
Ia-an-ti-na-ra-aḫ   242:2, 281:8
Ia-an-ti-nu-um, Ia-an-ti-num*
    1) s. of Ia-qu-ub-I[lum], 61:5
    2) f. of ᵈSin-a-ḫi-i-din-nam, 80:3*
Ia-ap-ḫu-ur-Li-im   281:5
Ia-qú-ub-I[lum]   f. of Ia-an-ti-nu-um, 61:6
Ia-ri-im-L[i-i]m   326:55 (R)
ˊIaˋ-ar-ˊza(?)ˋ   s. of ᵈAmur[ru-...], b. of ˊA-
    ḫuˋ-ši-na, b. of Ši-ˊnaˋ-nu, 309:7
Ia-ta-ru-um, Ia-ta-rum*
    1) f. of PN (not given), 109:5*
    2) 167:3
Ia-tum-mar-ṣa   169:11; 215:5
Íb...   f. of Sin-eri-ba-am, 324:2
I-ba-al-pi-e[l] (R)   1 (s); 56:19 (Y); 114 (s);
    115 (s); 116 (s); 131 (s); 233 (s); 298 (s)
Ib-bi-...   f. of ˊŠum-šu-imˋ-[ma-tim], 25:28
    (s)
I-bi-ᵈˊSinˋ   73:16 (R)
I-bi-ᵈAdad
    1) s. of Ku(?)-ur-ᵈSin, 162:8
    2) 169:10; 203:1; 204:1; 205:1; 206:1
Ib-bi-ˊiaˋ   f. of Da-bi-bu-um, 81:5
I-bi-ᵈIlaprat
    1) f. of Be-el-šu-nu, 64:16
    2) 207:1; 273:5; 323:7
I-[bi]-Ìr-r[a]   320:3ˊ
Ib-bi-Ištar
    1) f. of ˊIp(?)-qáˋ-tum, 305:27
    2) 162:10
Ib-bi-Sin, I-bi-Sin*, I-bi-ᵈSin**
    1) s. of ˊAwīl(?)ˋ-mu-ba-lí-iṭ, 225:rev. 1
    2) f. of Bur-ᵈSi[n], 29:29 (s)**
    3) f. of ᵈŠamaš-ra-bi, 306:3*
    4) 33:2 (w)**, 85:17 (w)*; 217:2**
I-bi-šu-ᵈMa-lik   130 (s) (R)
Ib-bi-tap-pí-šu,   Ib-bi-TAB.BA-e-šu*   24:
    18; 90:13; 91:18; 92:15*
Ib-ni...   22:2; 313:9
Ib-ni-ᵈ...   f. of Mār-ᵈšamaš, 310 ii:4ˊ
Ib-ni-ᵈAdad
    1) s. of Na-bi-ili(DINGIR)-šu, 30:20 (w)
    2) 33:6 (w); 90:3
Ib-ni-ᵈAmurru   305:42, 46

Ib-ni-ᵈEnlil,   Ib-ni-ᵈEN.LÍL.L[A]*   86:8*;
    183:4
Ib-ni-Ìr-ra
    1) f. of ˊIšˋ-bi-ᵈʳTišpak(?)ˋ, 118 (s); 121
        (s); 125 (s); 126 (s)
    2) 169 rev.:10ˊ
Ib-ni-ᵈIštar
    1) s. of Tu-..., 110:7
    2) f. of ˊA-zu-šumˋ(?), 73:6
    3) f. of Gu-lu-bi-ia, 73:15, (s)
Ib-ni-ia   s. of Ga-mi-[ilum], 70:4
Ib-ni-ᵈʳŠamašˋ   s. of Ia-am-ˊziˋ-Ilum, 296 (s)
Ib-ni-Še-rum   f. of ˊTu-ti-ruˋ, 320:10ˊ
I-da-ᵈSin   258:3
I-di-ia   s. of ᵈSin-še-mi, 45:18 (w)
I-di(?)-ia-tum   275:4
I-din-nam-ᵈŠamaš   162:7
I-din-Ilum
    1) s. of Warad-i-lí-šu, 58:10 (w); 64:14 (w)
    2) 107 i:29
I-din-Sin   s. of ..., 72:9 (w)
I-din-ᵈŠahan(MUŠ)   f. of ˊŠuˋ-ul-mu-da-
    mi-iq, 67:15
I-di-nu-ni-iš   f. of E-ri-ba-am, 43:20
I-di-šum   323:4
ᵈÍDₓ(A.SUK)-da-ia-an   255:5, 11
I-gi(?)-...   f. of Warad-ᵈS[in(?)], 83 rev.:4ˊ
Ig-mi[l(?)]-...   169:rev. (c)
Ig-mil-ᵈSin, Ig-mil-Sin*
    1) s. of ˊŠa-maˋ-ia-tum, 68:16 (w)*
    2) f. of ..., 132 (s)
    3) f. of ˊA-bi-zu-umˋ, l(s) 114 (s), 115 (s),
        116 (s)
    4) f. of ˊA-lí-bu-...ˋ, 231 (s)
    5) f. of ˊIn-bu-šaˋ 131 (s)
    6) 70:12 (w)*; 89:2*; 241:10*
ˊI-ka-biˋ...   f. of Ì-lí-ˊki-a-bi-iaˋ, 59:6
I-ku...   f. of Bur-ᵈ..., 244 (s)
ˊI-ku-un(?)-píˋ-...   167:12
I-ku-un-pî(KA)-ᵈAdad, I-ku-pí-ᵈAd[ad]*
    30:2, env.*
ˊI-ku-unˋ-pî-ᵈEN...   s. of ... ᵈSin, 60:15 (w)
I-ku-un-pî(KA)-i-lí   f. of Mu-na-wi-rum,
    30:21, env.
I-ku-un-pî(KA)-ᵈSin   26 (s), 300 (s)
I-ku-un-pí-šu
    f. of ᵈŠamaš-be-el-i-lí, 62:12
I-ku-pí   249:10
I-ku-pí...   172:2

2) s. of Sin-i-ia, 43:13 (w)*

3) f. of ᵈDa-mu-illassu (ILLAT-SU), 43:
12*

4) 165:3'*; 218:2*; 223:13*

Im-gur-ᵈŠamaš

1) s. of ..., 72:10 (w)

2) s. of ᵈŠamaš-..., 30:24 (w)

3) s. of ᵈNANNA ..., 30:24 env. (w)

4) 87:10

Im-gu-ru-um, Im-gu-rum*, Im-gur-rum**

1) s. of A-da-ia, 79:19 (w)*

2) s. of Na-ra-am-i-lí-šu, 43:4-6

3) f. of Ṣil-lí-ᵈIštar, 47:20; 58:13*, env.**

4) 85:18 (w)**; 143:8**

I-mi-ru 167:5

I-na-nu-um 179:2

I-na-qá-ti-ᵈŠamaš 241:5

In-ba-tum 92:4

[In-b]u-ʼIštar(?)ʼ 268:iii 10'

In-bu-ša

1) s. of Ig-mil-ᵈSin, 131 (s); 231 (s)

2) s. of Ma(?)-ni(?)-um, 320:8'

3) f. of ..., 307:rev. i 11'

4) f. of A-ḫu-wa-qa[r-r]u, 320:5'

5) f. of A-pil-i-lí-šu, 320:6'

6) f. of Warad-ᵈIštar, 305:44

7) f. of Warad-Ku-bi, 305:9

8) 59:11 (w); 90:12; 91:17; 92:14

I-ni-ir-ʼa-iaʼ-bi-šu, I-nir-a-ia-bi-šu* 139:
14*, 229:7

ᵈINNIN.MA.AN.SUM s. of ᵈSin-mu-ša-
lim, 179 (s)

I-pí-iq-ᵈ... 186:2

I-pí-iq-ᵈAdad

1) f. of ᵈSin-ma-gir, 94:9

2) 29:17 (R); 63:17 (R); 123 (s) (R);
185:2; 199:1; 205 (s) (R); 206 (s) (R);
232 (s) (R); 246 (s) (R)

Ipiq-(SIG)-ᵈAmurrim 7:11; 74:7 (w)

I-pí-iq-i-lí-šu

1) s. of Ṣé-eḫ-ri, 45:12 (w)

2) f. of Warad-[ᵈS]in, 235:9 (s)

I-pí-iq-Ìr-ra 242:22; 249:12; 262:12

I-pí-iq-Ištar, SIG-Ištar*

1) s. of Ì-lí-we-ʼdeʼ-ku, 34:15 (w)

2) 72:3, 77:14 (w), 78:8 (w)*, 108:5,
216:10, 269:9

I-pí-iq-Nu-nu 187:2

Ip-qá-a 32:2

Ip-qá-tum, ʼIp-qa-tumʼ*

1) s. of ʼI-biʼ-Ištar, 305:27

2) f. of ʼBu-ni-ṭà-a-bu-umʼ, 46:17*

3) 305:8

Ip-qu-ʼaʼ-... 268:i. 19

Ip-qú-ᵈNingal f. of Ilān (DINGIR.
DINGIR)-re-ʼšaʼ, 61:15

Ip-qú-ša

1) s. of Bur-Sin, 58:13a

2) s. of Ìl-lam-mi-lik, 34:20, (w) (s)

3) f. of Bur(!)-ri-ia 34:19

4) 268:i 10

I-ʼqaʼ-ru-za-... 273:2

Iqīš(BA)-Ištar s. of Mu-na-wi-rum, 30:
18 (w)

Iqīš(BA)-ᵈSin s. of Mu-na-wi-ru-um, 57:1

I-qi(!)-iš-ᵈTIŠPAK 33:13 (R)

Iq-ʼqáʼ-at-Ilim 268:iii 7'

Ìr-ra-ga-mi-il, Ìr-ra-ga-mil*

1) 34:1, 9*, 11*

2) 185:4; 186:3; 187:3; 188:3; 189:3

3) 243:11*

Ìr-ra-i-... 84:9 (w)

Ìr-ra-i-mi-ti 237:3

I-ra-šu-x-Sin 70:9 (w)

ʼÌr-ra-na-ṣirʼ f. of ..., 46:21

Ìs-ḫu-na-tum 90:7

I-si-mi-ʼlu(?)ʼ 16:1

I-ʼša-bi(?)ʼ h. of ʼA(?)-ḫa-tumʼ, 229:10

Iš-bi-Ìr-ra

1) f. of Ḫa-lí-ia, 34:14, (s) (also written
A-lí-ia)

2) 190:3, 191:4, 192:2, 4

ʼIš-bi-ᵈʼTišpak(?)ʼ s. of Ib-ni-Ìr-ra, 118 (s),
121 (s), 125 (s), 126 (s)

Iš-ḫi-Ilum-ma f. of Qi-iš-i-lí-šu, 151:6'

Iš-me-ʼᵈIMʼ f. of ᵈSin-a-bu-šu, 80:1

Iš-me-ᵈEnlil s. of Sin-be-el-i-lí, 88:4, 8

Iš-me-ᵈḪa-lí-ʼeʼ 211:1

Iš-me-Ilum (!) 50:11 (w)

Iš-me-Ìr-ra 189:2

Iš-me-ka(?)-ra-ab f. of E-ṭi-rum, 305:40

Ištar-gim-li-ni 158:5

Ištar-a(?)-sa-at 241:10

Ištar-ra-bi-at 158:6

It(?)-ti-ʼDINGIRʼ-ṣil-ʼluʼ 50:10 (w)

I-tu-li 107:i 27

I-túr-... f. of Warad-ᵈSin, 83:4

I-tur-Aš-du-ma f. of Im-gur-ᵈSin, 34:5

I-túr-Aš-du-um   f. of Sin-mu-ba-lí-iṭ,   62:5

I-túr(?)-ma-lik   271:4'

I-zi-ʿib-Ilumʾ   f. of Sà-ri-qum, 81:3

I-zi-Na-bu-ú
   1) s. of Me-ʿni(?)ʾ-ḫu-ʿumʾ, 62:13 (w)
   2) 95:8; 162:12; 214:4

I-zi-Su-mu-ú   5:3; 6:3; 7:3; 8:3

IZ-GÁN.NUN(?)   74:8 (w)

I-ʿxʾ-za   s. of A-bi-..., 152 (s)

ᵈKab-ta-ʿx xʾ   268: ii 14

ᵈKab-ta-ILLAT-su   94:4

Ka-ʿdi-irʾ-tum   268: ii 4

Ka-la-a   9:1; 10:1

Ka(?)-lí-...   162:4

Ka-li-Ilum   305:32

Ka-ʿluʾ-mi-ili, Ka-lu-mi-lí*   103:6; 169:8*

Ka-at-ri-ia   s. of Za-bu-lum 151:4'

Ki...   107: ii 12

Ki(?)-i-lu   s. of Su-um-ḫa-..., 61:12 (w)

ʿKi-di-in-Ištar(?)ʾ   268: ii 1

ᵈKi-ti-tum-um-mi   182:6

Ki-tum-li-zi-iz   268: iv 6'

Ku-ub-bu-lum

Ku-ub-bu-lum   s. of Ma-a-šum, f. of Mār-
   ᵈŠamaš b. of Ra-bu-ti-ʿiaʾ, 306: rev. 2

Ku-ub-bu-rum
   1) s. of Mār-il-tum, b. of Li-pí-it-ᵈTišpak,
     b. of KUR-Ḫi-it-ti-mu-uš-te-še-er, 305:
     15
   2) 322:9

Ku-bi-ia   s. of Ta-a[k]-..., 310: ii 6'

Ku-ku-li   85:11 (w)

Ku-ʿunʾ-na-ʿaʾ   270:8

KÙ.ᵈNA[NNA]   f. of ᵈSin-mu-b[a-lí-iṭ] 298
   (s)

Ku-nu-ub-tum   f. of ᶠPN (not given), 107:
   ii 17

Ku-nu-um, Ku-nu-ʿú-umʾ*
   1) f. of ᶠPN (not given), 7:4*
   2) f. of Pu-ḫa-nu-um, 151:9'
   3) 98: rev. 2'

Ku-ur-[ku-ú]r-ru-um   107: i 17

Ku-ri-tum
   1) d. of Be(?)-la-ia, 30:6
   2) m. of Ri-im-ᵈAdad, 89:4; 265:15

Ku-úr-ku-du   267:10

Ku-ru-um   s. of ..., 58:5

Ku-ur-ᵈSin   f. of I-bi-ᵈAdad, 162:9

Ku-ʿur-ṣiʾ-tu[m(?)]   307: rev. ii 17'

Ku-uš(?)-...   f. of ᵈŠamaš-ki-ma-..., 72:12

ʿKu-šu-bi(?)-mi(?)ʾ-...   137:7

La(?)-be-el-šu-nu   192:3

La-aḫ-bat   164:2

La-ṭà-bu-um   31: rev. 13 (w)

La-ḫu-ṭá-ba-at(?)   297:3 (s)

La-ma-sà-ni   23:12'; 97:3

La-ma-sí   90:5; 107: i, 20, ii 16

ᵈLa-qí-pu-um-ga-mi-il,   ᵈLa-qí-pu-ga-mil*
   129:2*; 182:7

ʿLiʾ-...
   1) f. of A-lí-..., 72:12
   2) 307: obv. ii 10'

Li-bur-na-di-ša   158:3

Li-pí-it-Ilim   s. of Ilum-ma 45:22 (w)

Li-pí-it-ᵈIštar, Li-pí-it-Ištar*
   1) s. of Awīl-ᵈʿAmurrumʾ, 46:13 (w)*
   2) s. of Mu-na-wi-rum, 30* (s)
   3) 271:5'*; 307: rev. ii 5'

Li-pí-it-ᵈTišpak   s. of Mār-il-tum, b. of
   KUR-Ḫi-it-ti-mu-uš-te-še-er, b. of Ku-ub-
   bu-rum, 305:13

Li-wi-ra-šum
   1) h. of ʿAʾ-ḫa-tum, 139:5
   2) 29:7; 98: rev. 4; 120: rev. 4'

Lu-da-ri   216:9

ʿLu(?)ʾ-da-ri-a-ʿat(?)ʾ   268: ii 13

Lu-mur-ša-ᵈŠamaš   152:2

LÚ.ᵈNANNA
   1) f. of Ì-lí-ù-ᵈŠamaš, 42:14
   2) 86:5, 269:1

LÚ.ᵈNIN.GÍR.SU   109:3
see also under Awīl-

Lu-ša-li-im, Lu-ša-lim*   248:7; 275:21*

Lu-zu-um
   1) f. of Pí-làḫ-Ilum 79:24
   2) 165:6'; 173:2; 175:2

M[a]-...   107: i 31

ʿMa-ḫiʾ-...   275:11

Ma-ki-ia-tum   107: i 14; 137:4; 150:2;
   229:13

Ma-n[i]-...   f. of Šu-ᵈSin, 310: ii 1'

Ma(?)-ni-um   f. of In-bu-ša, 320:8'

Ma-nu-um
   1) s. of ʿMas-suʾ(?)-qa-ni, 52:15
   2) s. of ᵈSin-ri-me-ni, 9:5
   3) f. of Ì(!)-ku-pí-ᵈAd[ad], 88:2
   4) 20:18; 127:2 (w); 223:6; 242:12; 243:8

Ma-nu-um-da-mi-iq 92:11

Ma-nu-um-ki-... f. of U-bar-ᵈŠam[aš], 83:
14

Ma-nu-um-ki-Sin 85:22 (w)

[Ma-nu]-um-ki-ˈmaˈ-ᵈAdad s. of ˈI-líˈ-ki-
ma-a-bi-ia, 311:obv. 5'

Ma-nu-um-ša-nin(?)-ˈšuˈ 85:9 (w)

Mārat-ᵈA-... 107:1 11

Mārat-GAB-ša-ˈPIˈ 270:5

Mārat-irṣitim (KI) w. of ᵈSin-na-ap-še-ra-
am, 64:7

Mār-il-tum f. of Li-pí-it-ᵈTišpak, KUR-Ḫi-
it-ti-mu-uš-te-še-eru and Ku-ub-bu-rum,
305:13

Mār-[Ištar] s. of Be-l[a-nu-um], 81:10, 17
(s) (w)

Mār-Sin 243:15

Mār-ᵈŠamaš

   1) s. of Ib-ni-ᵈ..., 310:ii 4'
   2) s. of Ku-ub-bu-lum, nephew of Ra-bu-
   ti-ia, and grands. of Ma-a-šum, 306:
   rev. 4
   3) h. of Ḫu-šu-tum, 72:5
   4) 85:21 (w); 268:iii 6'

Mār-Uríᴷᴵ f. of PN (not given), 109:4

ˈMas-suˈ(?)-qa-ni f. of Ma-nu-um, 52:16

Maš-pa-lu-um s. of Za-bu-lum, 151:5'

Ma-aš-qum 162:11; 308:10'

Ma-šum, Ma-a-šum*

   1) s. of Bur-Sin, 58:11
   2) s. of U-bar-rum, b. of E-ṭi-rum, 305:34
   3) f. of Ku-ub-bu-lum and Ra-bu-ti-ia,
   and grandf. of Mār-ᵈŠamaš, 306:rev. 2*
   4) 313:8

Ma-ta-ku(?)-ke(?)-el 323:6

Ma-ti-LÚ(?).ˈTU(?)ˈ.TA 163:6

Ma-ti-i-lí, Ma-ti-ili* 106:32; 269:2*

Ma-ti-ia-ia-tu-ˈumˈ 159:5

Me-ˈni(?)ˈ-ḫu-ˈumˈ f. of I-zi-Na-bu-ú, 62:
14

Me-ra-nu-um

   1) s. of Sú-ga-gu-um, 193:2
   2) 193:4; 194:3; 195:4; 264:2

Mi-nam-e-ˈpu-uš-ilumˈ 169:rev. 5'

Mi-ˈnam-eˈ-pu-uš-ˈšuˈ(!)ˈ s. of E-ri-ib-ᵈSin,
305:31

Mi-nu-na-tim m. of ˈḪaˈ-ri-il, 32:3

Mu-... 159:4

Mu-ḫa-di-tum 107:i 16, 28

Mu-ḫa-du-um f. of Sin-ri-me-ni, 183:3

Mu-uḫ-ra-am-mu h. of ˈPN (not given)
90:1

Mu-na-... 159:1

Mu-na-nu-um 12:rev. 5; 32:13 (w); 68:
18 (w); 70:13 (w); 71:13 (w); 82:10(w);
145:4; 242:5

Mu-na-wi-ru-um, Mu-na-wi-rum*

   1) s. of I(?)-k[u-u]n-pî(KA)-i-lí, 30:21*
   (w)
   2) s. of Ì-lí-Ku-ˈbiˈ, 35:18* (w)
   3) s. of ˈNa(?)ˈ-aw-ru-um, 161:2
   4) s. of Sa-li-ma-nu-um, 34:13* (w) (s)
   5) f. of Iqīš(BA)-Ištar, 30:18*
   6) f. of Iqīš(BA)-ᵈSin, 157:1
   7) f. of Li-pí-iṭ-Ištar, 30 (s)
   8) 100:7; 171:2; 242:14

Mu-ša-li-mu 88:3

ˈMu-taˈ-a-ˈaˈ f. of A-na-ᵈŠamaš-ták-[la-ku],
31:rev. 6 (w)

Mu-te-e-ra-aḫ 216:13

Na-... 242:16

Na-bi-... f. of Akšak-ˈxˈ..., 67:4

Na-bi-ᵈEnlil 267:7

Na-bi-i-lí-šu, Na-bi-ili-šu*

   1) f. of Ib-ni-ᵈAdad, 30:20 env.*
   2) 267:9

Na-bi-ᵈSin

   1) s. of We-ˈdiˈ-be-lum, 179:4
   2) 305:16

Nabu(ᵈPA)-ilum 168:10

Na-ma-arₓ(ḪAR)(?)-lu-mu-u[r] 270:10

Na-am-si-e-ᵈAdad 5:6

ᵈNANNA-...

   1) f. of [Im-gu]r-ᵈŠamaš, 30:24 env.
   2) 12:rev. 7; 281:9

Na-an-na-il-ˈtumˈ s. of ᵈSin-ma-ˈgirˈ, 60:
13 (w)

ᵈNANNA.ARḪUŠ ᵈNANNA.ARḪUŠ-
(!)ᴴᵁ·ᵁˢ* 53:5; 68:4*; 69:3; 70:3; 71:5;
95:6; 108:12-14

ᵈNanna-ma-ˈlikˈ f. of ᵈSin-e-ri-ba-am, 60:
12

ᵈNANNA.MA.AN.SUM

   1) s. of ᵈSin-mu-ša-lim, 47:21 (w); 179 (s)
   2) 50:4

ᵈNANNA.ME.DÍM, ᵈNANNA.ME.DÍM-
(?)*

   1) s. of ᵈŠamaš-mu-uš-te(!)-pí-iš, 34:6
   2) 45:24 (w)*; 47:4; 79:4*; 108:7-8

ʹNa-na-ruʹ-um   178:1

Na-na-t[um], ᵈNanna-tum*
1) s. of ᵈSin-..., 56:16 (w)
2) s. of Sin-ma-gir, 57:11 (w)*
3) 229:11*; 305:51*

Na-ra-am-i-lí-šu
1) f. of Im-gu-ru-um, 43:5
2) f. of ᵈSin/Sin-e-ri-ba-am, 232 (s); 265:10

Na-ra-am-ᵈSin   25:25 (R); 45:25 (R); 76:24 (R); 223:1; 267:5

Na-ra-am-tum
1) w. of ... nu, 46:10 (w)
2) 91:7; 158:1; 268:ii 10

Na-ar-ba-num   f. of Ḫa-zi-ru-um, 151:7'

Na-ʹarʹ-bi-ᵈIš-ḫa-ra   181:3

ʹNa(?)ʹ-aw-ru-um   f. of Mu-na-wi-ru-[u]m, 161:3

NE.NE...   156:rev. 2'

Ni-mi-lum   f. of [War]ad-ᵈŠamaš, 84:12

Ni-ši-ni-šu   d. of ᵈSin-ip-pa-ʹalʹ-sa, 55:6

ʹNuʹ-...   s. of [E]-ri-ʹba-amʹ, 46:18 (w)

Nu-ni-...   s. of ʹNu-úr(?)ʹ-Ku-ʹbiʹ, 79:15 (w)

Nu-nu-eriš(APIN)   281:7

Nu-úr-...   242:10; 268:ii 17

Nu-úr-ᵈAdad, ʹNuʹ(?)-ur-ʹᵈAdadʹ*   223:8; 241:10; 269:5*; 323:2

Nu-úr-Akšak   85:19 (w)

Nu-úr-ì-lí-šu
1) s. of ..., 51:12 (w)
2) f. of Awat(INIM)-ᵈEnlil, 44:5
3) 36:3

Nu-úr-ᵈIštar   f. of A-su-um, 45:17

Nu-úr-Ku-bi
1) s. of I-lu-šu-nu, 30:19 (w)
2) f. of Nu-ni-..., 79:16

Nu-úr-ᵈSakkud (SAG.KUD)
1) s. of Ìl-šu-ba-ni, 66:12 (w)
2) 136:3

Nu-úr-ᵈŠamaš
1) s. of Sin-i-din-nam, 43:15 (w)
2) s. of Ú-ṣur-pî(KA)-Ištar, 44:16 (w)
3) f. of [A-b]u-um-wa-qar, 311:obv. 6'
4) f. of Ri-iš-ᵈŠamaš, 69:5
5) f. of ..., ...NI, grandf. of ...A, 311:rev. 6'
6) h. of ... -ka(?)-súm, 107:i 30
7) 268:iii 18'

Nu-úr-ᵈʹTišpak(?)ʹ   128:2

Nu-ṭú-up-tum
1) w. of A-ia-ḫa-mu-ú, 53:6
2) 107:i 6, 25; 118:1; 216:8

Pa-di-...   242:8

Pí-làḫ-Ilum   s. of Lu-zu-um, 79:23 (w)

Pir-ḫu-um   b. of U-ba-rum, 305:19

Pu-ḫa-ʹdu(?)ʹ   268:i 11

Pu-ḫa-ʹlum(?)ʹ   167:14

Pu-ḫa-nu-u[m]   s. of Ku-nu-um, 151:9'

Pu-ḫu-um   s. of ʹQa-šuʹ-ub-tum, 80:2

Puzur-a-bi   275:3, 16

Puzur-Ištar   s. of Warad-ᵈSu[muqan] (GÌR?]), 79:13 (w)

Puzur-ᵈKi-ti-tum   90:11; 91:16; 92:13

Puzur-ᵈSakkud (SAG.KUD)   223:10; 241:8; 243:9

Puzur-ᵈSin, Puzur-Sin*
1) s. of .... 69:12* (w)
2) 269:6

Puzur-ᵈŠamaš
1) f. of ¹A-a-be-li-ʹitʹ-ma-ʹtimʹ, 77:8
2) 143:5

Qar-ʹra-adʹ-Ištar   146:2

ʹQà-aš-tumʹ(?)   107:ii 8

ʹQa-šuʹ-ub-tum   f. of Pu-ḫu-um, 80:2

Qí-ʹipʹ-ti-ba-al-ʹṭiʹ   159:6

Qí-iš-i-lí-a   192:1

Qi-iš-i-lí-šu   s. of Iš-ḫi-Ilum-ma, 151:6'

Qí-šu-ša   177:1

Qur-ru-ʹrumʹ(?)   272:8

Qur-ru-ʹdiʹ-im   19:1

Ra-bu-a-tum   221:1

Ra-ʹbuʹ-ti-ʹiaʹ   b. of Ku-ub-bu-lum, s. of Ma-a-tim, uncle of Mār-ᵈŠamaš, 306:rev. 2-4

[R]a-bu-ut-Sin   b. of ... 307:rev. ii 3'

Ra-ma-rum   91:3

Ra-šu-bi-tum, Ra-šum-É*   70:10* (w); 262:6

Ri-...   71:12 (w)

Ri-ib-ba-ʹtumʹ   275:15

Ri-im-ᵈAdad
1) s. of Ku-ri-ti-im, 89:3; 265:14
2) 241:11; 307:rev. ii 21'

Ri-iš-ᵈAdad   s. of E-ta-na, 30:16 (w)

Ri-iš-Ilum
1) s. of ʹṢí(?)-lí-iaʹ, 52:3
2) 143:3

Ri-iš-ᵈŠamaš
  1) s. of Nu-úr-ᵈŠamaš, 69:4
  2) f. of Warad-Ku-bi, 307:rev. ii 4'
  3) 91:4
Ri-iš-Tu-tu-ub s. of ...i-na-ma-ti 65:5
ᶠRu-bi-um(?) 107:i 26
Ru-bu-um (R) 61:16 (Y)
Sak-ka-ku(?) 271:6'
Sa-la-tum 21:3
Sa-li-ma-nu-um(?) f. of Mu-na-wi-rum, 34:13
Sa-li-ma-ti 163:4
Sal-li-ba(?)-nu(?)-um(?) 240:5
Sa-ma-ra-aḫ 271:rev. 3
ᶜSaᵓ-am-ma-tum 91:6
Sa-am-su-i-lu-na (R), 305:53; 314:22; 315:rev. 5'
Sa-ni-pí 236:4
Sà-ri-qu-um, Sà-ri-qú-um*, Sa-ri-qum**, Sà-ri-qum***
  1) s. of A-ᶜḫuᵓ-ṭà-bu-um(?), 62:15** (w)
  2) s. of Bu-ur-qa-nu-[um], 79:11** (w)
  3) s. of Ìl-šu-ba-ni, 65:13* (w)
  4) s. of I-zi-ᶜib-Ilumᵓ, 81:2***
  5) 76:3**; 127:3
Sa-si-ia f. of A-bi ..., 61:11
Si-bi-lu-um 262:2
ᵈSin-..., Sin-...*
  1) s. of ..., 151:2'*
  2) f. of A-ḫu-ni, 188:2*
  3) f. of Na-na-t[um], 56:17
  4) f. of Tab-bi-bu-um, 308:8'*
  5) f. of War[ad-...], 31:rev. 4
  6) 12:rev. 2; 24:5; 40:rev. 9 (w); 81:13; 83:17; 159:2; 170:1; 242:8; 273:1; 275:5; 300:6'; 307:rev. ii 18'
ᵈSin-a-... 50:5
ᵈSin-a-bu-..., Sin-a-bu-...* s. of Warad-Sin, 251:8*
ᵈSin-a-bu-um, Sin-a-bu-um*
  1) f. of ᵈSin-e-r[i-b]a-am, 84:14
  2) f. of ... -ba-ni, 40:rev. 6
  3) 46:3; 162:9*
ᵈSin-a-bu-šu, Sin-a-bu-šu*
  1) s. of ... -nu-um, 36:15 (w)
  2) s. of Iš-me-ᶜᵈAdadᵓ, 80:1
  3) 44:20f. (R)*; 77:15 (w); 268:iv 7'*; 271:3'
ᶜᵈSin-a-ḫa-am-i-din-namᵓ 54:12 (w)

ᵈSin-a-ḫi-i-din-nam, Sin-a-ḫi-i-din-nam*
  1) s. of ᶜIa-an-tiᵓ-num, 80:3
  2) 78:10* (w)
ᵈSin-an-dùl-lí 106:38; 242:21; 267:6
ᵈSin-ba-ni
  1) s. of A-da-a-a, grands. of ᶜṬà-ab-ṣíl-ᶜla-šuᵓ, 31:4f
  2) f. of Ì-lí-we-de-ku, 34 (s)
  3) 13:10; 156:4
ᵈSin-be-el-ap-li 179:1
Sin-be-el-i-lí f. of Iš-me-ᵈEnlil 88:5
Sin-da-ia-an 108:2
ᵈSin-dannum (KALAG.GÁ), Sin-dannum* 273:9; 319:9; 323:9*
ᵈSin-en-nam
  1) f. of ᶜIaᵓ-aḫ-su-uk-Ilum, 151:10'
  2) f. of ᵈSin-e-ri-ba-am, 31:rev. 8
ᵈSin-e-ri-ba-am, Sin-e-ri-ba-am*, ᵈSin-eri₄-ba-am** ᵈSin-e-ri-ba***
  1) s. of Be-el-šu-nu, 194:1*
  2) s. of Íb-..., 324:2**
  3) s. of ᵈNanna-ma-ᶜlikᵓ, 60:11 (w)
  4) s. of Na-ra-am-i-lí-šu, 232 (s); 265:9*
  5) s. of ᵈSin-a-b[u]-um, 84:13 (w)
  6) s. of ᵈSin-en-nam, 31:rev. 7 (w)
  7) s. of ᵈS[in-i]-qí-ša-a[m], 42:15 (w)
  8) s. of ᵈŠamaš-mu-uš-te-pí-iš, 64:4
  9) s. of PN (not given), 14:2***
  10) f. of A-bu-um-ilum, 68:6; 71:10**
  11) f. of Ì-lí-qa-ti-ṣa-ba-at, 77:4
  12) f. of É.BABBARₓ(UD.UD).RA-lu-ᶜmurᵓ, 45:21
  13) b. of ᵈSin-ri-me-ni, 13:3
  14) 12:rev. 9*; 15:1; 25:1, 8, 10, 12; 28:5', 9', 14'; 45:5; 94:21; 110:11; 230:2***; 232:3 (s); 234:9; 268:iv 17'*; 269:4; 307:rev. ii 16'
Sin-ga-mi-il, ᵈSin-ga-mil*, Sin-ga-mil**
  1) s. of Tap-pa(?)-li-su 85:13** (w)
  2) f. of ᶜAᵓ-lí-ia, 76:9*
  3) 196:5; 197:3; 198:1; 269:8*
Sin-i-din s. of Tu-tu-..., 324:1
ᵈSin-i-din-nam, Sin-i-din-nam*, ᵈSin-i-di-nam**, Sin-i-din-am***,
  1) s. of [A-p]il-ì-lí-šu, 265:20*
  2) s. of Sin-i-qí-ša-am, 231:4*
  3) s. of ᵈŠamaš-ᶜsu-mu-umᵓ, 9:3
  4) f. of A-pil-ì-lí-šu, 67:19
  5) f. of Be-el-šu-nu, 75:11*

7) 31:6; 83:2; 94:11; 156:2'; 162:6*;
227:2, 7, 10**
ᵈSin-ˈweˈ-de-e-ku, ᵈSin-we -de-ku*
1) s. of ᵈSin-mu-ba-li-iṭ, 55:14 (w)
2) 28:11'*
Sin-ta-ˈaˈ-ia-ar   18:21
Si-ir-si-ri-tum   47:5; 66:4
Su-ˈx-niˈ   316:4
Sú-be-lim(?)   143:10
Su-bi-ra(?)   s. of Bu-ur-Sin, 65:15 (w)
Sú-ga-gu-um
1) f. of Me-ra-nu-um, 193:3
2) 38: rev. 5', 169:7
Su-ka-li-ia
1) f. of A-ḫu-wa-qar, 63:6
2) 271:2'
Su-um-ḫa-...   f. of Ki-i-lu, 61:13
Su-mu-a-bi-ia-ri-i[m]   27:8' (R)
Su-mu-a-bu-um   281:4
ˈSu-mu-ᵈAdadˈ   103:7
Su-mu-bi-na-šu   281:2
Su-mu-le-el-du-ri   281:3
Su-mu-nu-um-ḫi-im   326:47, 50, 53 (R)
ˈSú-pa-píˈ-im   f. of Il-ta-ˈtumˈ, 57:6
Ṣé-eḫ-ri   f. of I-pí-iq-i-lí-šu, 45:13
Ṣi-il-Be-el-ga-še-ˈerˈ   259:3
Ṣil-lí-...   f. of ᵈŠamaš-na-..., 35:20
Ṣil-lí-ᵈ...   309:13
Ṣil-lí-a-...   268:i 17
ˈṢí(?)-lí-iaˈ   f. of Ri-ˈiš-Ilumˈ, 52:4
Ṣil-lí-ᵈAdad   f. of Ap-pa-an-ilim, 64:13
Ṣil-lí-ᵈIštar
1) s. of Im-gur-rum, Im-gu-rum*, 47:19
(w); 58:12*, env. (w)
2) s. of Ši-ˈnaˈ(?)-nu, grands. of ᵈAmu[rru-
...], nephew of Ia-ar-za(?) and A-ḫu-ši-
na, 309:9
Ṣil-lí-ᵈLa-qi-ip-ˈpuˈ   85:23 (w)
Ṣil-lí-ᵈNanna(?)   268:i 13
Ṣil-lí-Sin   f. of ..., 69:17
Ṣil-lí-ša   308:11'
Ṣil-lí-ᵈŠamaš   f. of ...-du, grandf. of ...ˈniˈ,
307:i 8'
Ṣ[í]-iṣ-ˈṣú- na-wiˈ-ra-at   s. of ᵈSi[n]-ri-me-ni,
44:10 (w)
ˈŠaˈ-ilim   184:2
Ša-ì-lí-šu   160:1; 168:4, 9, 12
Ša-ir-mu-uš-ši   167:4
Ša-ka-ap-ḫu   216:12

Ša-al(?)-du(?)-ra-mu   216:15
Ša-ma-...   268:ii 16
Ša-ma-ia   s. of A-píl-Ku-bi, 62:17 (w)
ˈŠa-maˈ-ia-tum   f. of Ig-mil-Sin, 68:17
ᵈŠamaš-...
1) s. of A-ˈmurˈ-na-ar-bi-[šu], 123 (s)
2) f. of Im-gur-ᵈŠamaš, 30:24
3) f. of ...-na, 52:14
4) 268:iv 10'
ᵈŠamaš-...-ˈtimˈ   268:iii 3'
ˈᵈŠamaš-aˈ-...   273:3
ᵈŠamaš-a-bi-ˈliˈ
1) s. of Ba-ˈdiˈ-ia, 44:14 (w)
2) 269:11
ᵈŠamaš-a-bu-um   7:10; 139:10; 229:9
ˈᵈŠamaš-ˈaˈ-bu-ˈniˈ   169: rev. 3'
ᵈŠamaš-a-ia-ba-aš   323:1
ᵈŠamaš-ˈapˈ-ti (?)   275:5
ᵈŠamaš-ba-ni   51:4; 267:8
ᵈŠamaš-be-el-i-lí   s. of I-ku-un-pi-šu, 62:
11 (w)
ᵈŠamaš-dajjan(DI.K[U₅])   242:15
ᵈŠamaš-ga-ˈmilˈ   270:4
ˈᵈˈŠamaš-gim-ˈlaˈ-an-ni   275:2
ᵈŠamaš-ˈḫa-zi-irˈ   s. of ˈᵈSinˈ-mu-ba-lí-ˈiṭˈ,
42:11 (w)
ᵈŠamaš-i-din-nam, ᵈŠamaš-ˈi-dìˈ-nam*
216:6; 268:i 8*
ᵈŠamaš-id(!)-na-an-ni   111:4
ᵈŠamaš-ilum
1) s. of A-da-rum, 79:21 (w)
2) 139:12
ᵈŠamaš-ˈkiˈ-...   242:15
ᵈŠamaš-ki-ib-ˈriˈ   s. of Warad-Tu-tu-ub(?),
63:15 (w)
ᵈŠamaš-ki-ma-...   s. of Ku-uš(?)-..., 72:12
(w)
ᵈŠamaš-ma-gir   308:9'
ᵈŠamaš-ma-ˈlikˈ   48:6
ᵈŠamaš-ˈmaˈ-ti   8:20
ᵈŠamaš-mu-uš-te-pí-iš, ᵈŠamaš-mu-uš-te(!)-
pí-iš*, ᵈŠamaš-mu-ˈuš-te(?)-pi-išˈ**
1) s. of Ú-še-pí 25 (s); 45:6
2) f. of Awīl-ᵈNIN.A.ZU, 73:11
3) f. of ᵈNANNA.ME.DÍM, 34:7*
4) f. of ᵈSin-e-ri-ba-am, 64:5
5) 65:4; 130 (s)**; 142:5; 237:6
ᵈŠamaš-na-...   s. of Ṣil-li-..., 35:19 (w)
ˈᵈˈŠamaš-na-ˈaḫˈ-ra-ri   169: rev. 13'

U-ˈx-x-el-lumˈ 146:3
ˈU-bar-x xˈRA^KI 311:rev. 4'
U-ba-ar-Lim f. of Za-ri-ru-um, 55:17
U-bar-^dŠamaš
    1) s. of Im-di-^dS[in], 44:18 (w)
    2) s. of Ma-nu-um-ki-..., 83:13 (w)
    3) f. of ^dSin-mu-ba-lí-iṭ, 58:11b
U-bar-rum
    1) f. of E-ti-rum and Ma-šum, 305:33
    2) b. of Pir-ḫu-um, 305:18
ˈÚ-kà-aš-ši-idˈ-ŠU-RA-AN(?) f. of ^dSin-na-ap-še-ra-am, 64:6
Ú-ul-lu-ša-mu 158:6
ˈUm-miˈ-... 169:12
Um-mi-ṭà-ba-at 158:5; 268:ii 7
ˈÚ-mu-ta-ˈmarˈ f. of A-ḫu-ni, 154:3
Up-... 275:6
Ú-ˈqaˈ-i-la f. of Warad-^dŠamaš, 47:14
Ur-^dKab-ta 21:1
Ur-Sa-ma-na 223:16; 241:16; 243:13
Ú-ṣi-na-wi-ir s. of Be-el-šu-nu, 46:4
Ú-ṣur(?)-pî(KA)-Ištar f. of Nu-úr-^dŠamaš, 44:17
Ú-ˈṣur(?)ˈ-šam-ša-ti 268:ii 3
Ú-ṣur-šu 216:5
Ú-še-pí
    1) f. of ^dŠamaš-mu-uš-te-pí-iš, 25 (s); 45:7
    2) 85:3
Uš-ˈtap(?)ˈ-pí(?)-ru 107:i 13
Uš-ta-aš-ni-Ilum 155:1
ˈÚ-ta-tumˈ 107:i 21
Ú.TU.I-... 83:rev. 1' (w)
Ú-túl-Ištar
    1) s. of Ba-si-ia, 79:5
    2) f. of Be-el-šu-nu, 305:11
    3) 162:1; 181:2
^dUTU.ZI.MU 33:4 (w)
Wa-ki-il-ì-lí 248:10; 249:4
Wa-qar-tum 270:1
Warad-...
    1) s. of ^dSi[n]..., 31:rev. 3 (w)
    2) 31:rev. 2 (w)
ˈWarad(?)ˈ-...-ˈḫuˈ-... 309:11
ˈWaradˈ-...šu 272:1
Warad-^dAdad 80:13 (w); 103:4
Warad-ˈA-la-mu-ušˈ(?) 256:2
Warad-^dAmurrim 8:5; 133:6
Warad-Ba-ri 139:19
Warad-^dEnlil f. of Warassa(ARAD-sà), 30:23

Warad-^dIlaprat
    1) f. of Warad-Ku-bi, 306:rev. 6
    2) 106:30
ˈWarad-Ilimˈ 213:1
Warad-ì-lí-šu
    1) s. of Ìl-šu-ba-ni, 45:14 (w)
    2) f. of I-din-Illum, 58:10; 64:14
    3) 26:2; 33:1 (w); 231:2; 241:2; 264:1; 270:3
Warad-^dIŠ 164:4
Warad-^dIštar, Warad-Ištar*
    1) s. of Ia-an-...-nu, 67:12 (w)
    2) s. of In-bu-ša, 305:44
    3) f. of ... -šu, 307:rev. i 7'
    4) f. of [Ḫu(?)]-za-lum, 307:rev. ii 7'
    5) 260:4*; 320:rev. 4'*
Warad-ˈKi-išˈ-ṣum 82:3
Warad-Ku-bi
    1) s. of Warad-^dIlaprat, 306:rev. 6
    2) s. of In-bu-ša, 305:9f
    3) s. of Ri-iš-^dŠamaš, 307:rev. ii 4'
    4) 54:10 (w); 308:6'
Warad-^dMa-mi 265:2
Warad-^dNanna 156:1; 268:i 2
Warad-^dSin, Warad-Sin*
    1) s. of I-túr-..., 83:15 (w)
    2) s. of I-pí-iq-ì-lí-šu, 235:8 (w)
    3) s. of Zi-kir-^dˈŠamašˈ, b. of A-wi-ˈliˈ-ia, 306:9*
    4) f. of Sin-a-bu-..., 251:9*
    5) 156:3; 168:3*; 179:8; 216:2*
Warad-^dSum[uqan(GÌR)(?)] f. of Puzur-Iš[tar], 79:14
Warad-^dŠamaš
    1) s. of Né-mé-lum, 84:11
    2) s. of Ú-ˈqaˈ-i-la, 47:13
    3) f. of Ḫu-za-lum, 71:2; 82:2
    4) 70:15 (w); 103:3; 257:11; 262:10
Warad-^dTišpak 31:16 (w); 106:25
Warad(?)-ˈTu(?)ˈ-... 315:rev. 8'
Warad-Tu-tu-ub(?) f. of ^dŠamaš-ki-ib-ˈriˈ, 63:16
Warassa (ARAD-sà)
    1) s. of Warad-^dEnlil, 30:22 (w)
    2) 119:6; 157:3
Wa-ar-du-um(-di-im)
    1) f. of Be-ˈlaˈ-nu-um, 305:12
    2) 222:3
We-di-be-lum
    1) f. of Na-bi-^dSin, 179:4

2) f. of ᵈSin-mu-ba-li-iṭ, 179:3
ᵈWi-ir-x-ˈxˈ 216:4
ᵈWi-ir-a-bu-šu 305:23
ᵈWi-ir-ˈba-niˈ 10:3
ˈWiˈ-ir-ba-ni-šu 11:1
ᵈWi-ir-da-ia-an 107:i 22
Wu-súm-ˈtumˈ 270:6
Za-... 48:4
Za-bu-lum f. of Ka-at-ri-ia and Maš-pa-lu-um, 151:4', 5'
ˈZaˈ-lu-pa-tum 268:ii 11
Za-ar-ḫu-... 307:rev. ii 14'
Za-ri-ru-um d. of U-bar-Li-im, 55:16 (w)
Za-ar-rum f. of Sin-mu-ba-lí-iṭ, 57:14
Za-tu-ˈma-ANˈ f. of ᵈSin-ri-me-ˈniˈ, 87 (s)
Zi-ia-tum f. of ... ˈNIˈ-ir-a-lum, 305:37
Zi-ˈkirˈ-Sin 178:2
Zi-kir-ᵈˈŠamašˈ f. of A-wi-li-ia and Warad-Sin, 306:rev. 8
Zi-ˈim-ra-tum(?)ˈ 112:12
Zi-im-ri-Ku-ku 264:3
Zi-ta-ˈanˈ-nu-um 252:3
ˈZuˈ-ba-... f. of A-ia-ˈḫaˈ-..., 214 (s)

...ᵈSin b. of A-pil-ᵈSin, b. of [AN]-ˈKAˈ-EŠ₄DAR 18:1
ˈxˈ-ᵈŠamaš 19:5
...li... 19:6
...ˈbaˈ-ni... 25 (s)
...am-mu-šu ˈxˈ 31:obv. 17
...tum(?) 32:5
...ru-mu-um 32:11 (w)
...ˈmaˈ-am PA 32:13 (w)
...-mi-il 32:14 (w)
...ˈkiˈ-el 32:15 (w)
ᵈ...bu s. of Šu-ᵈSin, 35:15 (w)
...nu-um f. of ˈᵈSinˈ-a-bu-šu, 36:16
ˈx-KA-iaˈ 37:3
...-ba-ni s. of ᵈSin-a-bu-[um], 40:rev. 5 (w)
...ḫa-tum... 41:rev 2' (w)
...ˈnuˈ s. of ˈE-ri-ba-amˈ, h. of Na-ˈra-am-tumˈ, 46:11
...ˈniˈ f. of ˈA-pil-ᵈENˈ..., 52:6
...na... f. of ᵈŠamaš ..., 52:13 (w)
ᵈˈxˈ-ta-x s. of Bi-ˈxˈ-Ilum, 55:12 (w)
...um s. of ᵈˈSin-pu-uṭ-rˈ[a-am], 56:6
...ᵈSin f. of ˈI-ku-unˈ-pí-ᵈEN..., 60:16
...i-na-ma-ti f. of Ri-iš-Tu-tu-ub, 65:6

...ˈišˈ-me-an-n[i] s. of ᵈˈŠamašˈ-na-ṣir, 68:14 (w)
...[i]-lí-šu 82:8 (w)
...ᵈˈŠamaš 82:9 (w)
...-ta-num f. of A-pil-Sin, 85:25
...bu-um 86:9 (w)
...ˈmuˈ-da-ni-iq 106:37
SAL ˈxˈ.[ÈŠ].NUN.NAᴷᴵ 107:i 19
...ˈtumˈ 107:ii 13
...ᵈ-NIN.A.ZU 108:9, 110:10
ᵈ... 127:13
...-Sin 129:3
...ˈliˈ 130:2
...ru f. of ... bi-ru-um, 151:11'
...bi-ru-um s. of ...ru, 151:11'
...a-tum 158:7
...-Akšak 160:5
...-ṣir 160:6
ˈx-ma(?)ˈ-ia 162:2
...ḫi-si 169:1
ᵈ... 169:rev. (d)
...nu-rum 226:rev. 1'
...-ša-mi-i 229:14
...-šar-rum 229:15
ˈxˈ-ta-ˈkuˈ-ru f. of ... ša ..., 233 (s)
...ˈbiˈ-KALA 237:7
ˈxˈ-ma-i-lí-ˈšuˈ s. of ˈx x'-Éˈ..., 246 (s)
ˈx x'-Éˈ... f. of ˈxˈ-ma-i-lí-šu, 246 (s)
...-gamil 268:i 5
...-kum 268:i 6
ˈx x'-ma-ra-aṣ 268:iii 9'
...kum 268:iii 11'
...-ma 268:iii 13'
...nu-um 268:iii 14'
...ˈáš-gaˈ-nu-um 268:iii 16'
...bil 268:iii 17'
...-Ištar 268:iii 19'
...-Ištar 268:iv 14'
...bi 271:rev. 5
...-ram 272:2
ˈᵈˈ...ni 272:3
...num 272:5
...mi 272:10
ˈxˈ-LUGAL 275:6
ᵈEN... 300:2', 4'
...ˈILLATˈ-tí 305:26
...ˈNIˈ-ir-a-lum s. of Zi-ia-tum, 305:37
...ᵈ... 307:obv. i 1'
...NE f. of PN (not preserved), 307:obv. i 3'

...e...   b. of PN (not preserved), 307: obv.
  i 4'

...me-Sin f. of PN (not preserved), 307
  obv. i 5'

...ᵈTISPAKˈ 307: obv. i 9'

...šu   b. of [A(?)]-ˈlum(?)ˈ-wa-qar, 307: rev. i
  5'

...šu   s. of Warad-ᵈIštar, 307: rev. i 7'

...du   s. of Ṣíl-lí-ᵈSamaš, f. of ... ni, 307: rev.
  i 8'

...ni   s. of ...ˈduˈ, grands. of Ṣíl-lí-ᵈSamaš,
  307: rev. i 9'

...ib...   307: rev. ii 9'

...na   s. of ᵈIlaprat-a-bu, 309: 1

...ˈANˈ   f. of ˈA-pilˈ-ᵈSamaš 309: 15

ᵈx-x-um(?)-ti-x-x   f. of PN (not preserved),

f. of ...na-ṣir, grandf. of ...še-mi, 311:
  obv. 2'

...na-ṣir   s. of PN (not preserved), grands. of
  ᵈx x-um(?)-ti-x-x, 311: obv. 3'

...-še-mi   s. of PN (not preserved), grands.
  of ᵈx-x-um(?)-ti-x-x, 311: obv. 4'

...NI   s. of ˈNu-úrˈ-ᵈSamaš, b. of ..., uncle
  of ...A, 311: rev. 7'

...A   s. of ..., grands. of ˈNu-úrˈ-ᵈSamaš,
  nephew of ... NI, 311: rev. 8'

...-iš-me   s. of ... ᵈSin 312: 4

...-ᵈSin   f. of ... iš-me 312: 5

...ˈeˈ-ri-iš   312: 6

...ra-at   s. of ..., b. of [A]-ˈtaˈ-kal-ši, 312: 10

...-ma-ra-aṣ   313: rev. 2'

...tu...   321: 1

II. INDEX OF TITLES AND PROFESSIONS

AGA.UŠ   23: 2', 4'

AŠGAB   162: 9

DAḪ   306: 2, rev. 3, 9; 307: obv. ii 2', 4',
  9', rev. ii 8', 10', 12', < <15'> >, 17',
  21'; 308: 4', 9'; 309: 7, 12; 310: ii 7'; 314:
  1, 12; 316: 1; 318: 2

DAM.QAR   85: 18; 305: 18, 21

DI.KU₅   9: 4; 25: 5, 28; 26: 3; 268: iv 2', 8'

DIRI(SI), DIRI*   307: obv. ii 5', rev. ii 18',
  22'*; 309: 8; 313: 9f*; 315: rev. 14'*; 316:
  1*; 317: obv. ii 2'; 318: 3.

DUB.SAR   12: rev. 9; 20: 18; 30: 22; 31:
  16; 45: 24; 49: 14; 52: 18; 68: 18; 70: 13;
  71: 13; 76: 11; 81: 14; 82: 10; 169: 11;
  270: 9

DUMU É ṭup-pí   60: 14; 305: 15, 51

É.GI₄.A É   5: 1; 6: 1; 7: 1

EN   106: 36

ERÍN, ṣa-ba-am*   4: 13*; 17: 16; 151: 13';
  305: 6, 9, 11, 13; 306: 11; 313: 9-12; 314:
  8, 14, 16, 17, 18; 315: rev. 7', 9', 10',
  11', 12'; 316: 2; 317: obv. ii 1'; 318: 1

ERÍN ḪUN (?)   305: 24

ERÍN KÁ É.ˈGALˈ   313: 2; 315: rev. 9'

ERÍN.SAG, (ERÍN).SAG*   305: 48; 316:
  1*

ERÍN um-ma-tim   313: 3

GAL.MAR.TU   23: 7'

GÌR.NITÁ   24: 16; 68: 10; 70: 3, 9

GÚ.GAL, GU.GAL*   226: 2*; 268: iii 18'

GURUŠ   4: 14, 19, 24; 275: 17

GURUŠ É   274: 1

GU.ZA.LÁ(!)   91: 8

ik-ka-ru-um, ik-ka-ri*   4: 8*; 261: 8

ˈKA.KIˈ, ka-ki(!)-k[u₈-<um>]*   118 (s);
  121 (s); 125 (s); 126 (s); 168: 3*

LÚ.BAPPÍR (ŠIM)   31: rev. 13; 133: 6

LUGAL   17: 16; 24: 13; 30: 15; 32: 9; 35:
  14; 36: 14; 90: 16 (Y); 91: 21 (Y); 294: 6';
  305: 53 (Y); 314: 22 (Y) 315: rev. 5' (Y);
  320: obv. 14'

LÚ.ḪUN.GÁ, LÚ.ḪUN*, ḪUN**   234:
  2; 242: 16**; 272: 11; 273: 9; 274: 2, 3;
  308: 3-4*; 323: 8

LÚ KU₆.ÚS.SA   41: rev. 3'; 94: 12

LÚ.ŠÀ.GUD   137: 5

LÚ.TÚG   179: 2; 216: 7

LÚ.TU(?).TA   163: 6

LUKUR   87: 3, env.

LUKUR ᵈUTU, na-di-tum ša ᵈUTU*   30:
  6f; 45: 4; 77: 8*

MÁ.LAḪ₄, ma-la-ḫi-im*   128: 4*; 169: 6

MAŠ.EN   187: 4; 188: 4; 191: 3; 192: 5;
  196: 5; 197: 3

MAŠ.KAK.EN, MAŠ.EN.KAK*, 16: 13*;
  183: 5; 184: 3; 185: 3; 186: 4; 189: 5; 190:

III. INDEX OF DIVINE NAMES*

IV. INDEX OF PLACE NAMES*

* The GNs in no. 319 have not been included in the
index; they appear to be part of a scribal school
list, similar to the Harmal Geographical Lists and the
list cited by Jacobsen in OIP 43 128⁴³. See now also
Hh XXI, MSL 11 8-20, 34-63.

...ᵗtu-tuᴷᴵ᾽ 307: obv. i 2'
...ᵗpa-šumᴷᴵ᾽ 307: obv. i 6'
...ᵗsu(?)-si(?)-niᴷᴵ᾽ 307: rev. i 10'
...ᵗa-tuᴷᴵ᾽ 310: i 6'
...ᵗᴷᴵ᾽ 311: rev 2', 9'
x x LUGAL 314:19

...tum 316:3
...bi-ta-aš-šu-ulᴷᴵ 317: obv. i 2'
...ši(?)-ni-a-tumᵗᴷᴵ᾽ 317: obv. i 3'
...úḫ(?)-nu-umᵗᴷᴵ᾽ 317: obv. i 4'
...riᴷᴵ 317: rev. 8'
...ᵗᴷᴵ᾽ 317: rev. 10'

V. INDEX OF MONTH NAMES

ITU A-bi-i, A-bu-ú* 91:19; 133:4; 146:
8*; 147:10; 152:7; 252:7
ITU BARAG.ZAG.GAR 314:21
ᵗITU DIRI ša᾽ Ki-in-kum 42:19
ITU ᵈDUMU.ZI 90:14; 117:4; 121:6;
133:2
ITU E-lu-num, 125:3; 128:8
ITU Ki-in-kum 74:9; 76:12; 78:11; 81:
15; 114:4; 130: rev. 1; 231:6
ITU Ki-nu-nu-um, Ki-nu-nu*, Ki-nu-nim**,
Ki-nu-ni*** 46:6**; 113:4*; 132:6**;
140:5**; 145:9*; 148:12; 179:12*; 228:
9***; 232:4**
ITU Kir-ri-tim 93:2; 120:2; 123:1
ITU Ki-is-ki-súm, Ki-is-ki-si* 95:9*; 118:
5; 126:3; 149:10; 215:6
ITU Ma-aq-ra-tum, Ma-aq-ra-tim* 92:16;
219:4*; 225: rev. 3*
ITU ᵈMa-mi, ᵈMa-am-mi* 29:14; 115:4;
131:6; 273:11*

ITU Ma-am-mi-tim 323:10
ITU MÁ.AN.NA 98: rev. 6'
ITU Maš-kán-nim 76:7
ITU Na-ab-ri-i, Na-ab-ri*, Na-ab-ru-ú**
43:8; 44:7; 45:8**; 93:7, 9; 112:13; 119:
7*; 274:5
ITU Níg-gal-lim 96:6; 129:4; 136:16;
137:15; 236:5
ITU SIG₄.A 326:55
ITU Ša-ad-du-tim 49:7; 74:5; 81:7
ᵗITU ŠE.KIN᾽.KUD 305:52
ITU Tam-ḫi-ri, Tam-ḫi-ru*, Tám-ḫi-ri-i**
93:4; 106:38**; 116:4; 140:6, 13; 214:
6*; 233:6*; 272:13*
ITU Za-ḫa-ra-tum, Za-ḫa-ra-tim* 93:4*;
134:6; 181:5*; 228:4
ITU Zi-ᵗib᾽-num 138:12

PLATES

The tablet copies presented here represent the joint efforts of the writer and Thorkild Jacobsen. Prof. Jacobsen began working on the purchased Ishchali tablets shortly after their acquisition (see Preface, Introduction); he generously made these copies available to the writer for incorporation into this book. The copies were re-edited by the author, who takes full responsibility for errors. Prof. Jacobsen's copies are : nos. 2-3, 6, 8, 15, 22-25, 29 (obverse), 33, 34 (envelope), 35, 43-45, 48-49, 51, 55, 57, 60-61, 63-68, 70-71, 73-74, 76, 78 (reverse), 79-82, 84, 90-94, 108, 110, 117, 132, 136, 138, 140, 143, 145, 148-150, 153, 158, 163, 217, 220, 228-229, 243, 247, 263, 305-306, 307 (reverse), 308-314, 316, 318-325 — i.e., 82 total copies plus 4 partial copies. All other copies and all seal impressions are the work of the author.

1

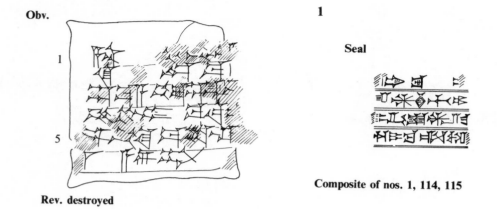

Obv.

1

5

Rev. destroyed

Seal

Composite of nos. 1, 114, 115

2

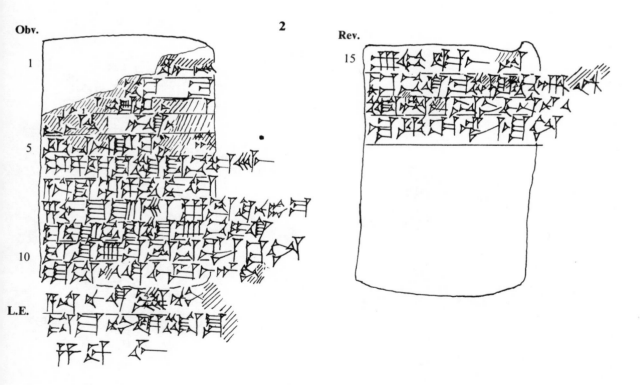

Obv.

1

5

10

L.E.

Rev.

15

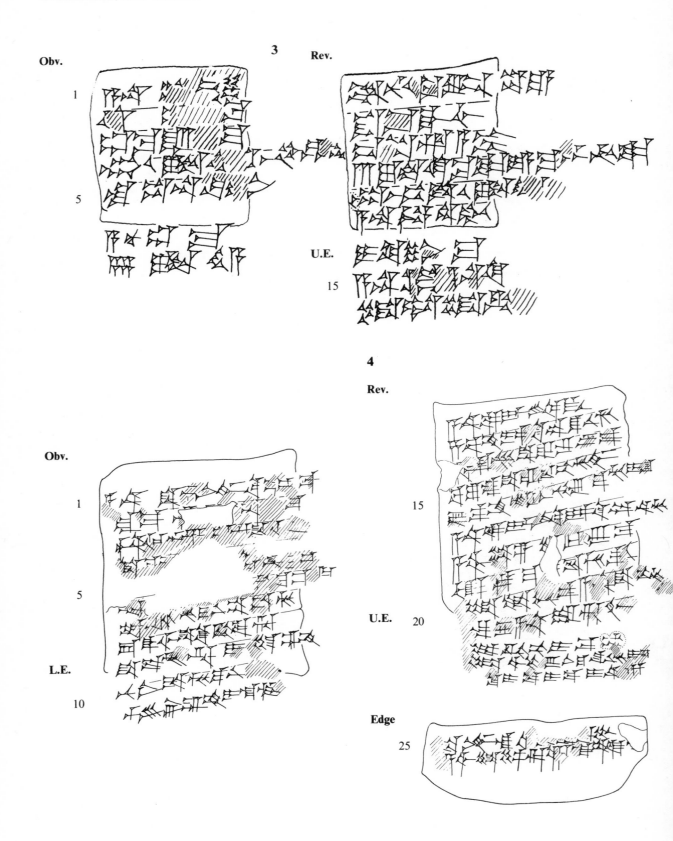

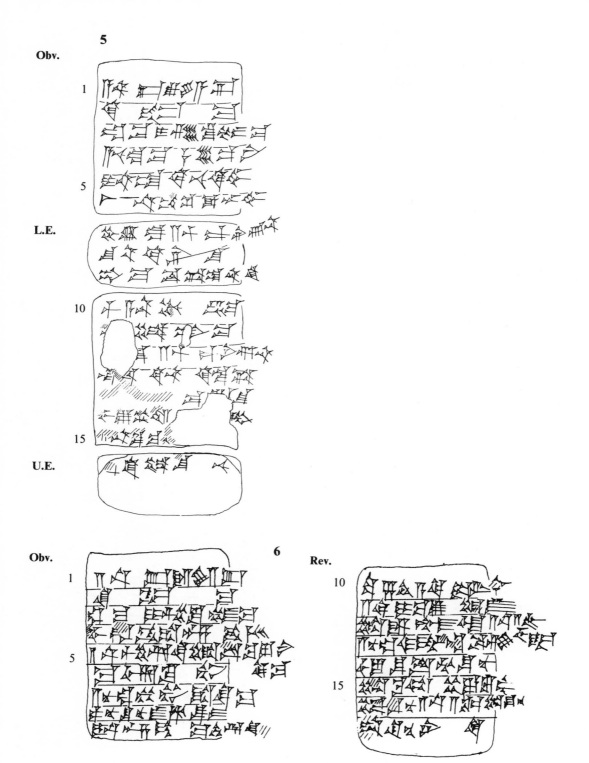

Obv.

7

1

5

Rev.

10

U.E.

15

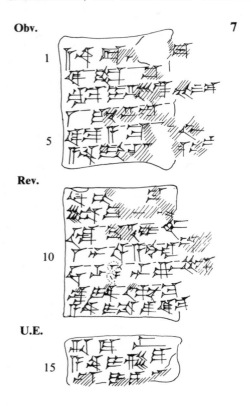

8

Obv.

1

5

L.E.

Rev.

10

15

U.E.

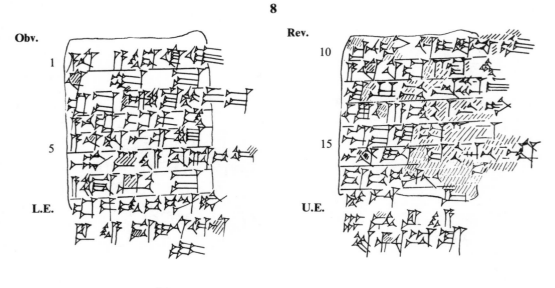

Edge

20

9

Obv.

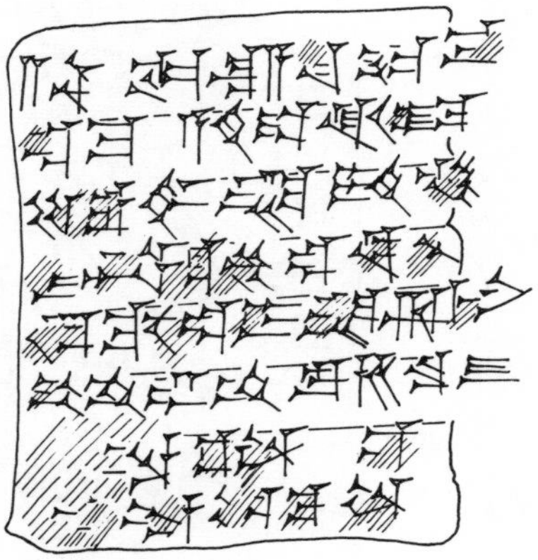

1

5

L.E.

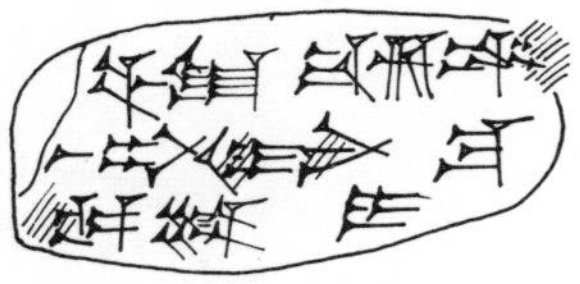

10

Rev.

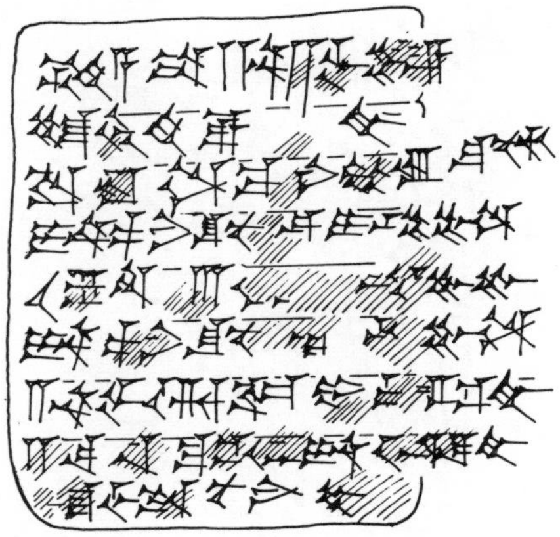

15

20

U.E.

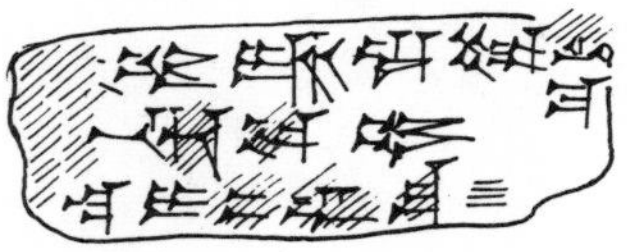

Edge

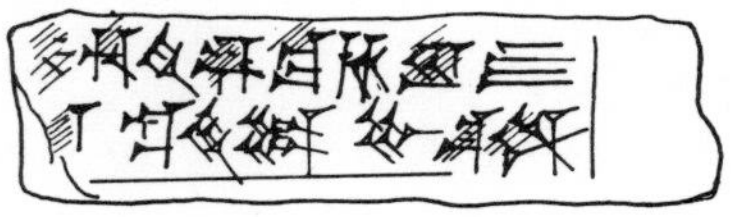

25

10

Obv.

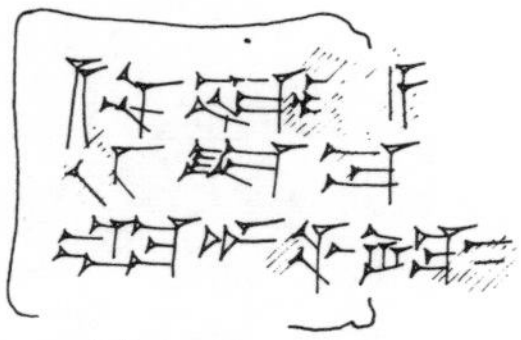

1

L.E.

5

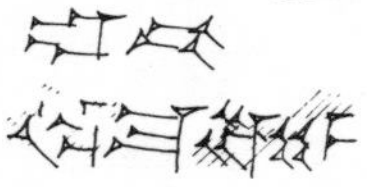

Rev.

U.E.

11

Obv.

Rev.

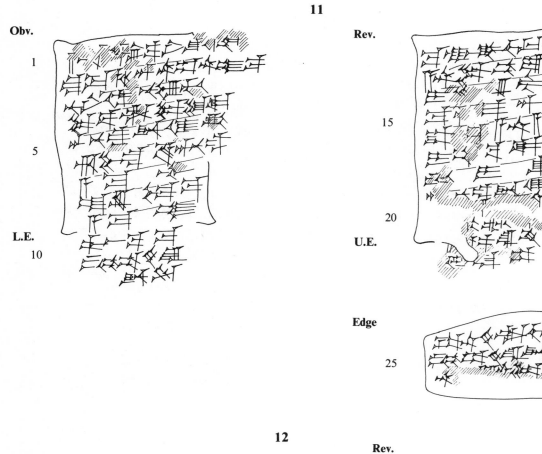

1

5

L.E.

10

15

20

U.E.

Edge

25

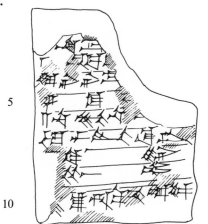

12

Obv.

Rev.

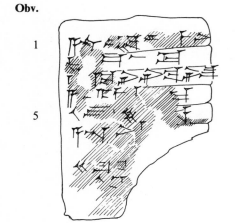

1

5

5

10

13

Obv.

1

5

10

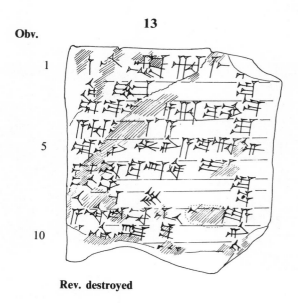

Rev. destroyed

14

Obv.

Rev.

1

5

10

1′

5′

10′

U.E.

15′

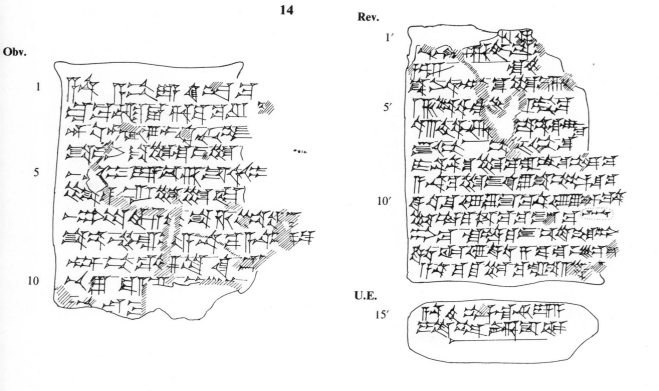

15

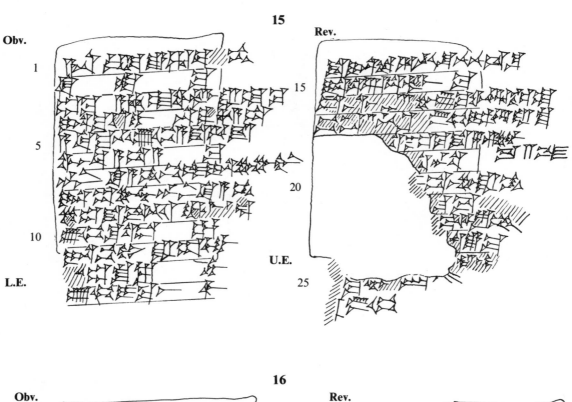

16

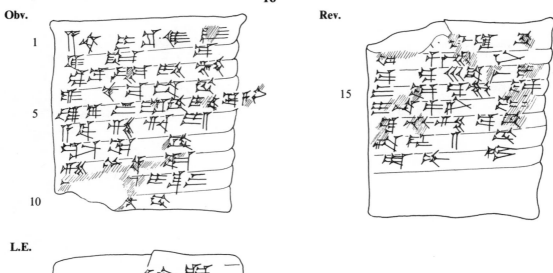

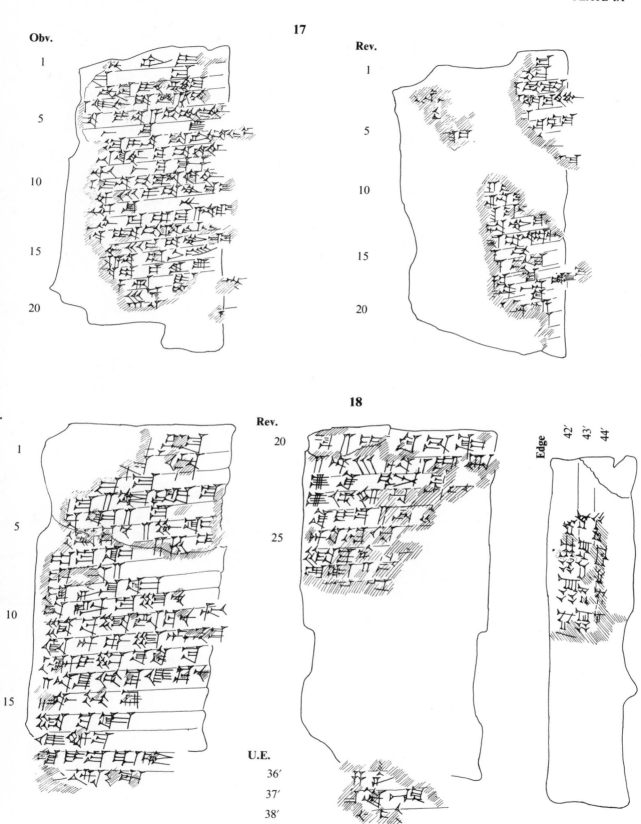

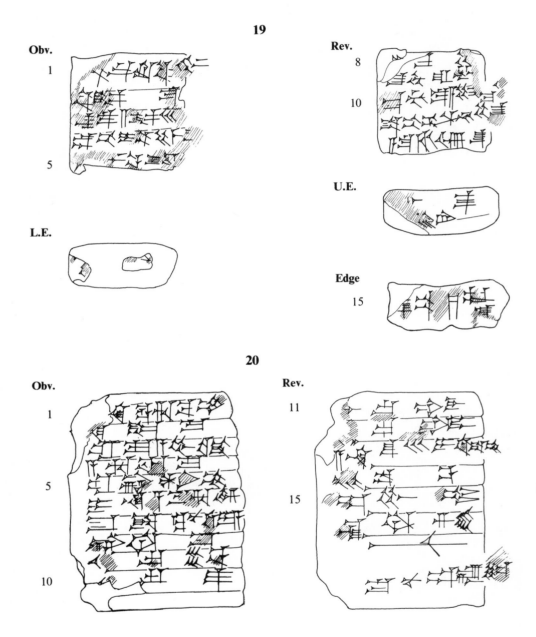

19

Obv.

Rev.

L.E.

U.E.

Edge

20

Obv.

Rev.

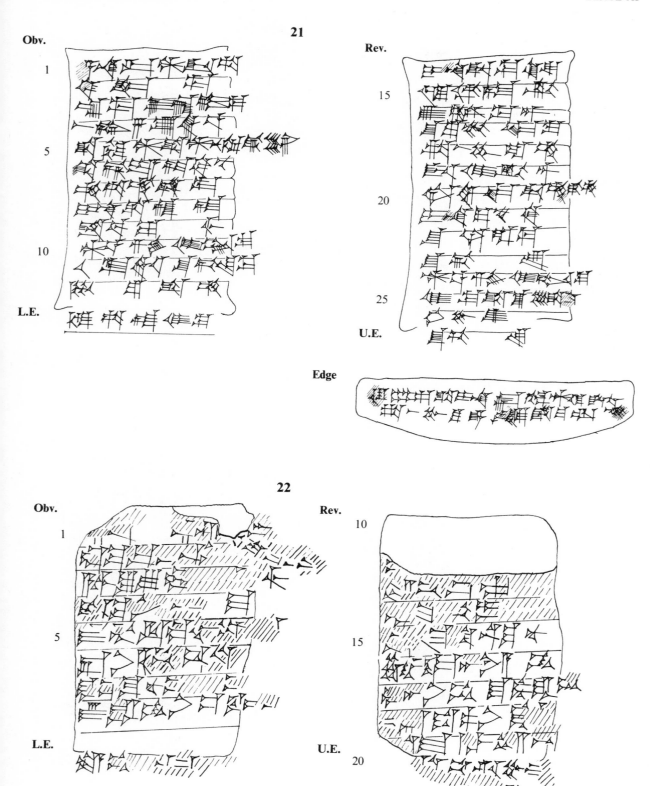

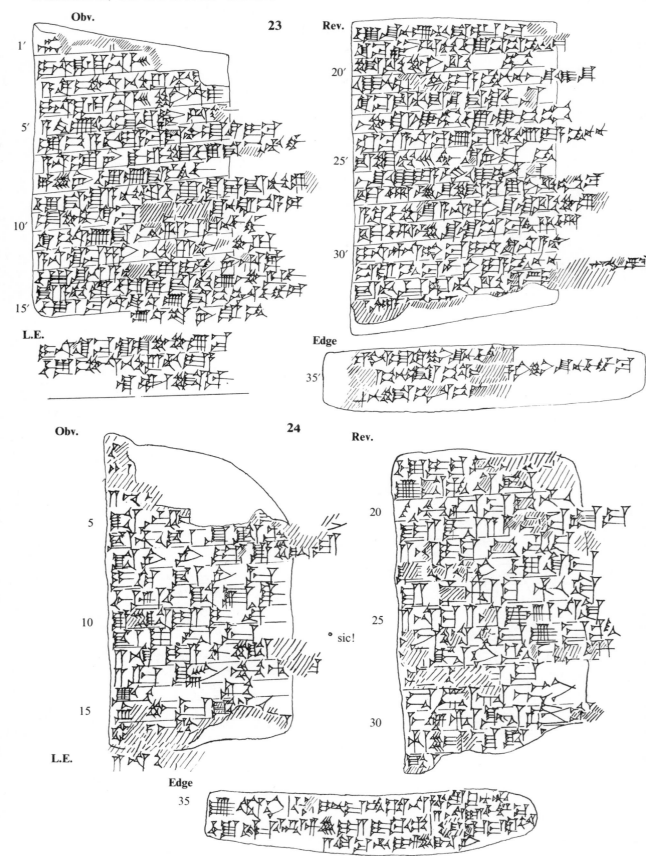

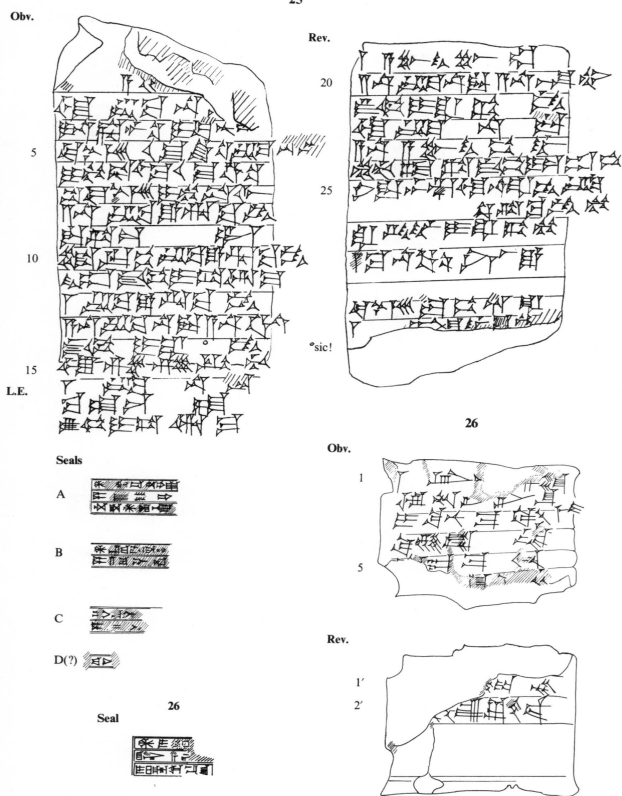

25

Obv.

Rev.

20

5

25

10

°sic!

15

L.E.

26

Obv.

1

5

Seals

A

Rev.

B

1′

C

2′

D(?)

26

Seal

Composite of nos. 26, 300

27

Obv.

1′

5′

Rev.

10′

L.E.

10

28

Obv.

1′

5′

Rev.

8

10′

15′

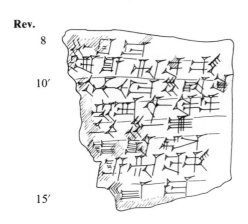

29

Obv.

1

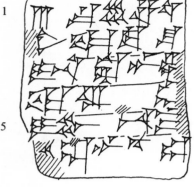

5

Env. frag.

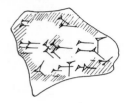

Rev.

7

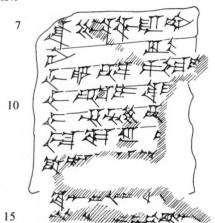

10

15

Edge

Seal

composite

30

Obv.

Env. variants

1

5

L.E.

10

Seals

A

B

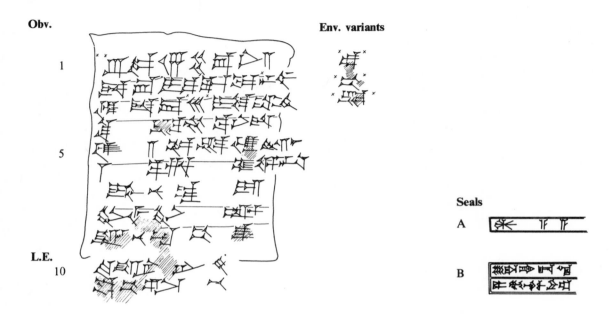

Rev.

15

20

U.E.

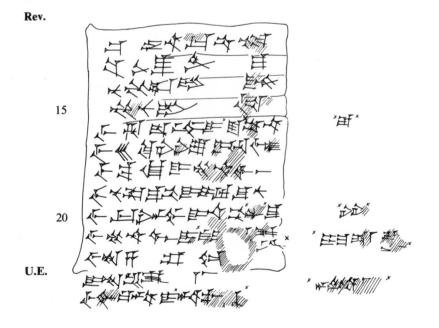

31

Obv.
1

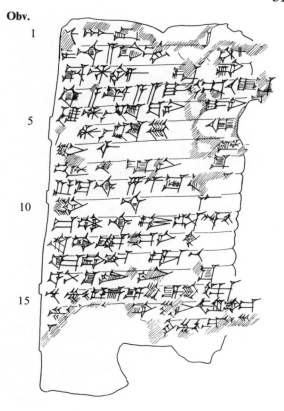

5

10

15

Rev.
1

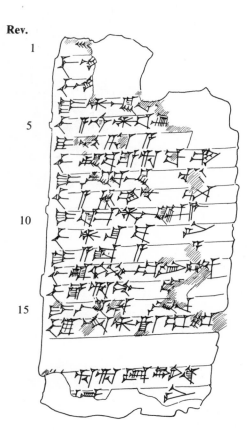

5

10

15

32

Obv.
1

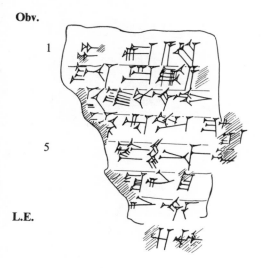

5

L.E.

Rev.
9

10

15

33

Obv.

Rev.

U.E. 15

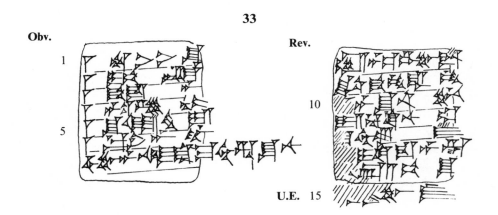

34 Tablet

Obv.

Rev.

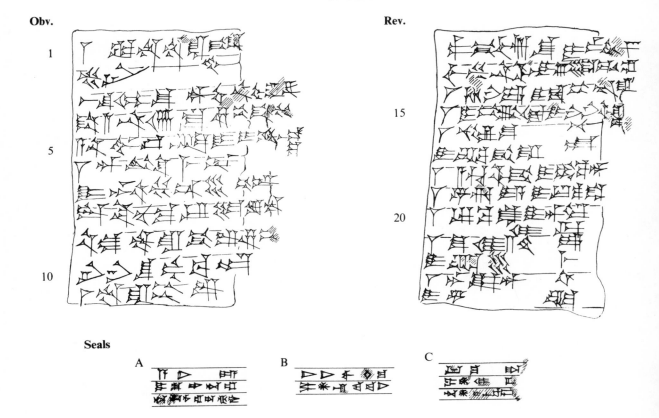

Seals

A

B

C

34 Envelope

Obv.

Rev.

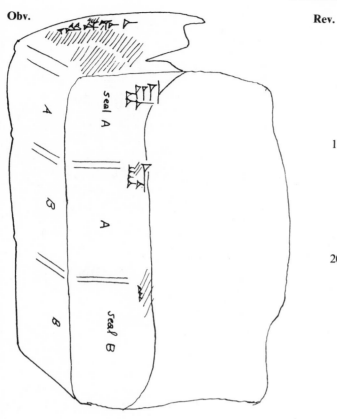

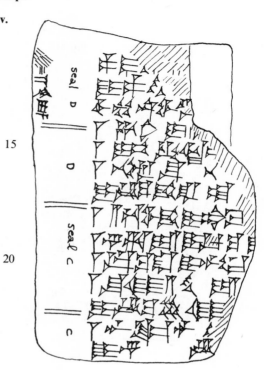

35

Obv.

Rev.

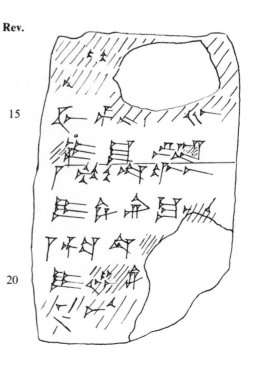

36

Obv.

Rev.

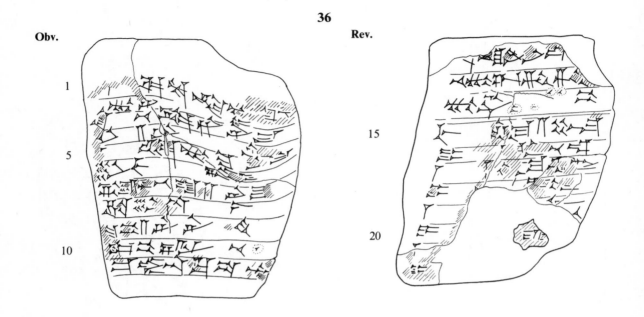

37

Obv.

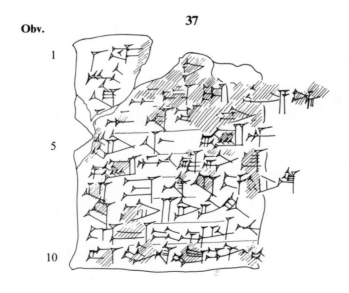

Rev. uninscribed

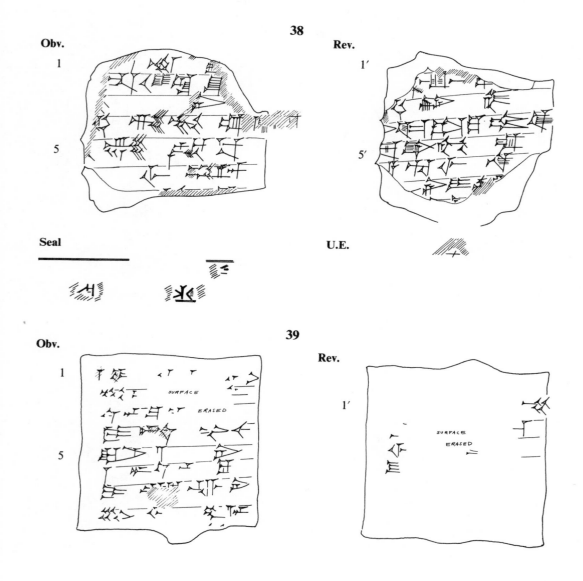

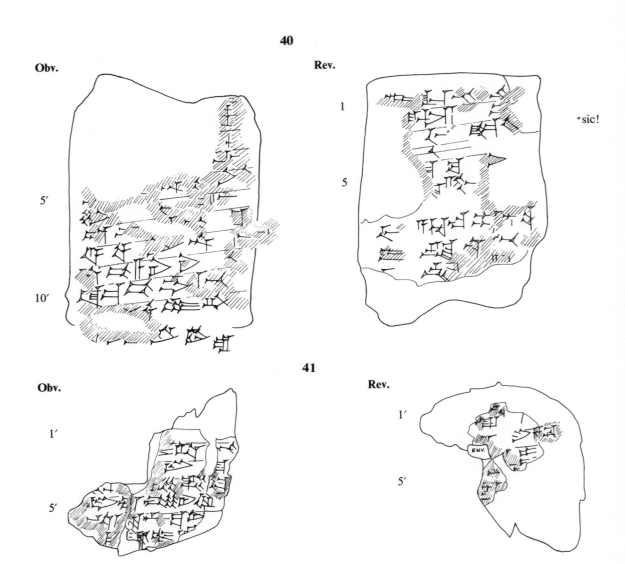

40

Obv.

Rev.

1

5

°sic!

5′

10′

41

Obv.

Rev.

1′

1′

5′

5′

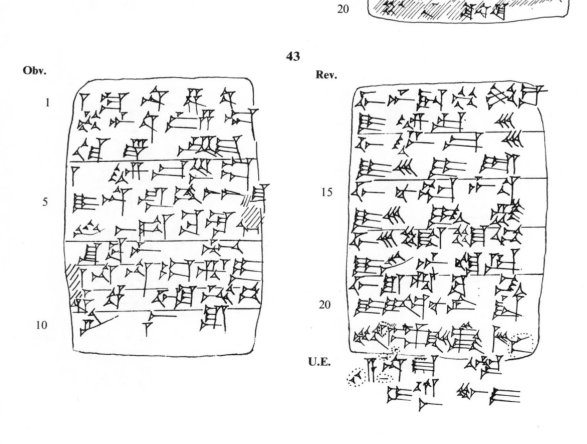

44

Obv.

20

1

5

Rev.

10

15

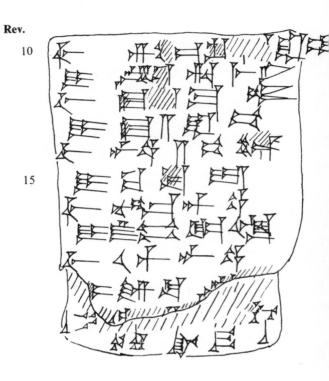

45

Obv.

1

5

10

L.E.

° sic!

Rev.

15

20

U.E.

25

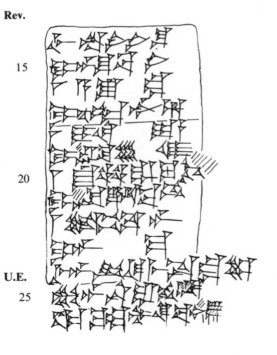

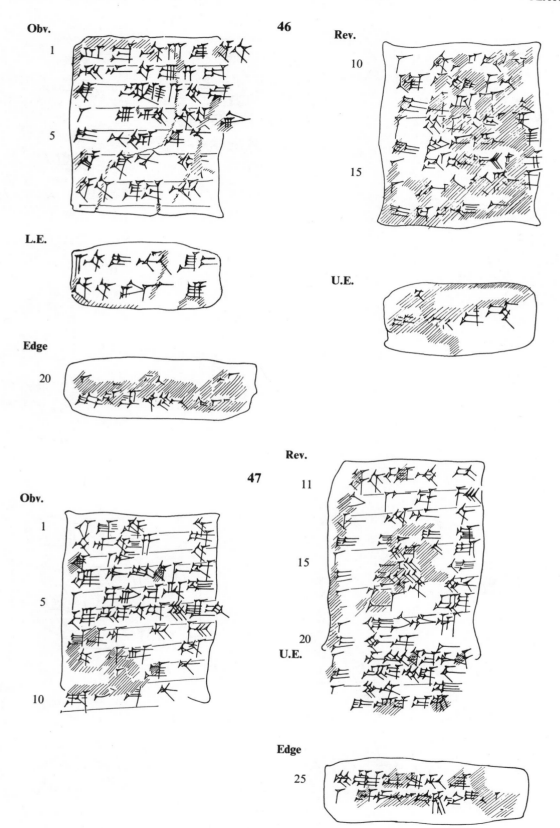

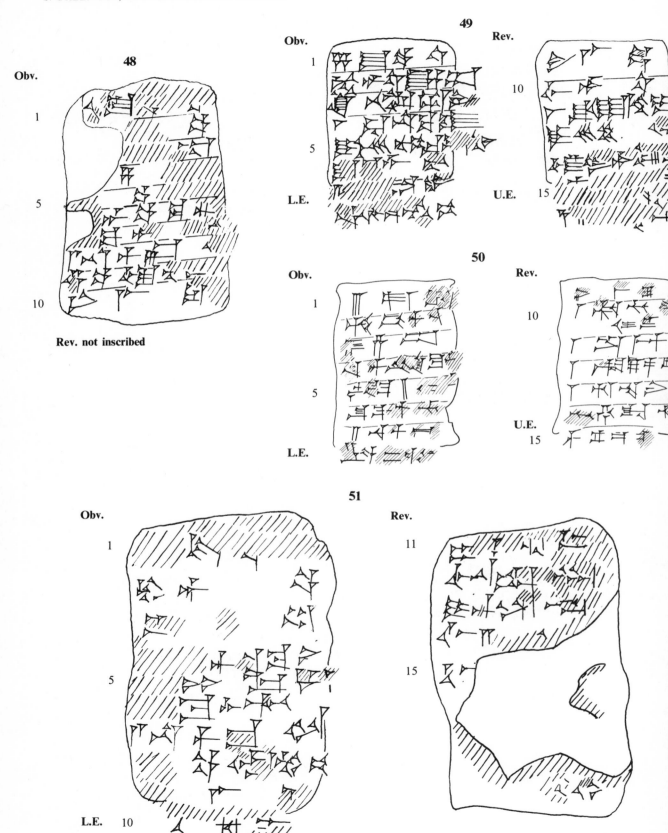

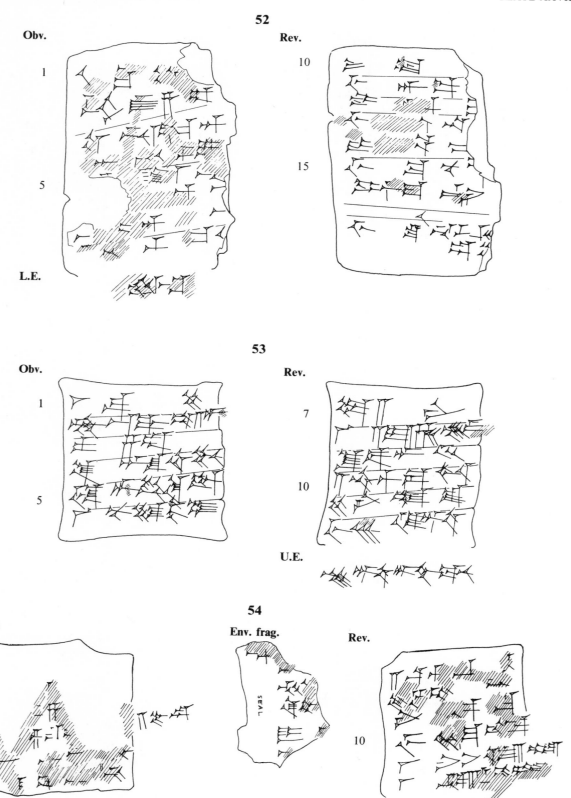

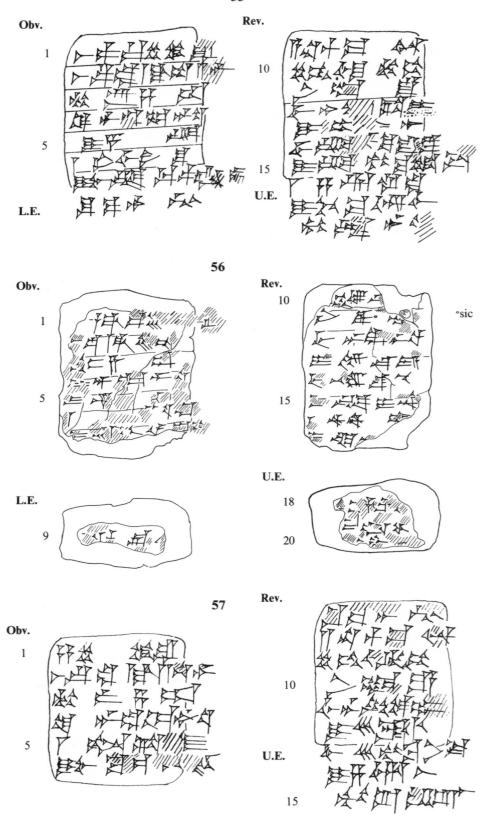

58

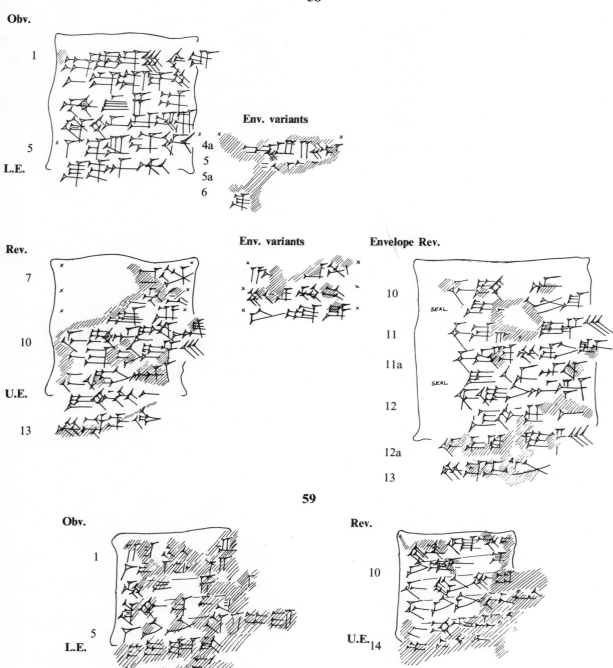

Obv.

1

5

L.E.

Env. variants

4a
5
5a
6

Rev.

7

10

U.E.

13

Env. variants

Envelope Rev.

10

SEAL

11

11a

SEAL

12

12a

13

59

Obv.

1

5

L.E.

Rev.

10

U.E. 14

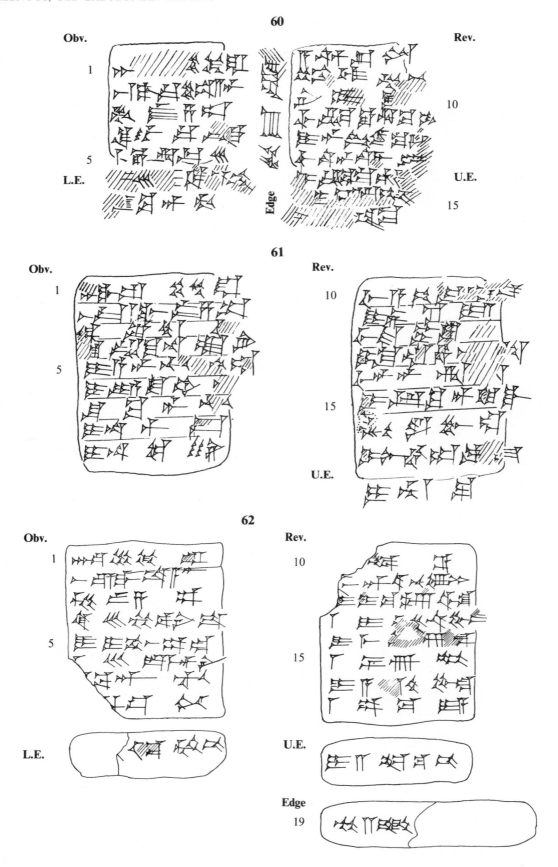

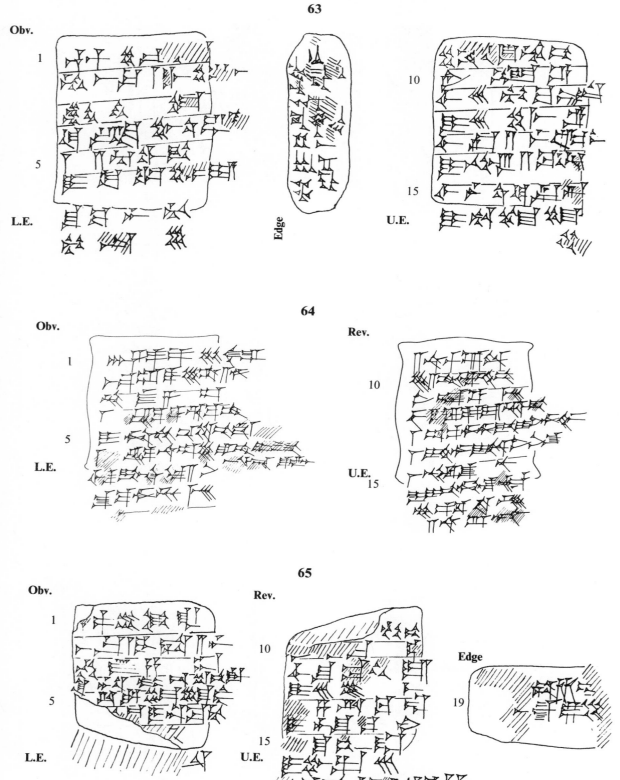

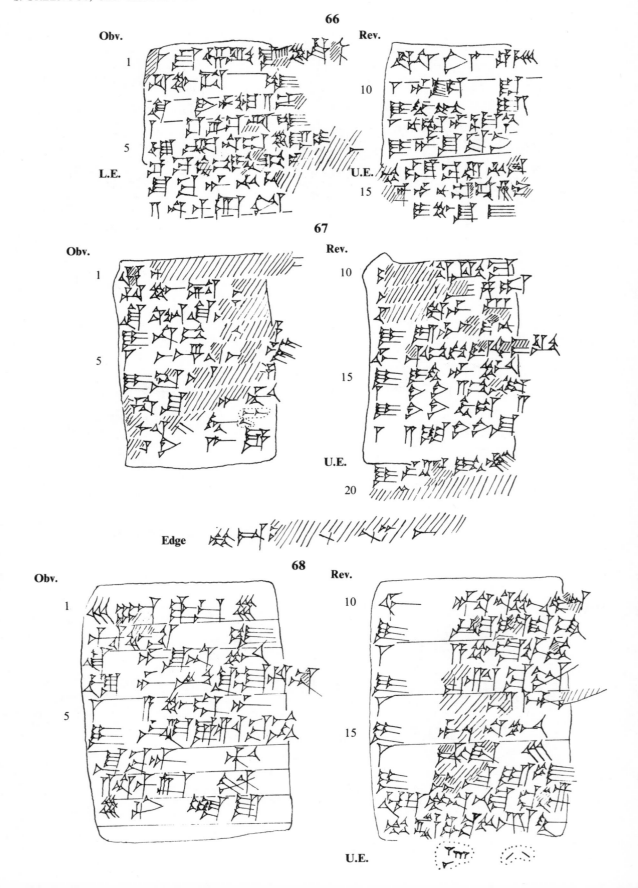

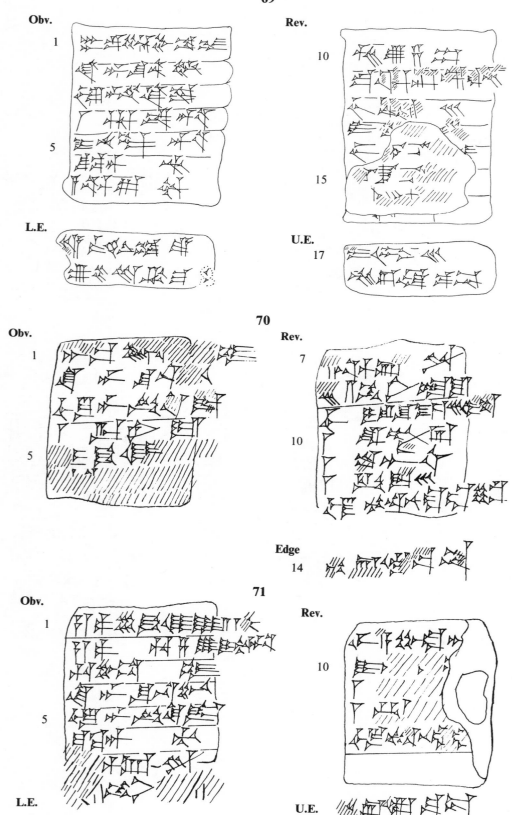

72

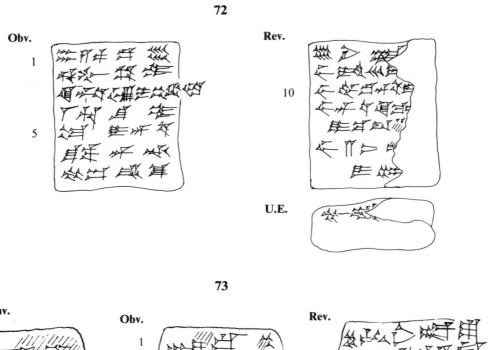

73

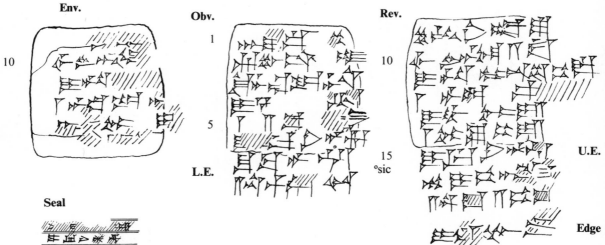

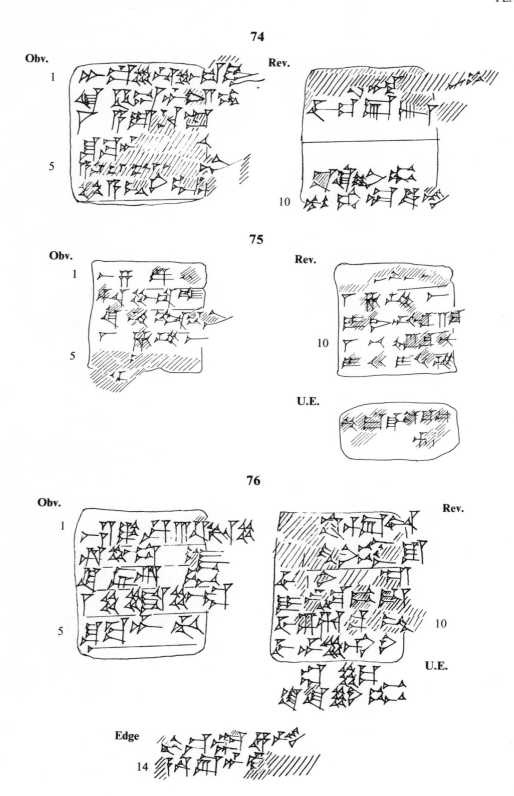

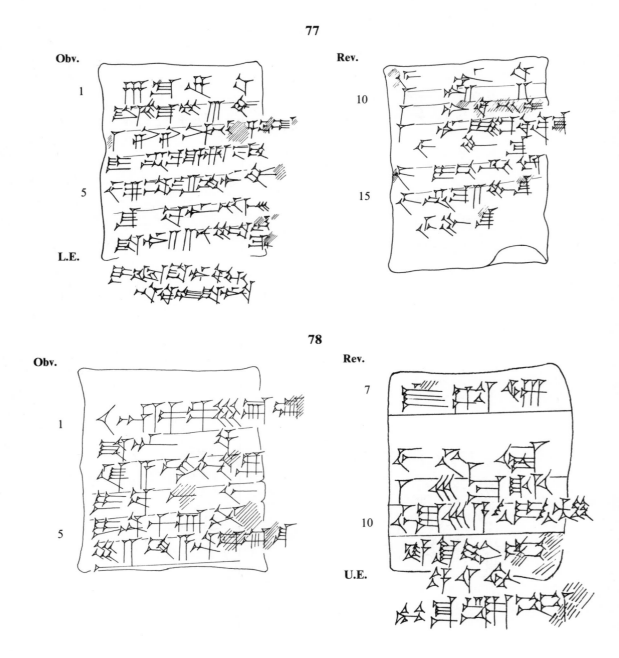

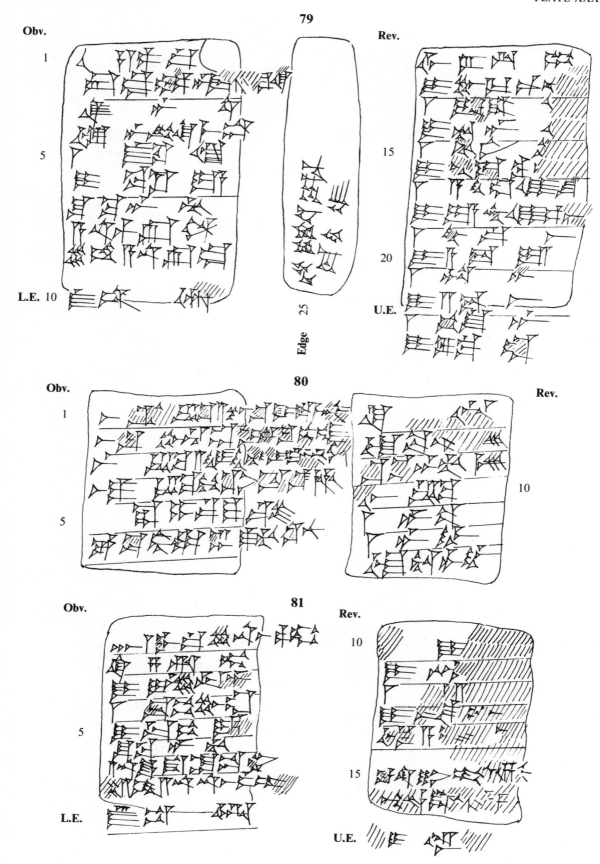

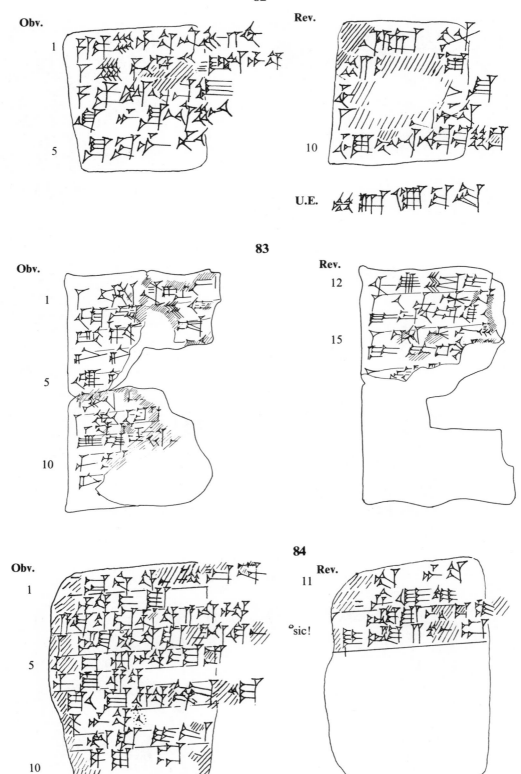

85

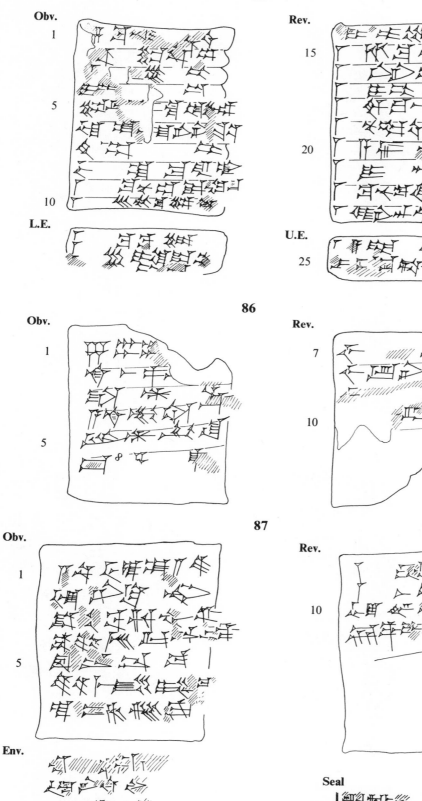

87

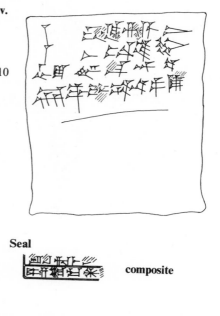

composite

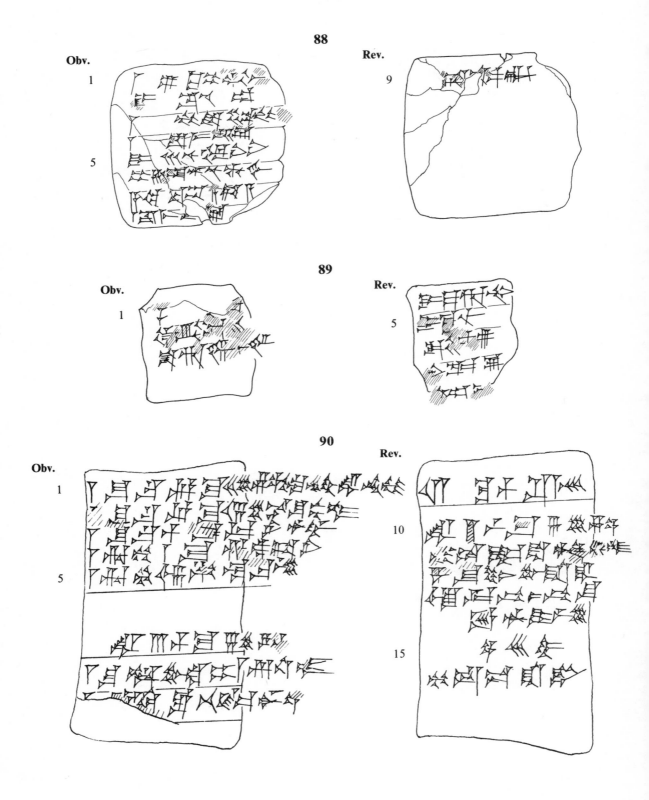

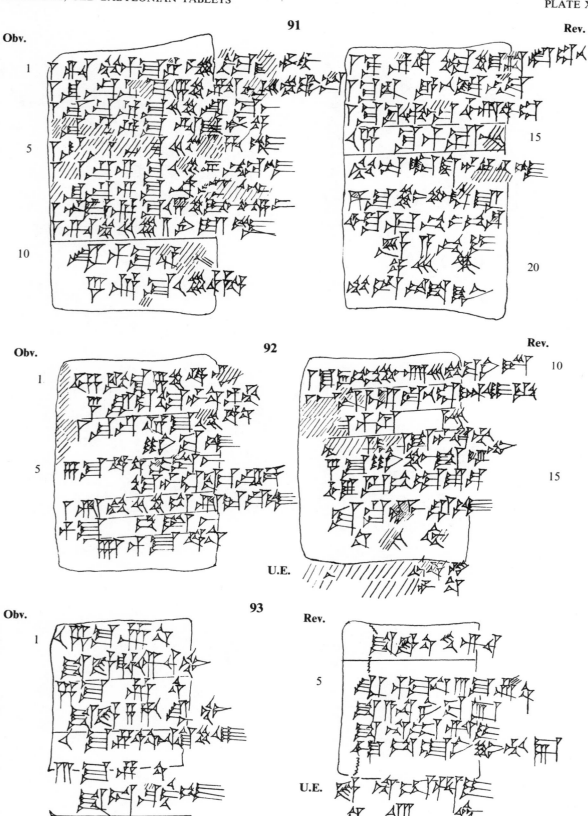

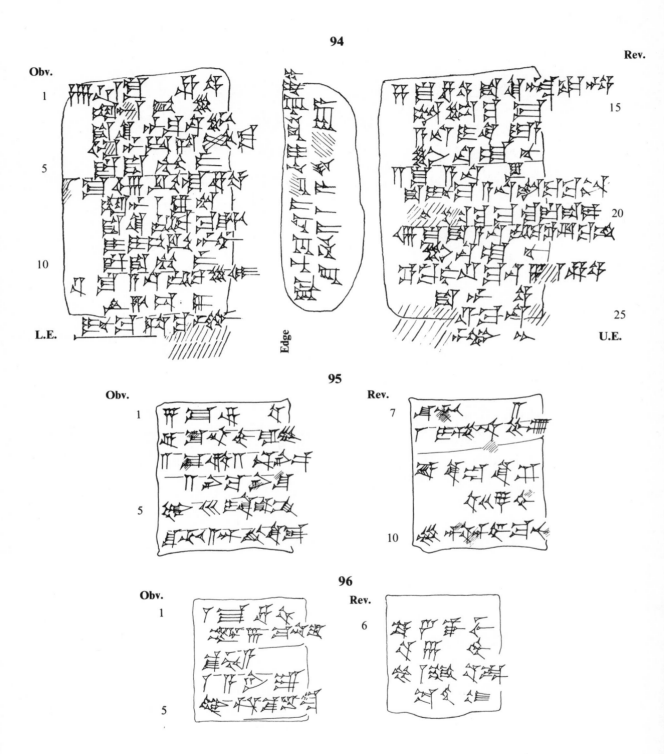

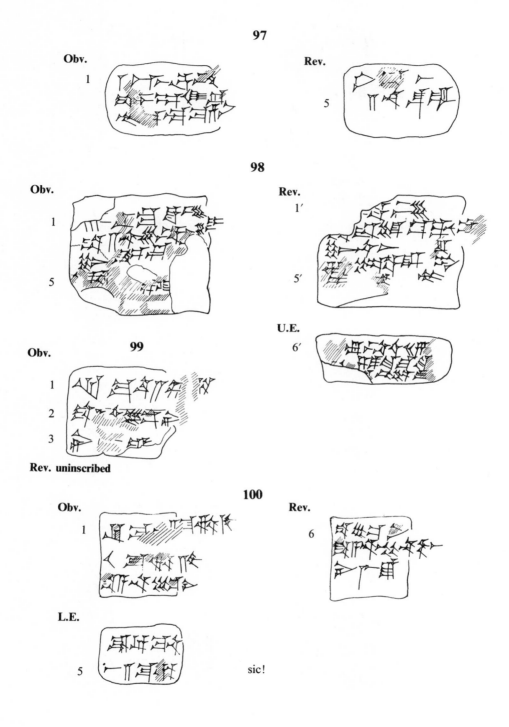

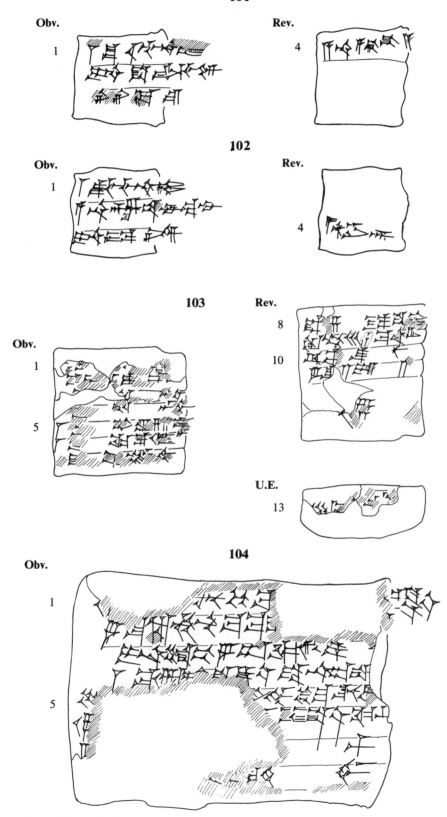

101

Obv.

1

Rev.

4

102

Obv.

1

Rev.

4

103

Rev.

8

10

Obv.

1

5

U.E.

13

104

Obv.

1

5

Rev. not inscribed

105

Obv.

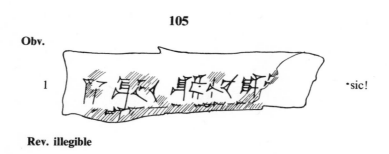

1

·sic!

Rev. illegible

106

Obv.

Rev.

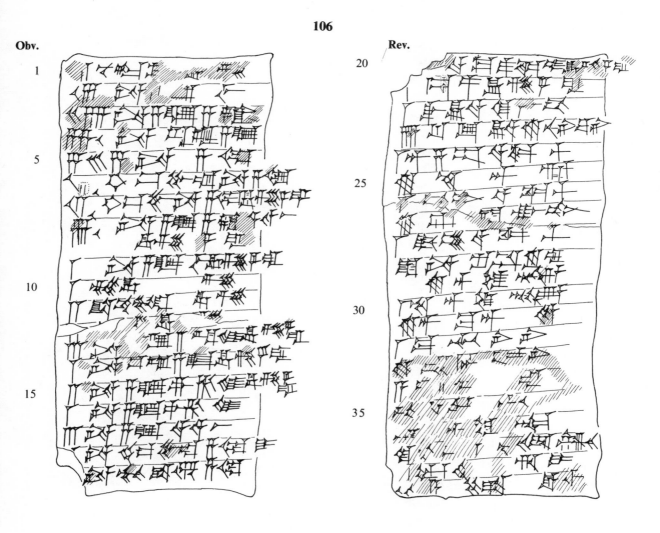

107

Obv.

col. i

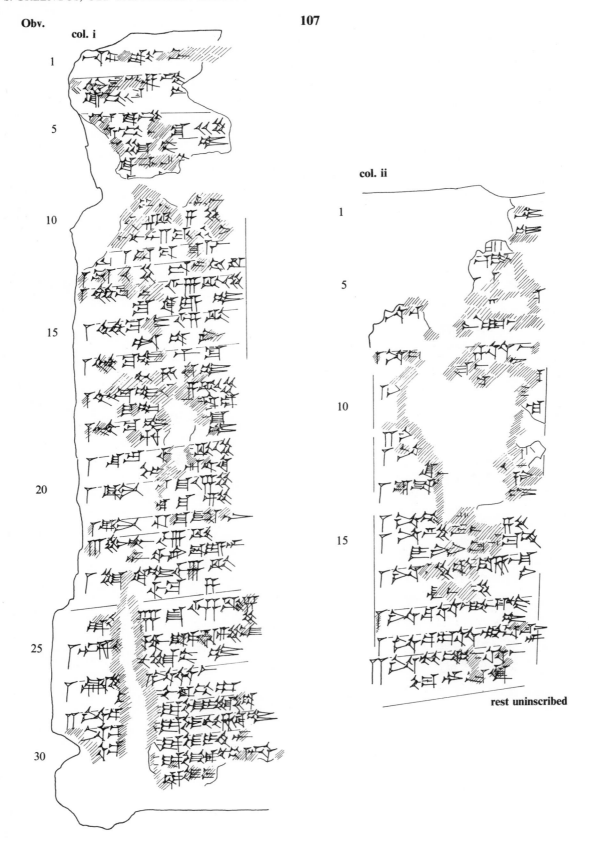

col. ii

rest uninscribed

108

Obv.

Rev.

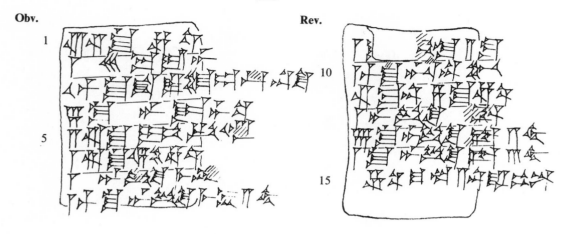

109

Obv.

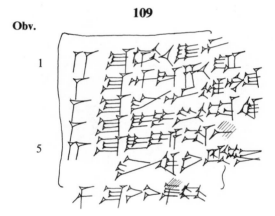

Rev. uninscribed

110

Obv.

Rev.

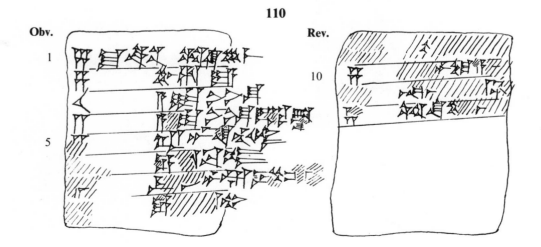

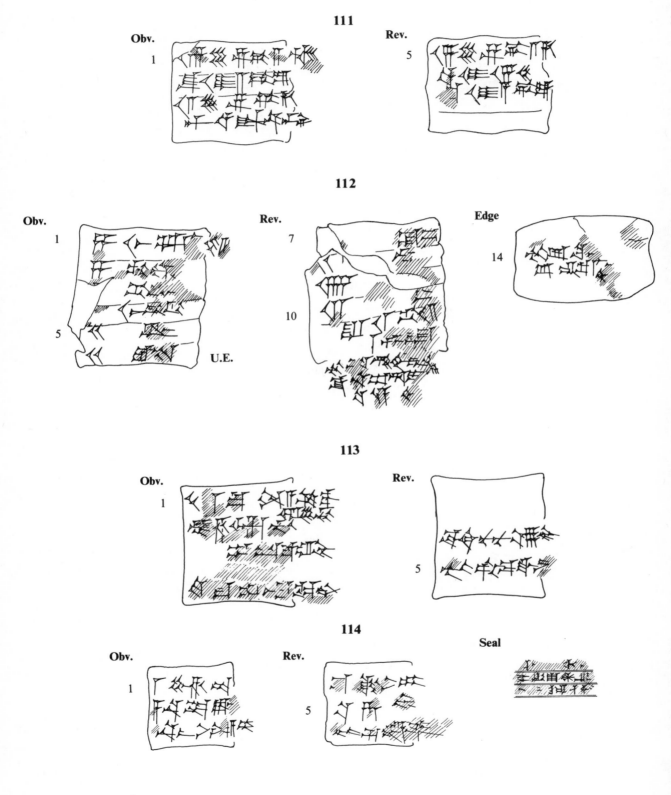

115

Obv.

1

Rev.

5

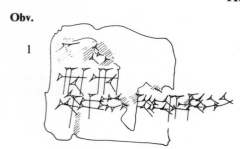
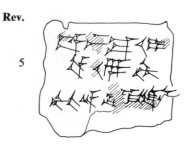

116

Obv.

1

2

Rev.

3

4

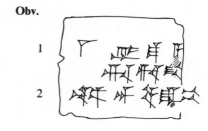

117

Seal

Seal

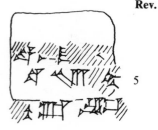

Obv.

1

Rev.

5

118

Obv.

1

Rev.

5

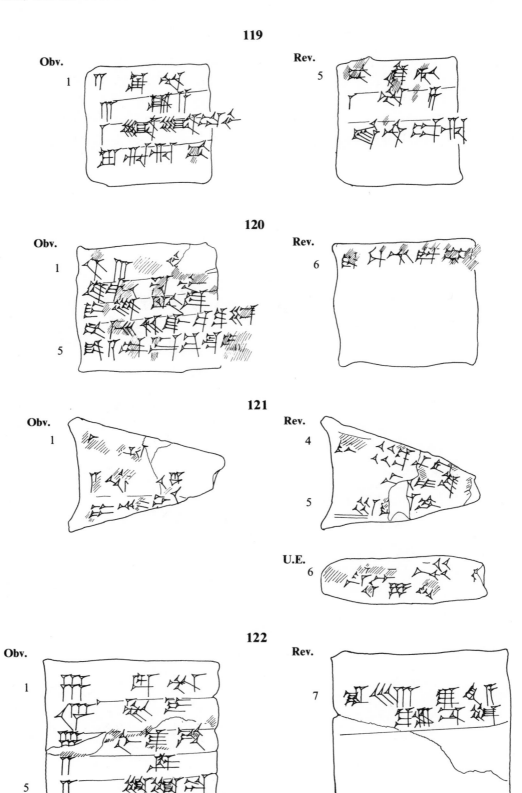

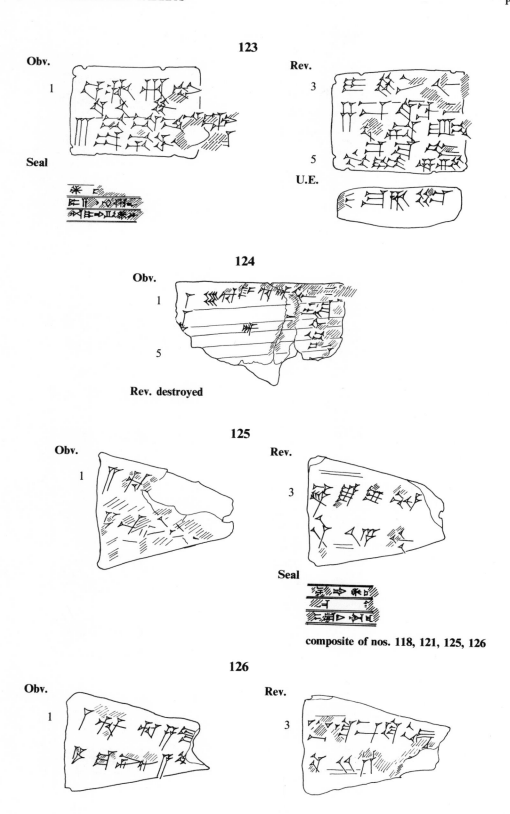

123

Obv.

1

Seal

Rev.

3

5

U.E.

124

Obv.

1

5

Rev. destroyed

125

Obv.

1

Rev.

3

Seal

composite of nos. 118, 121, 125, 126

126

Obv.

1

Rev.

3

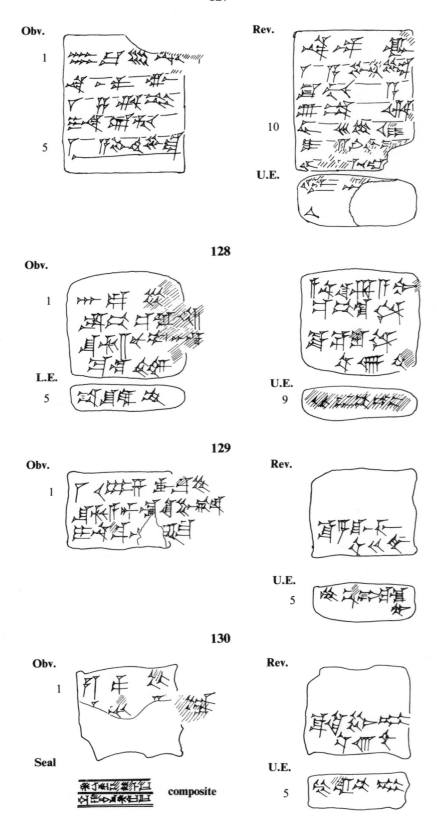

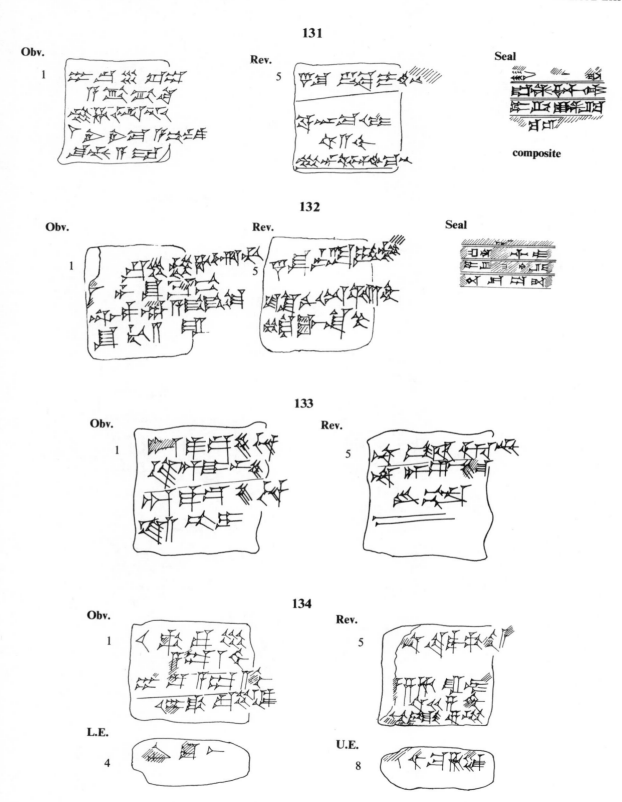

131

Obv.

Rev.

Seal

composite

132

Obv.

Rev.

Seal

133

Obv.

Rev.

134

Obv.

Rev.

L.E.

U.E.

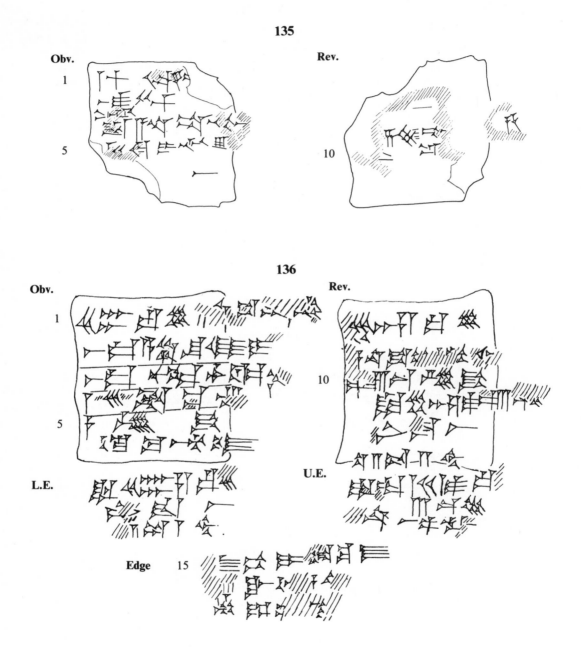

137

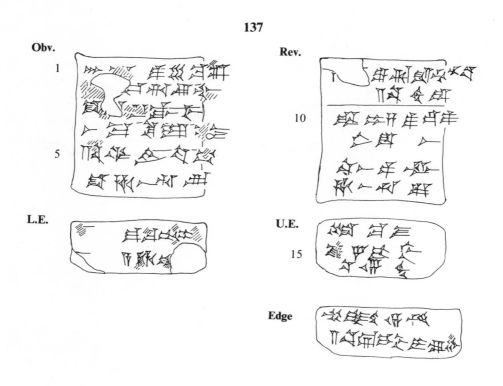

138

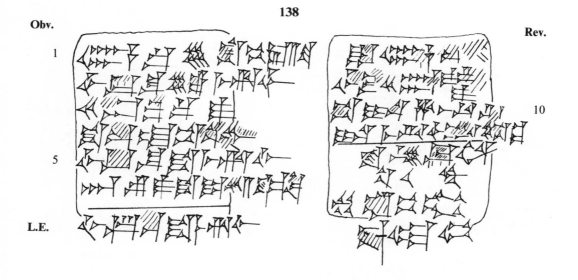

139

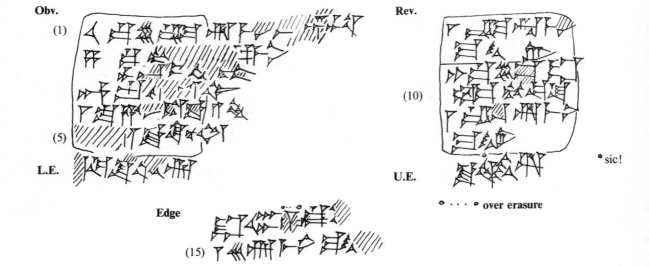

140

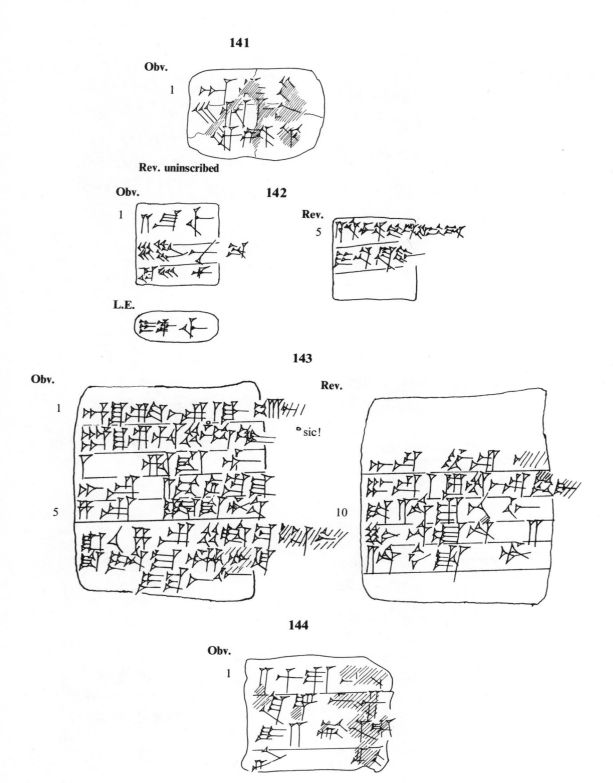

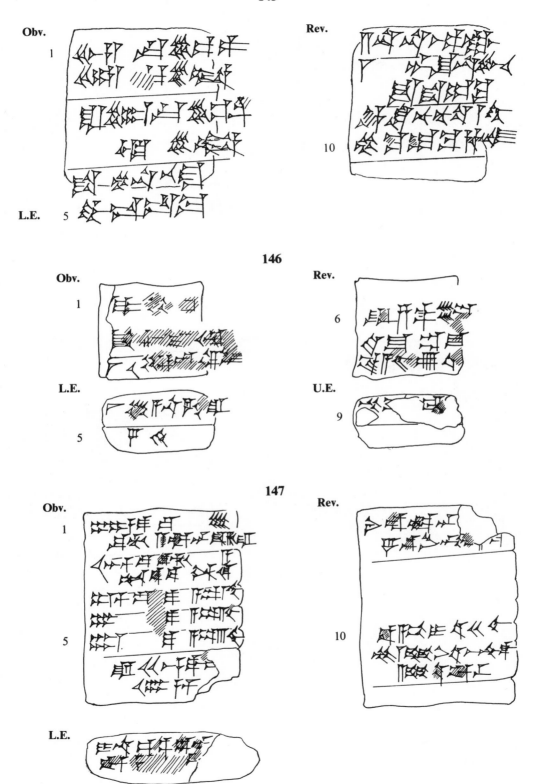

148

Obv.   Rev.

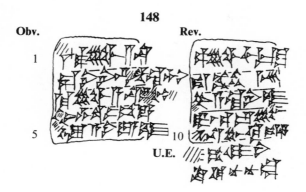

U.E.

149

Obv.   Rev.

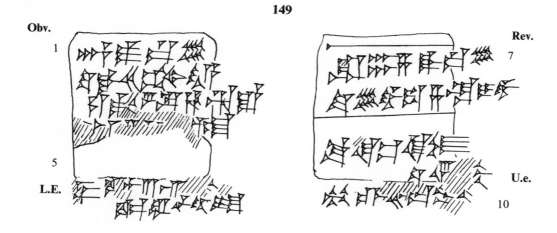

L.E.   U.e.

150

Obv.   Rev.

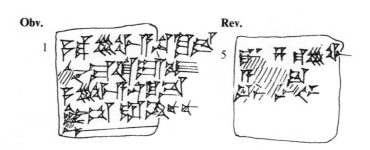

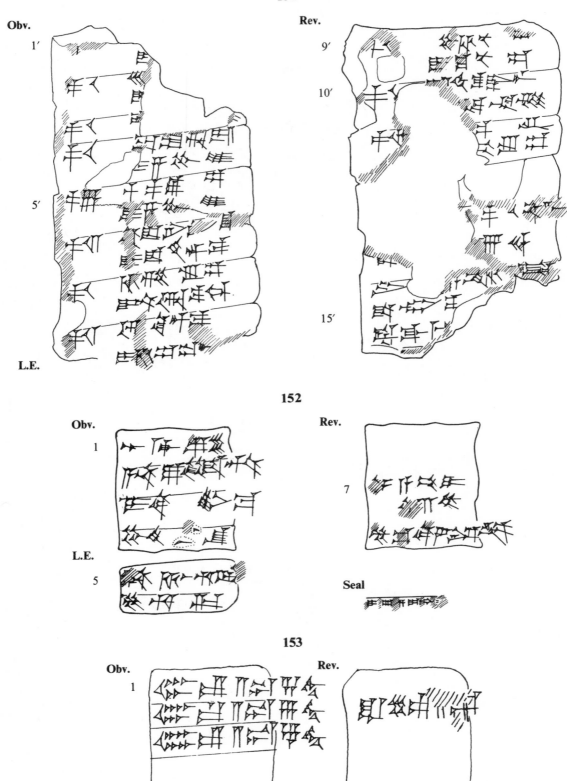

154

Obv.

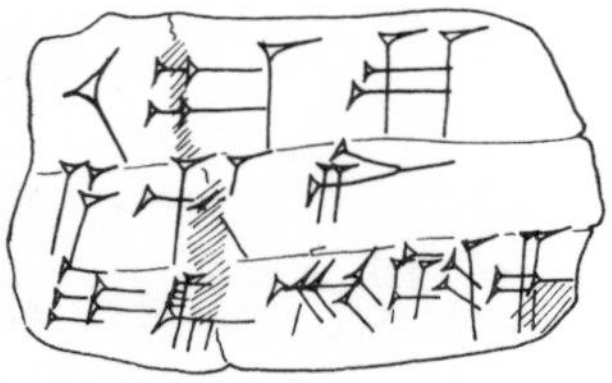

Rev. uninscribed

155

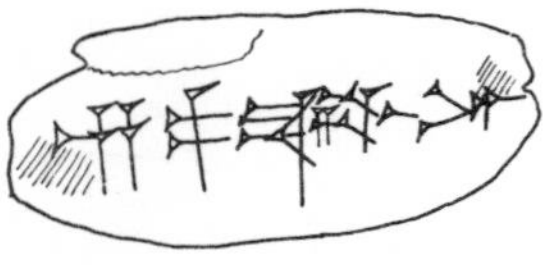

156

Obv.

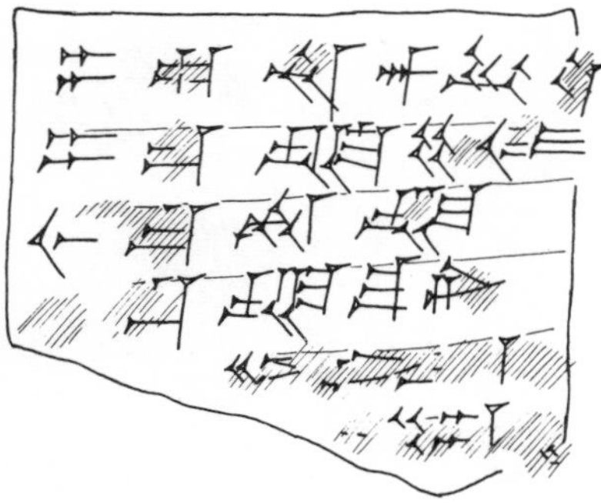

Rev.

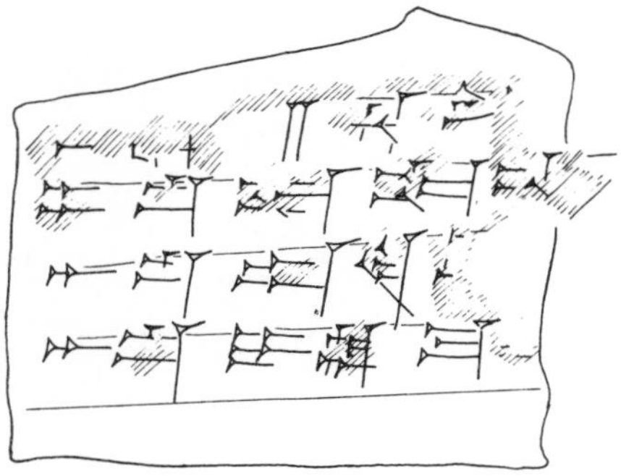

157

Obv.

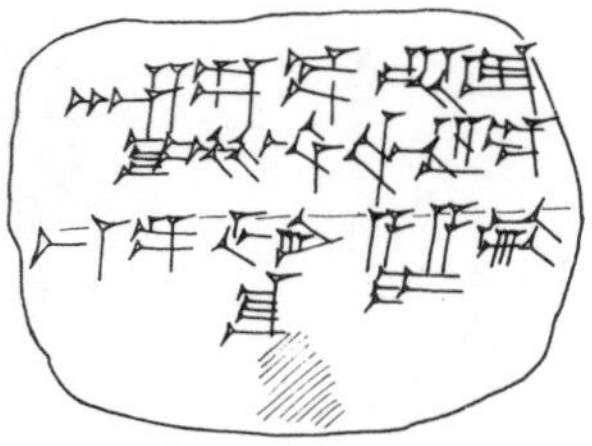

Rev.

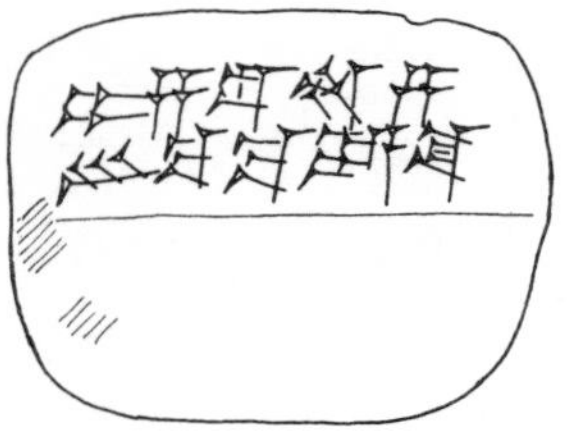

158

U.E.

Obv.

Rev.

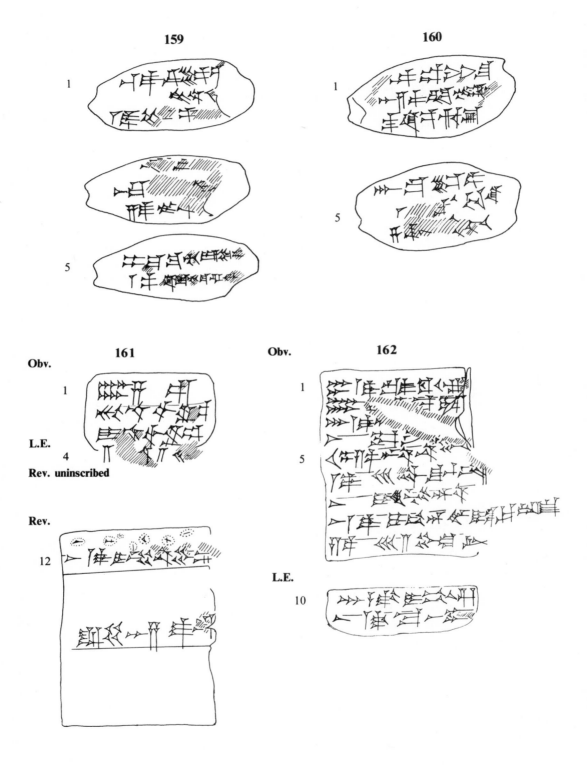

163

Obv.   Rev.

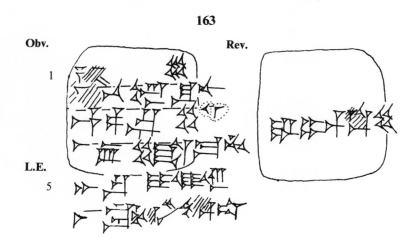

164

Obv.   Rev.

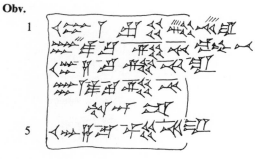

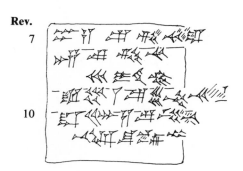

L.E.

166

Obv.

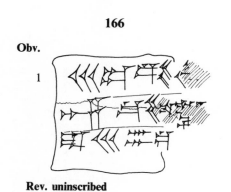

Rev. uninscribed

165

Obv.

Rev. uninscribed

167

Obv.

Rev.

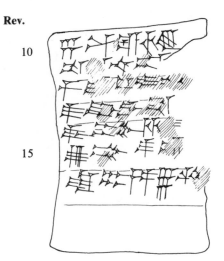

168

Obv.

Rev.

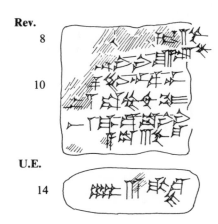

L.E.

U.E.

169

Rev.

Obv.

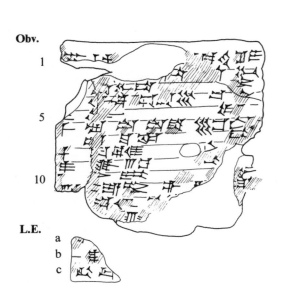

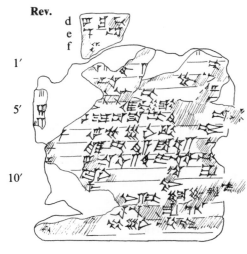

L.E.

U.E.

170

Obv.

1

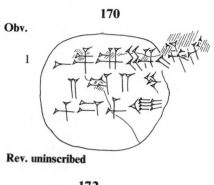

Rev. uninscribed

171

Obv.

1

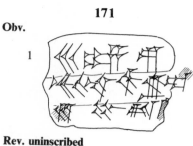

Rev. uninscribed

172

Obv.

1

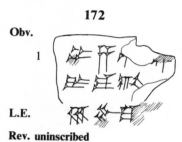

L.E.

Rev. uninscribed

173

Obv.

1

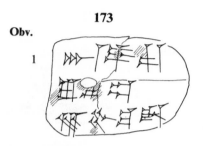

Rev. uninscribed

174

Obv.

1

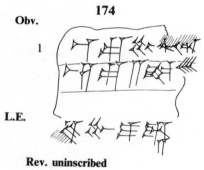

L.E.

Rev. uninscribed

175

Obv.

1

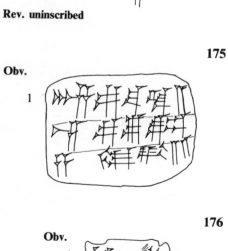

Rev.

4

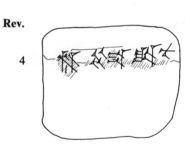

176

Obv.

1

Rev.

3

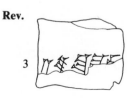

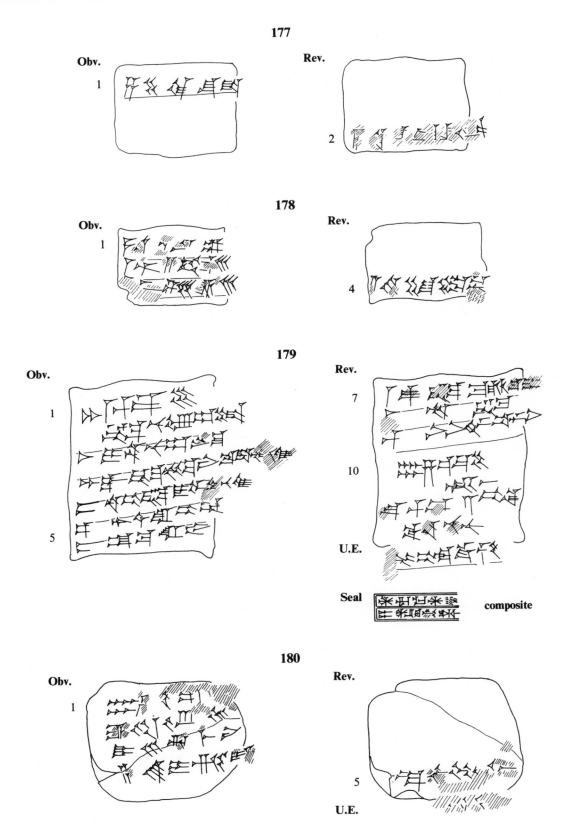

181

Obv.

1

Rev.

5

"sic

182

Obv.

1

Rev.

5

183

Obv.

1

4

Rev.

5

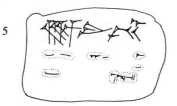

184

Obv.

1

Rev. uninscribed

185

Obv.

1

Rev.

4

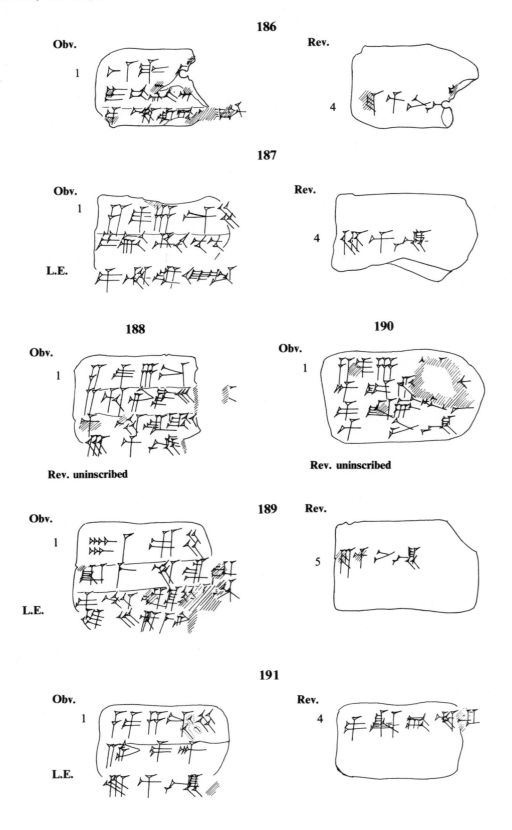

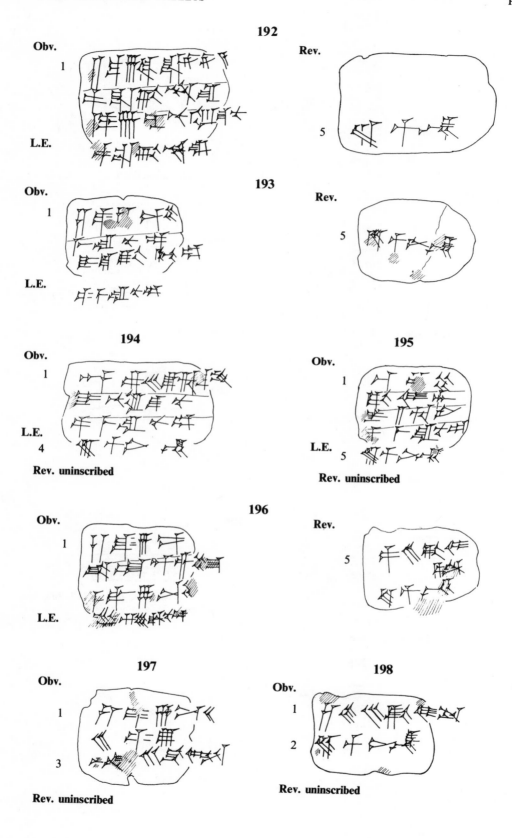

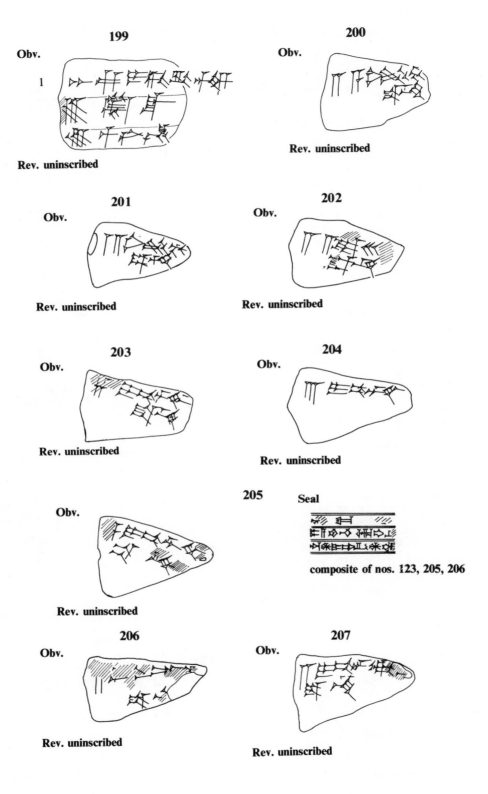

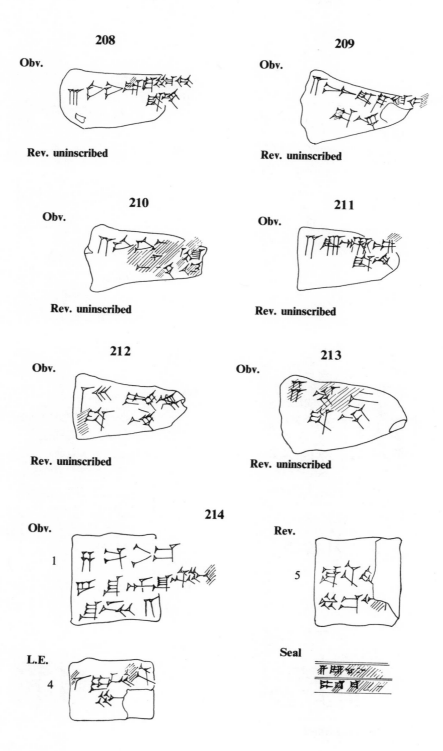

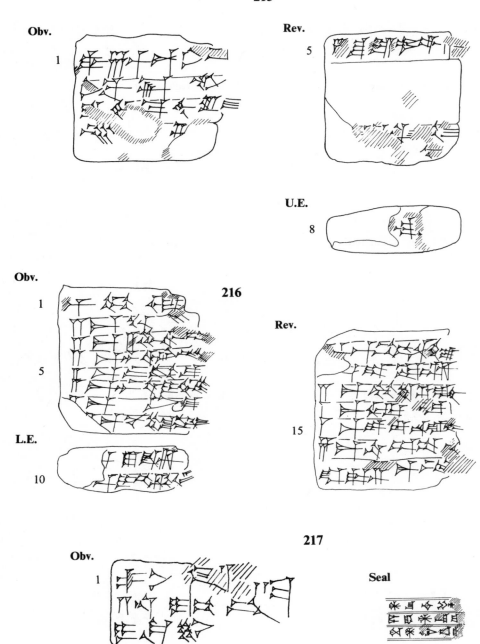

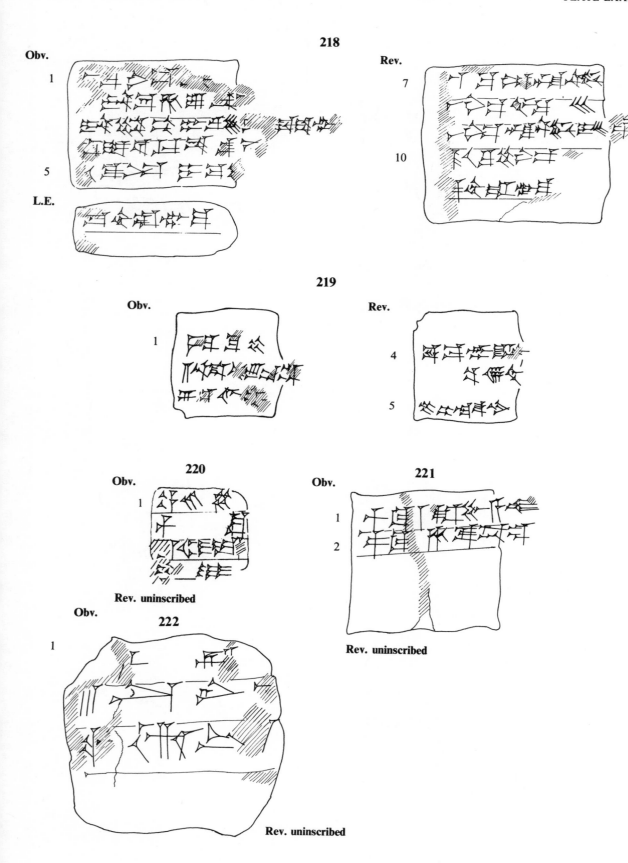

223

Obv.

Rev.

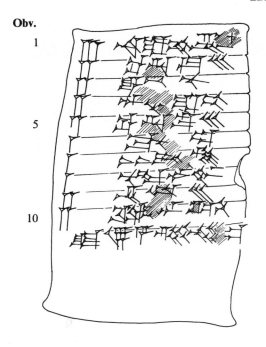

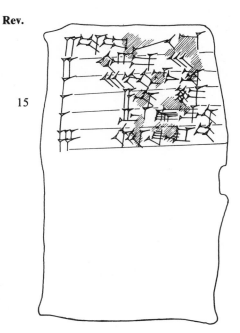

224

Obv.

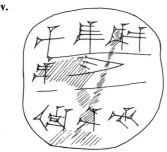

Rev. uninscribed

225

Obv.

L.E. destroyed

225

Rev.

U.E.

226

Obv.

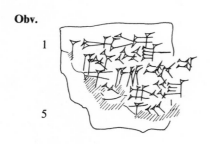

Rev.

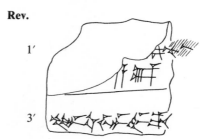

227

Obv.

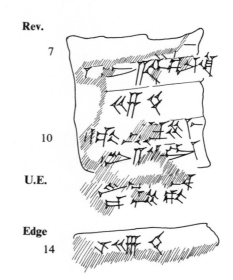

Rev.

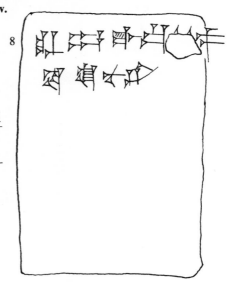

228

Obv.

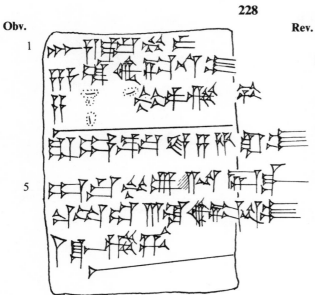

Rev.

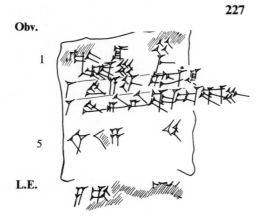

229

Obv.

Rev.

1

5

10

15

U.E.

Edge

20

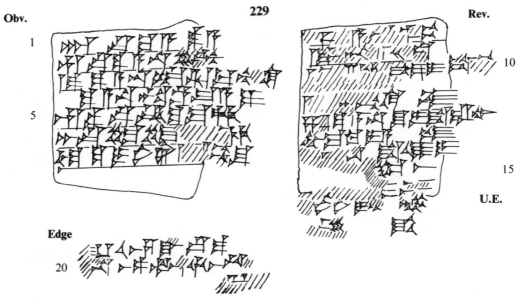

230

Obv.

Rev.

1

5

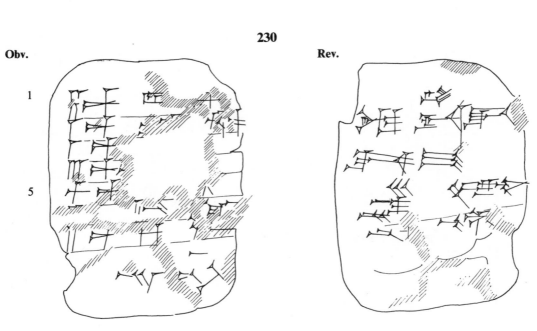

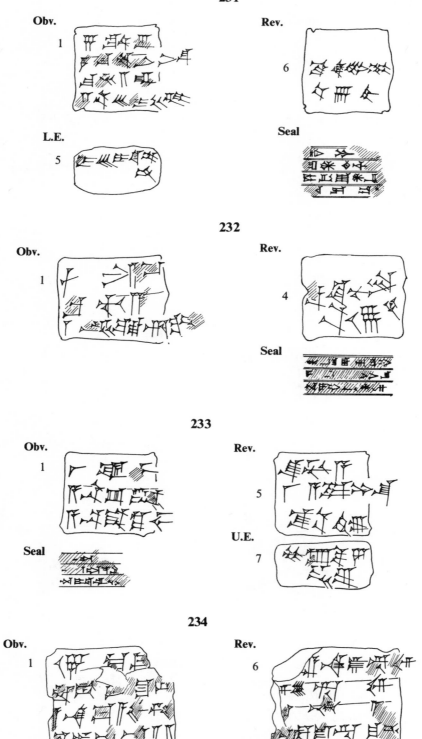

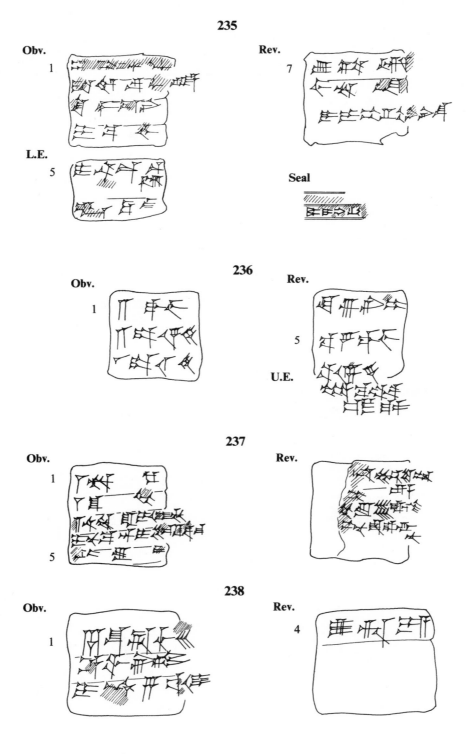

239

Obv.

Rev.

240

Obv.

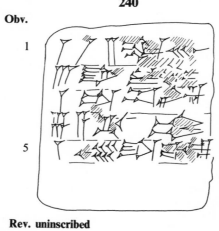

Rev. uninscribed

241

Obv.

Rev.

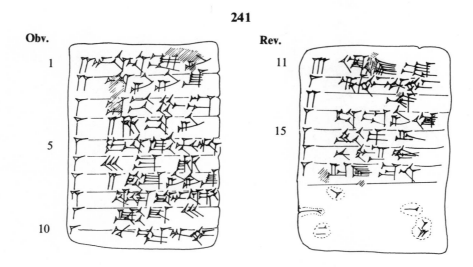

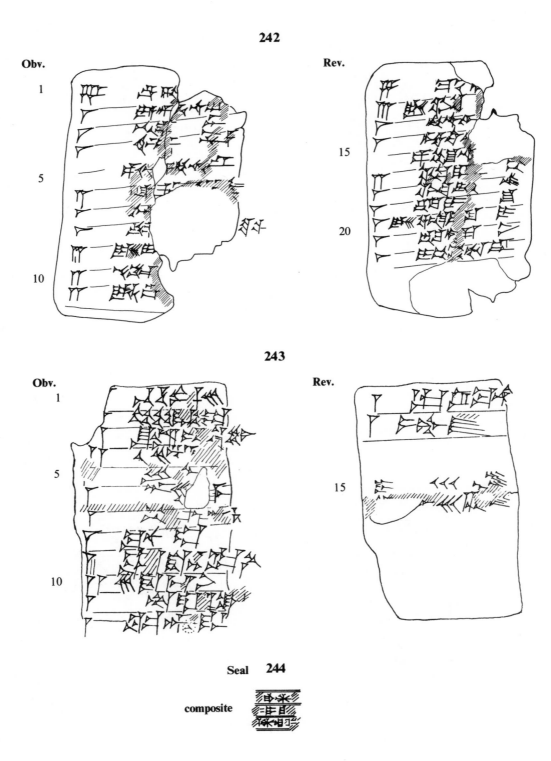

242

Obv.

Rev.

243

Obv.

Rev.

Seal 244

composite

245

Seal

246

Obv.

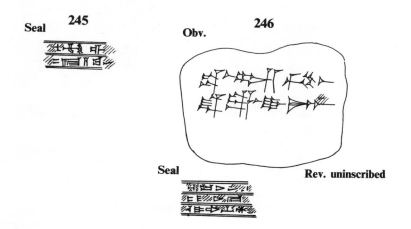

Seal

Rev. uninscribed

247

Obv.

Rev.

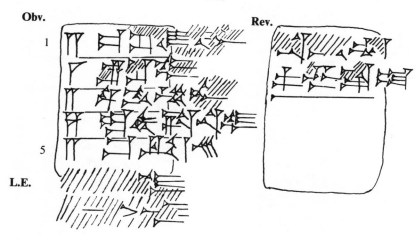

1

5

L.E.

248

Obv.

Rev.

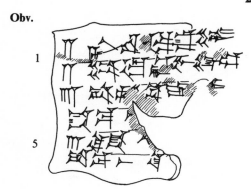

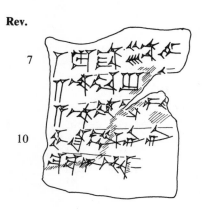

1

5

7

10

249

Obv.

Rev.

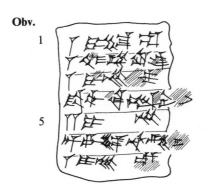

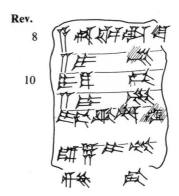

250

Obv.

Rev.

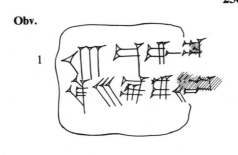

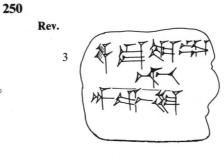

251

Obv.

Rev.

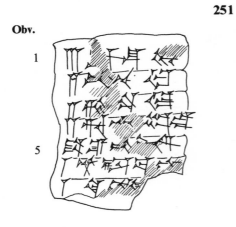

252

Obv.

Rev.

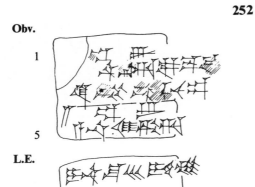

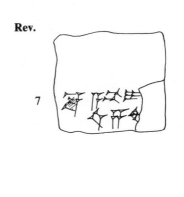

L.E.

253

Obv.

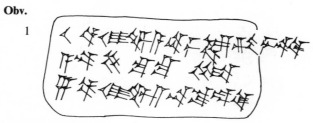

Rev. uninscribed

254

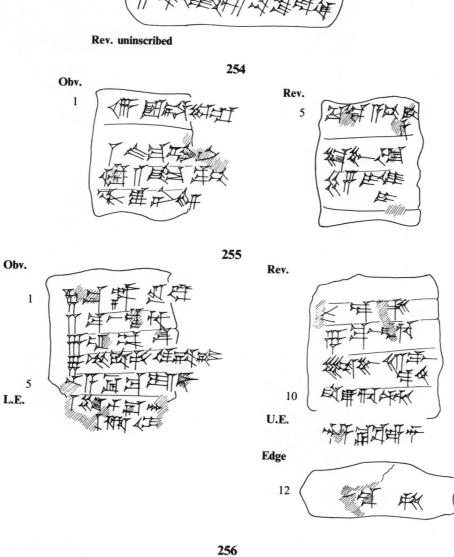

255

256

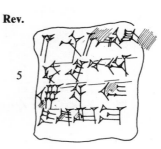

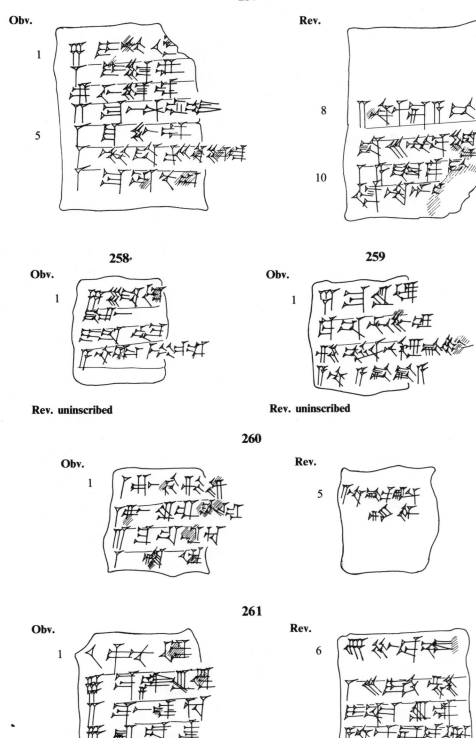

257

Obv.

Rev.

258

Obv.

Rev. uninscribed

259

Obv.

Rev. uninscribed

260

Obv.

Rev.

261

Obv.

Rev.

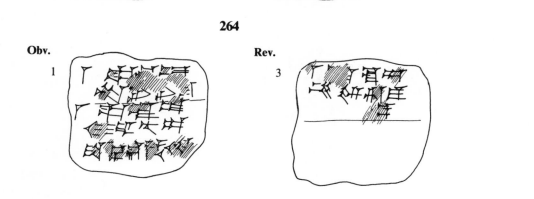

262

263

264

265

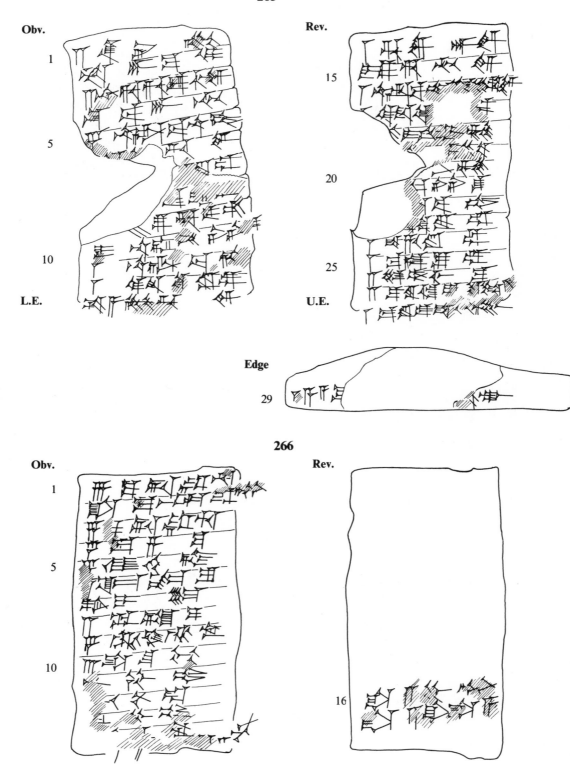

266

267

Obv.

Rev.

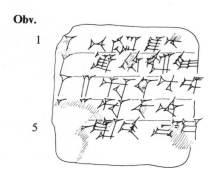

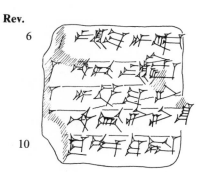

268

Obv. col. i

Obv. col. ii

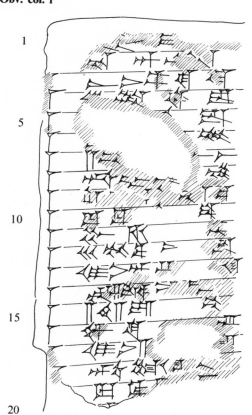

rest of col. i   destroyed

rest of col. ii   destroyed

PLATE LXXXVIII

268

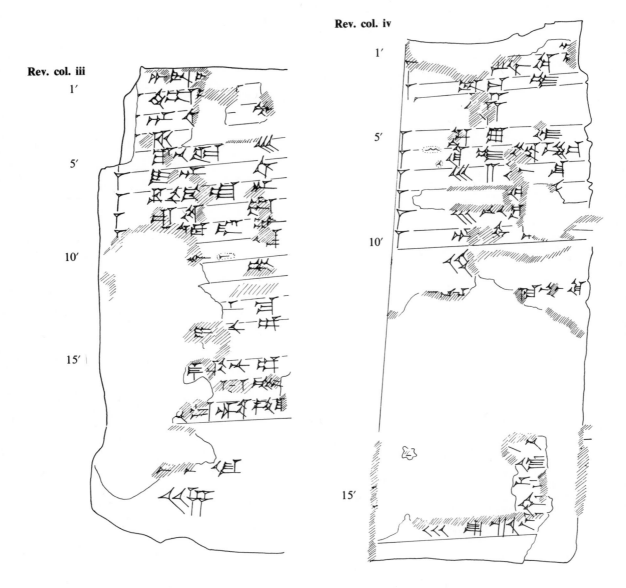

Rev. col. iii

Rev. col. iv

269

Obv.

1

5

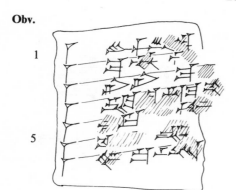

Rev.

10

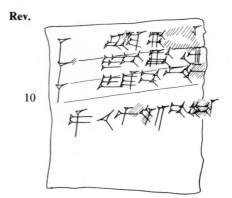

270

Obv.

1

5

10

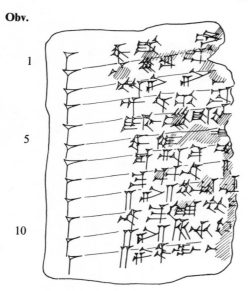

Rev.

15

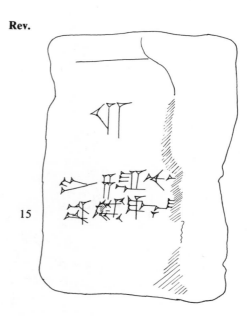

271

Obv.

1'

L.E.

5'

Rev.

1

5

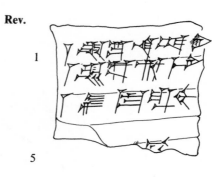

Edge

6

272

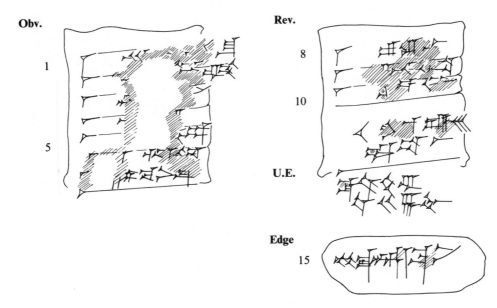

273

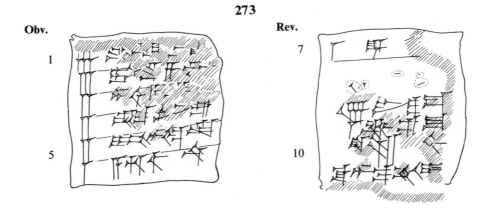

274

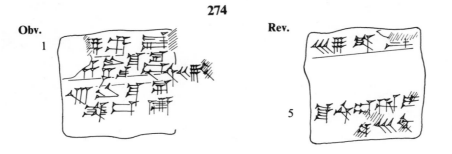

275

276

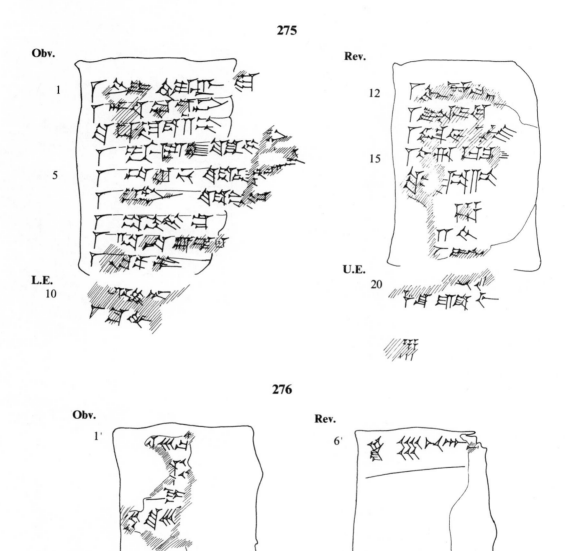

277

Obv.

Rev.

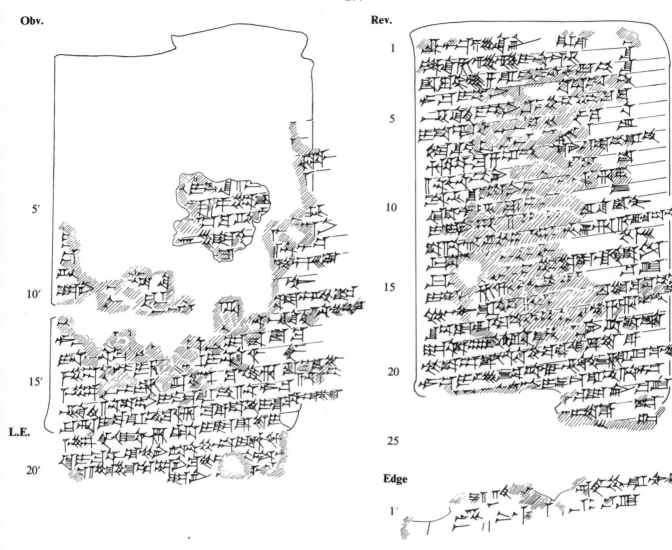

5'

10'

15'

L.E.

20'

1

5

10

15

20

25

Edge

1'

278

Obv. col. i

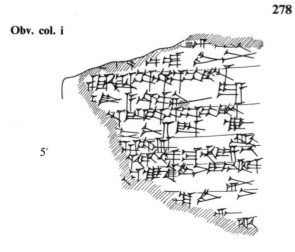

5'

Rev. col. ii

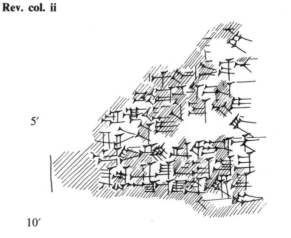

5'

10'

278

Obv. col. ii

Rev. col. ii

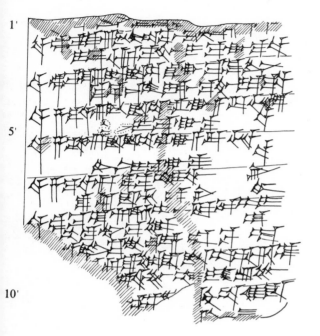

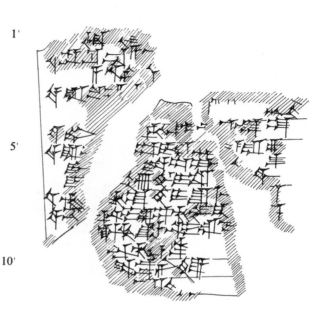

Obv. col. iii

Rev. col. iii

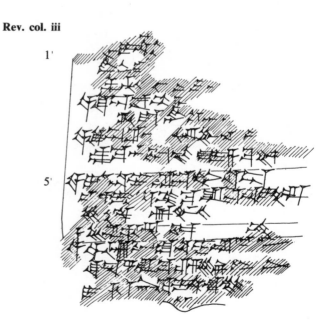

279

outer face

bottom

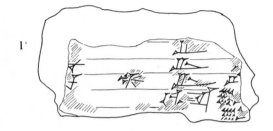

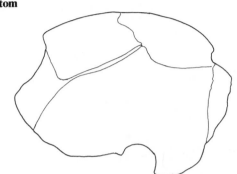

280

Obv.

Rev.

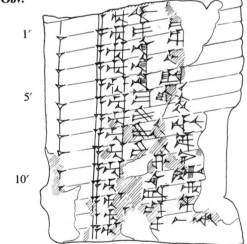

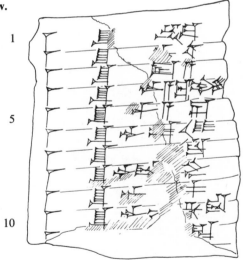

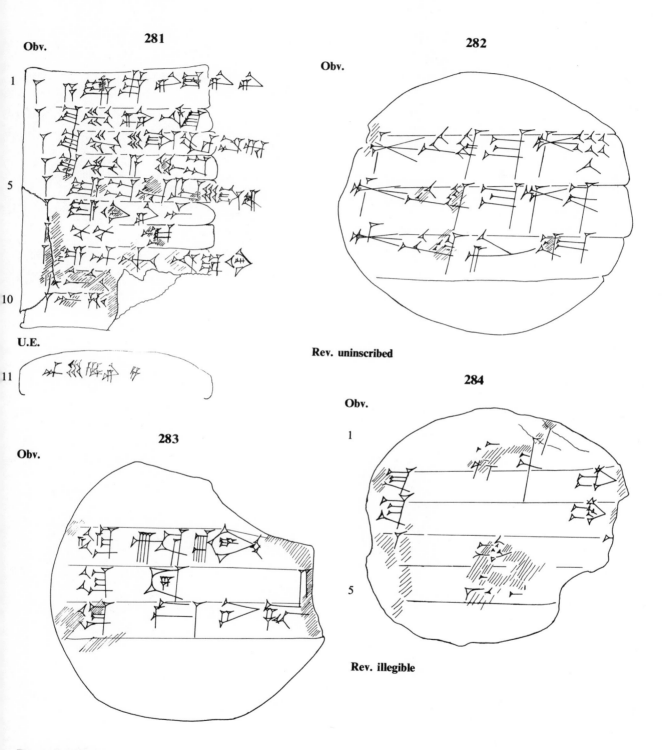

281

Obv.

U.E.

282

Obv.

Rev. uninscribed

283

Obv.

Rev. uninscribed

284

Obv.

Rev. illegible

285

Obv.

Rev.

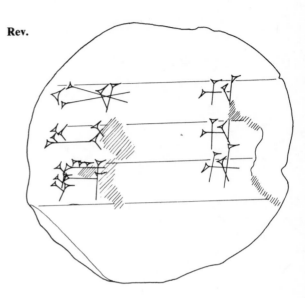

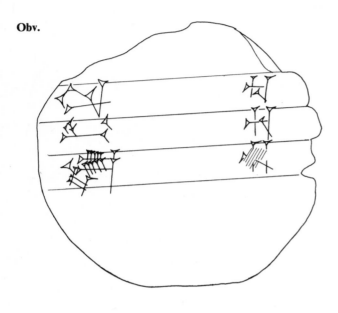

286

287

Obv.

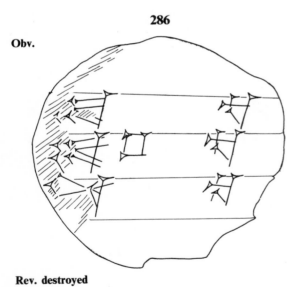

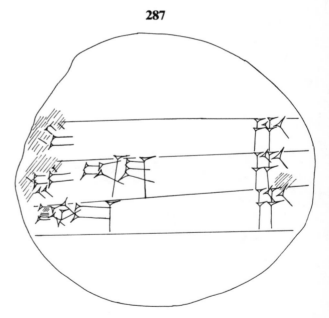

Rev. destroyed

Rev. uninscribed

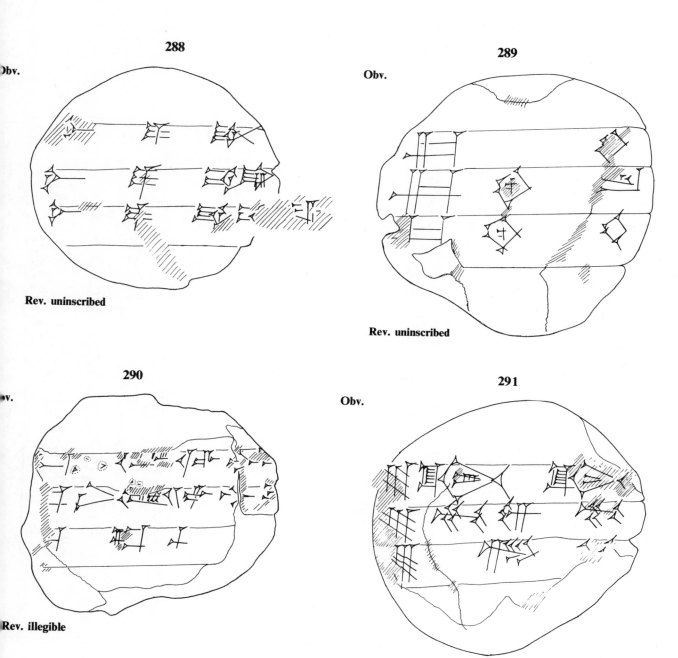

288

Obv.

Rev. uninscribed

289

Obv.

Rev. uninscribed

290

Obv.

Rev. illegible

291

Obv.

Rev. uninscribed

292

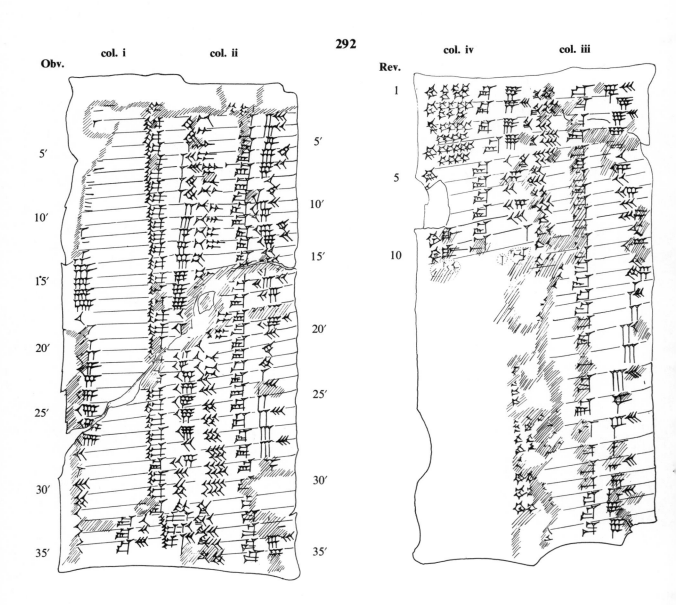

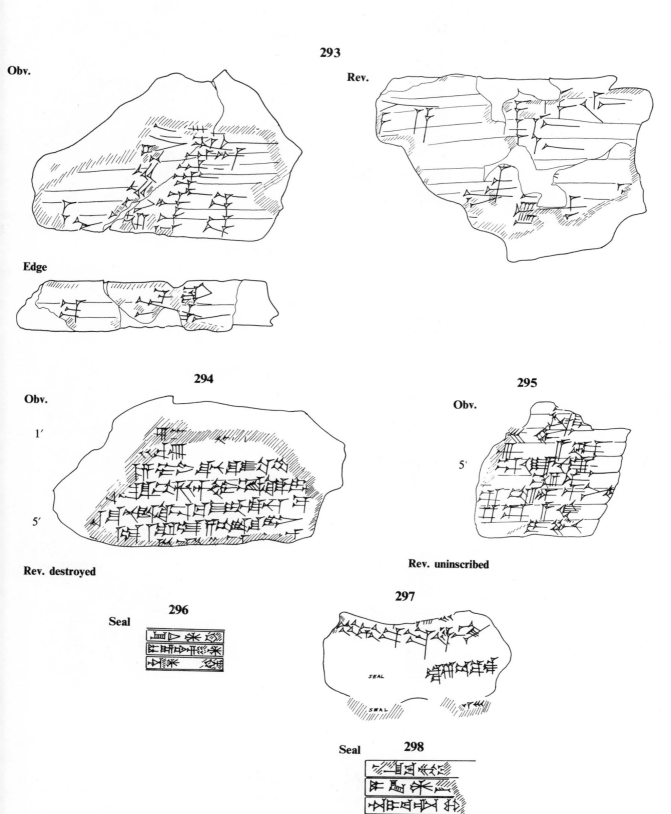

293

Obv.

Rev.

Edge

294

Obv.

1′

5′

Rev. destroyed

295

Obv.

5′

Rev. uninscribed

296

Seal

297

SEAL

SEAL

298

Seal

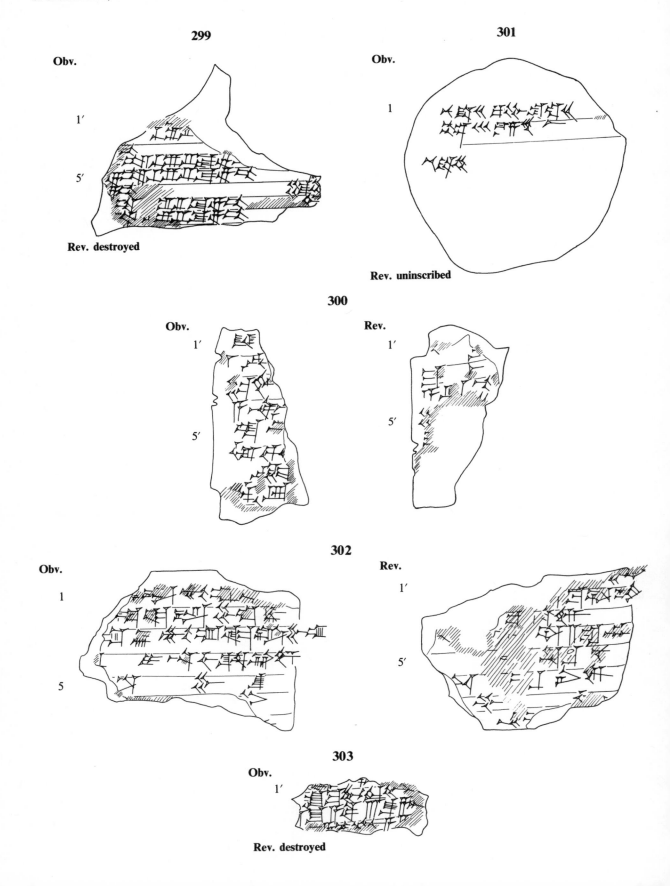

304

Obv.

Rev.

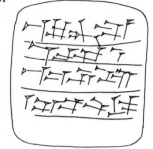

305

Obv.

1

5

10

15

20

Rev.

30

35

40

45

50

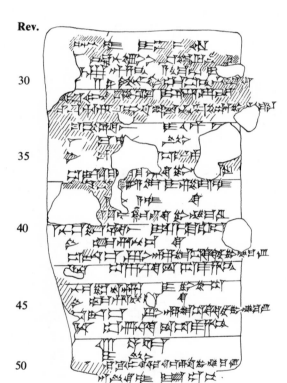

L.E.

25

U.E.

Edge

55

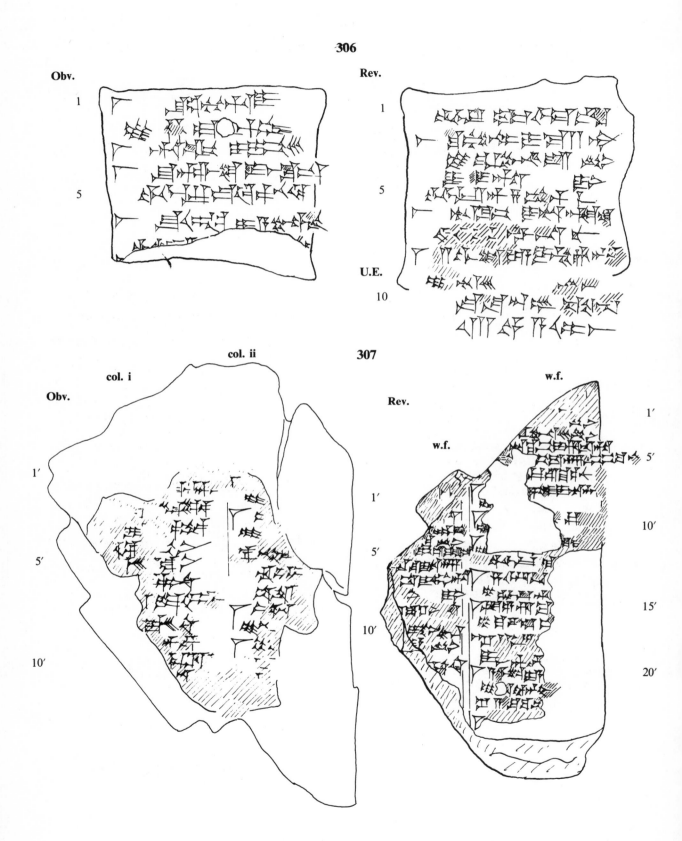

308

Obv.

Rev.

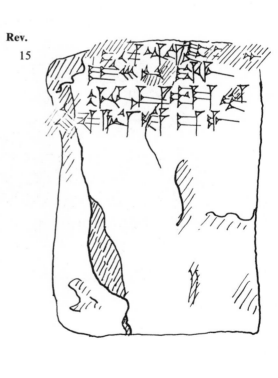

309

Obv.

Rev.

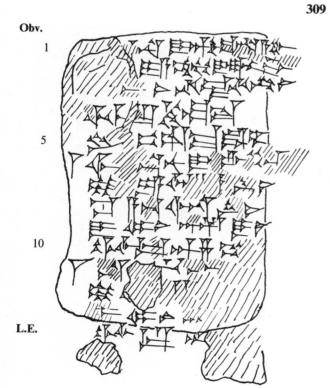

310

Obv. (?)

col. i   col. ii

1′

1′

5′

5′

other side destroyed

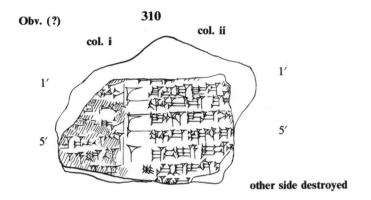

311

Obv.

Rev.

1′

1′

5′

5′

10′

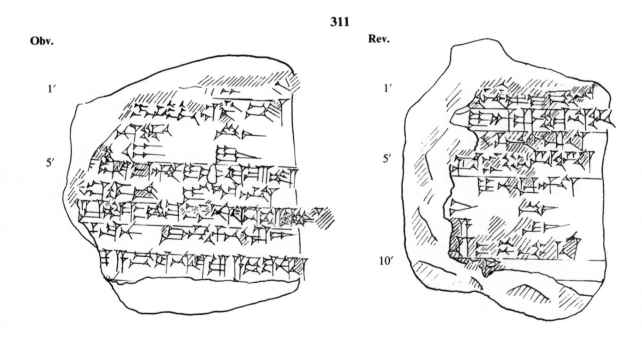

312

Obv.

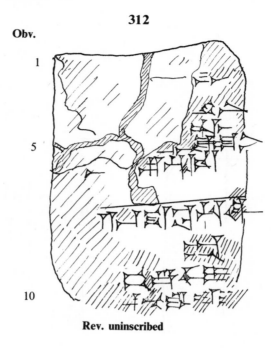

Rev. uninscribed

313

Obv.

Rev.

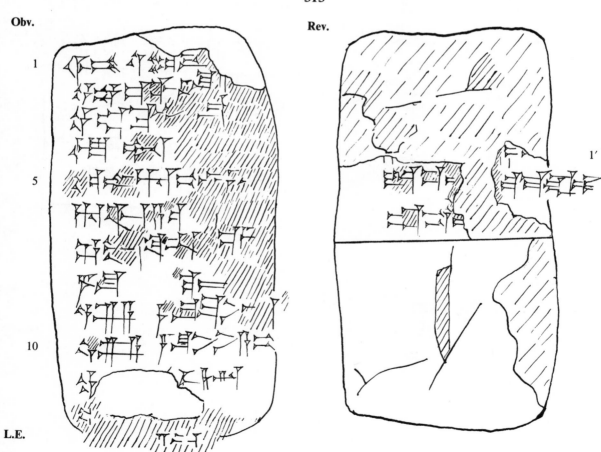

L.E.

314

Obv.

Rev.

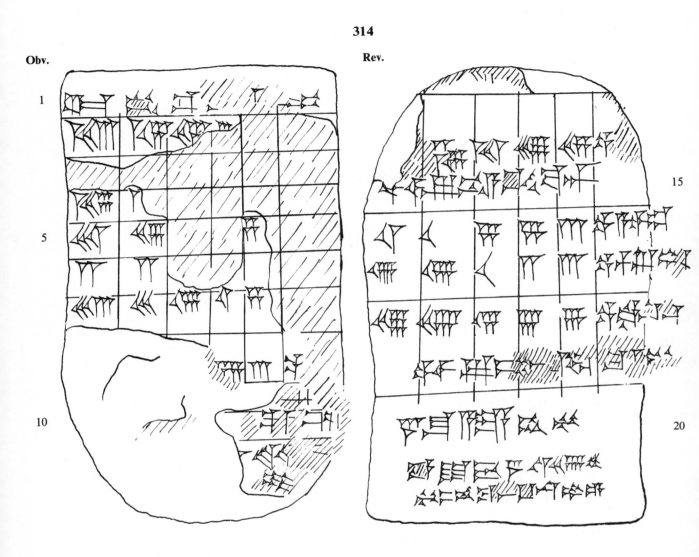

U.E.

315

Obv.

Rev.

1′

5′

10′

15′

20′

L.E.

1′

5′

10′

15′

20′

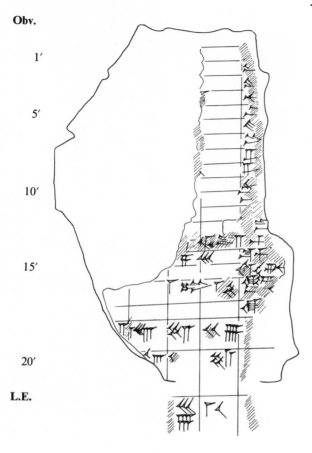

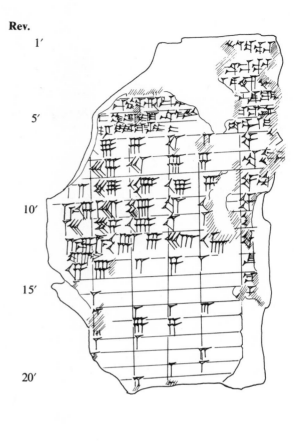

Obv.

316

1

5

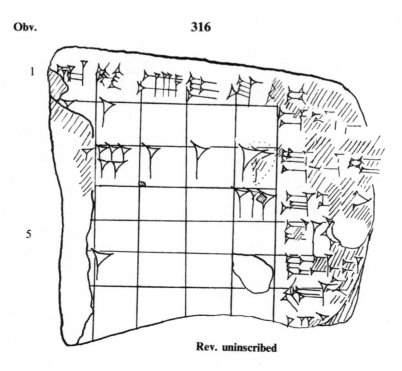

Rev. uninscribed

PLATE CVIII

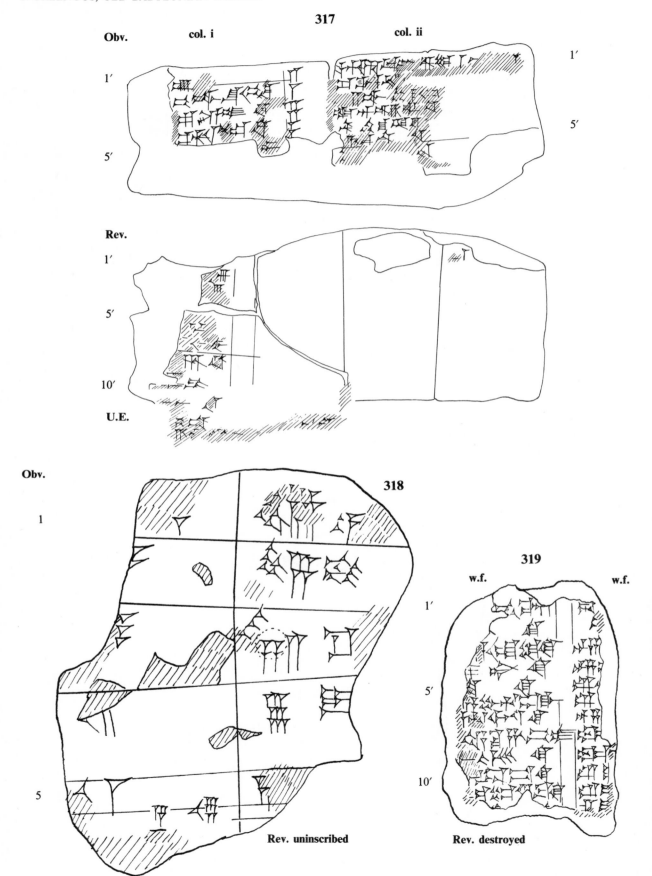

317

Obv.

col. i   col. ii

1′

5′

1′

5′

Rev.

1′

5′

10′

U.E.

Obv.

1

318

319

w.f.   w.f.

1′

5′

5

10′

Rev. uninscribed   Rev. destroyed

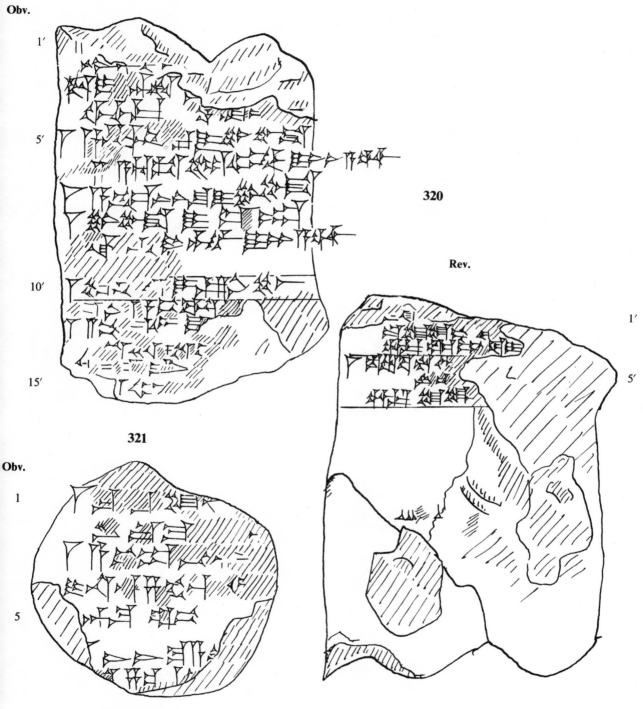

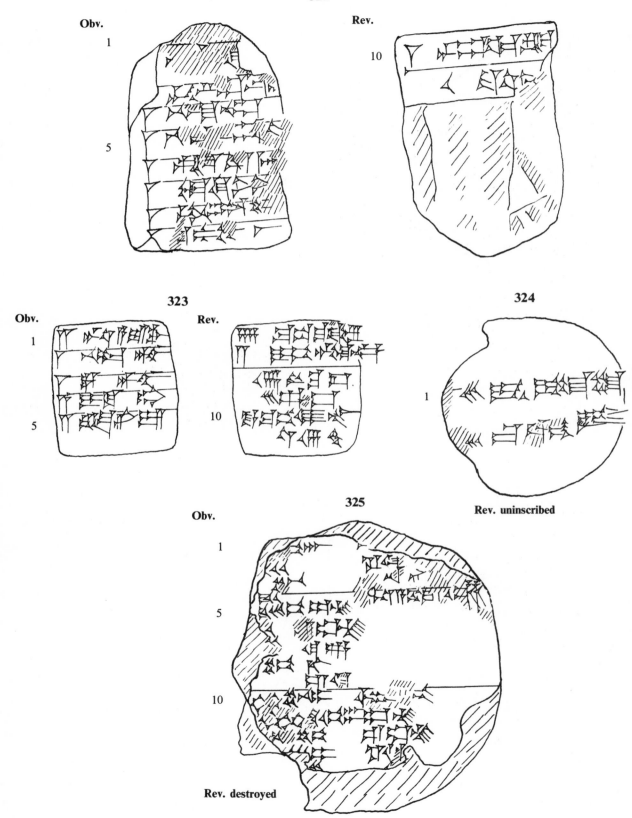

322

Obv.

Rev.

323

Obv.

Rev.

324

Rev. uninscribed

325

Obv.

Rev. destroyed

326

Obv.

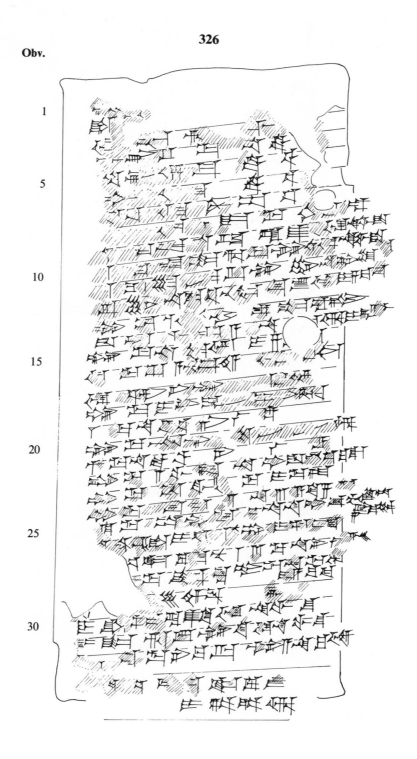

326

Rev.

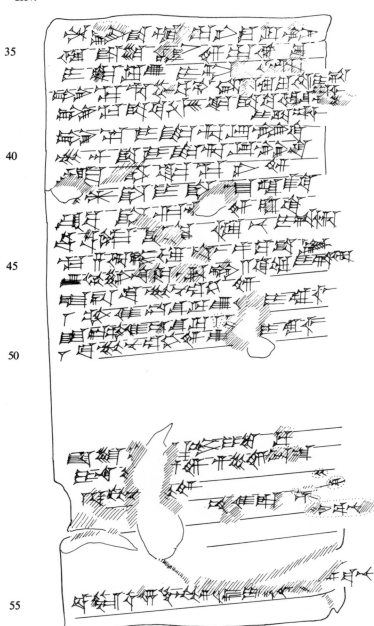

35

40

45

50

55

Imprimerie Orientaliste, P.O. Box 41, 3000 Louvain (Belgium)

DATE DUE

GAYLORD			PRINTED IN U S A